T0267959

What in Me Is Dark

What in Me Is Dark

The Revolutionary Afterlife of Paradise Lost

ORLANDO READE

First published by Jonathan Cape, Great Britain in 2024

Astra House
A Division of Astra Publishing House
astrahouse.com

Library of Congress Cataloging-in-Publication Data
Names: Reade, Orlando, author.
Title: What in me is dark : the revolutionary afterlife of Paradise lost / Orlando Reade.
Description: First U.S. edition. | New York : Astra House, 2024. | Includes bibliographical references and index. | Summary: "What in Me Is Dark tells the unlikely story of how Milton's epic poem came to haunt political struggles over the past four centuries, including the many different, unexpected, often contradictory ways in which it has been read, interpreted, and appropriated through time and across the world, and to revolutionary ends"-- Provided by publisher.
Identifiers: LCCN 2024040081 (print) | LCCN 2024040082 (ebook) | ISBN 9781662602795 (hardcover) | ISBN 9781662602801 (epub)
Subjects: LCSH: Milton, John, 1608-1674. Paradise lost. | Milton, John, 1608-1674.--Influence. | Politics and literature.
Classification: LCC PR3562 .R365 2024 (print) | LCC PR3562 (ebook) | DDC 821/.4--dc23/eng/20240903
LC record available at https://lccn.loc.gov/2024040081
LC ebook record available at https://lccn.loc.gov/2024040082

First U.S. edition, 2024
10 9 8 7 6 5 4 3 2 1

Design by Jouve (UK), Milton Keynes
The text is set in Bembo Book MT Pro.
The titles are set in Bembo Book MT Pro.

It is exactly because it is dark that it wants to be understood.

Paul Celan, 'On the Darkness of Poetry'

Everybody talks about Paradise Lost *and nobody reads it.*

Unknown, late nineteenth century

Contents

Introduction

Dark Writing

Norfolk Prison Colony, Massachusetts, 1948

Two men sit down at a table to talk. They are brothers, both in their early twenties. The younger, Reginald, is sharply dressed. His older brother Malcolm wears a uniform of coarse white cloth with black code printed on it. They have recently joined a new religion, learning a new account of how the world was created, and how one race came to rule over another. They have been changed, and this is visible in the way they hold themselves: with pride and discipline. Reginald had been the one to initiate Malcolm, telling him: 'I'll show you how to get out of prison.'[1]

On this day, Reginald is visiting, hoping perhaps to impress his older brother with newly learnt rhetorical skills, to share news from the movement and the teachings of their leader.[2] But Malcolm wants to talk about something else. In the prison library, he has discovered a book that appears no less than prophetic. It's a work of literature by one of the most famous authors in Western history: a title that would intimidate most readers. Not this one. Malcolm is a man of exceptional mental energy. He lays out his theory in the visiting room in front of his impressed, uncertain brother. He must know that what he is about to say runs against the received wisdom of his time. Malcolm tells Reginald that this book, written three centuries ago, confirms what they have been taught: America is governed by the Devil.

Two decades later, Malcolm X recalled that moment. It is described in *The Autobiography of Malcolm X*, published in 1965, shortly after his assassination. He read John Milton's *Paradise Lost* at a time when he hadn't yet exchanged his 'slave name' for an X, and his role as the most controversial Black leader in America was still in the distant future. *Paradise Lost* provided a surprising illumination, confirming what he had learnt about white supremacy from Elijah Muhammad, leader of the Nation of Islam, the unorthodox Muslim sect sect that Malcolm and his brother had recently joined.[3] In his *Autobiography*, Malcolm remembers telling Reginald that 'Milton and Mr Elijah Muhammad were actually saying the same thing'.[4] If it seems like an astonishing interpretation of a Christian poem written three centuries earlier, that it spoke to the radical needs of the present, Malcolm wasn't alone.

Paradise Lost, first published in 1667, might be the most influential poem in English. Its subject is the Fall of Adam and Eve, but not as you read about it in the Bible. *Paradise Lost* is modelled on the epic poems of ancient Greece and Rome. Homer's *Iliad*, *Odyssey*, and Virgil's *Aeneid* are stories of heroes and gods, catastrophic wars, harrowing journeys, tragic seductions, and the founding of great empires. *Paradise Lost* is about the founding of the human race by God, and it also describes what happened before the creation of the world, when one angel leads an uprising in Heaven against God's authority. After the uprising is defeated, and the rebel angels fall down to Hell, they debate what to do. Their leader volunteers to travel up to the world that God has just created, intending to ruin it by tempting the new humans to disobey their Creator. We then see the fatal consequences of that decision.

Paradise Lost is not only a work of art. It is also an important political document. Like Thomas Hobbes, John Locke, and Jean-Jacques Rousseau – the most influential political philosophers of the seventeenth and eighteenth centuries – Milton offers an account of human origins to make a political argument. The poem explains how an infinitely just and loving God could have created a world full of sin, suffering, and death. To do so, it argues that God gave humans free will so they could choose to obey or disobey him. This is not only a point of theology: freedom is the natural condition of humanity, and the fundamental value on which societies should be built. The political vision of *Paradise Lost* went on to influence readers embedded in revolutionary struggles in America, France, Haiti, and elsewhere. It became part of the modern imagination, used by readers to understand the best and worst parts of their world. To read *Paradise Lost*, therefore, is to learn about the modern world, its culture and its politics. But in order to understand how it came to have this extraordinary career, we need to know how it was written in the ashes of a failed revolution.

If you had walked out of London on a fine day in the early 1660s, before the great plague arrived, passing through Cripple Gate in the ancient city walls, and turning alongside Artillery Gardens, you might have seen a grey-haired man in a cloth coat sitting outside one of the houses. There would have been birdsong in the air, which would have smelt fresh after the reek of the city. If you had come in the early morning, you would have found him inside, in a first-floor room hung with rusty green fabrics, dictating to a young man long, serpentine sentences. The young man would then read the lines back to the older man. He would think a while, then recite the lines again, only this time more compact, like a great cat about to leap. This is the place in which John Milton spent the last years of his life, and where *Paradise Lost* was revealed to him. He had come up with the idea of writing a poem about the Fall of Adam and Eve twenty years before. But he hadn't written it then. The reasons behind this delay, and what happened to Milton in the meantime, are essential to understanding his epic.

Milton was born one midwinter morning in 1608 at his family home in Bread Street, London.[5] We know little of his mother, Sara, except that she wore glasses. His father, also John, had been disinherited by his Catholic father for reading the Bible in English. He was a self-made man, who worked as a scrivener, or legal clerk, and his prudence made his family financially comfortable. He was an amateur musician and composer, and sent his two sons to St Paul's School, in the churchyard of the great cathedral where the dean was the poet John Donne, whose sermons drew meanings out of scripture like rabbits from a hat. At the age of twelve, Milton was already showing signs of an exceptional mind, devouring classical literature late into the night. The boys of St Paul's were trained to read Latin and Greek so well that when they arrived at university, they often felt superior to other students.[6] In 1625, aged sixteen, Milton went to Christ's College, Cambridge, where he first distinguished himself for reasons other than his mind. Within his first year, he was whipped and temporarily expelled. This was unusual for a student and must have been deeply embarrassing.[7]

At that time, political tensions were rising throughout England. In 1625, King Charles I had married a French Catholic princess, Henrietta Maria, and many feared that he would convert to Catholicism himself. England had become Protestant in the early sixteenth century, under King Henry VIII. During the reign of Elizabeth I (1558–1603), the Church of England had established a cautious middle course between Catholicism and the more extreme forms of Protestantism. What was at stake in the nation's religion was not just doctrine or ritual, but also political autonomy from the Pope. Then, in the 1630s, the new Archbishop of Canterbury began to introduce reforms that seemed to many suspiciously close to Catholicism. As a young man, Milton conformed to the state religion, his heresies still to come. On graduating, however, he decided not to become a clergyman, a comfortable career for someone with his gifts. Instead, he went back to his parents' home, where he taught himself mathematics and wrote increasingly ambitious poetry. In 1637, he composed an elegy called 'Lycidas', for a Cambridge student who had died in a shipwreck. At the end of the poem, Milton announces his intention to move on to 'pastures new'. A year later, he embarked on a tour of Italy, something that young men intending to learn modern languages did in pursuit of a diplomatic career. Thanks to his connections, Milton was able to meet some famous writers and thinkers, including the blind scientist Galileo, then living under house arrest for insulting the Pope. While he was there, news arrived that a war had broken out between the English King and the Scottish bishops over issues of religious autonomy. Milton later claimed that he vowed to return home and take up the fight for liberty. In reality, he took his sweet time, lingering in Rome, returning to Florence, and visiting Venice.

By the time Milton arrived back in England, the country was deeply divided. The success of Scottish resistance to the King's reforms had given courage to England's radical Protestants. In 1641, Milton joined a controversy between the Church of England bishops and a group of anonymous Presbyterians, who believed the bishops were exercising a tyrannical control over Protestants. The young poet had been radicalised. He didn't want England to become like Catholic Italy, where free thinkers like Galileo were oppressed. To be a great poet, he had to be free to hold up bad ideas against good ones, questioning orthodoxies as much as heresies.[8] At the same time, he was thinking about a new work of literature. He boasted that his friends said that he was capable of producing 'something so written to aftertimes, as they should not willingly let it die' – in other words, a masterpiece that would survive for centuries.[9] He came up with almost a hundred potential titles, including 'Paradise Lost'.[10] It was to be a tragedy. (But how to stage a play about naked people?) Only he didn't write it then. Instead, in a world-historical act of procrastination, Milton put literature to one side and threw himself into politics. He believed that the God who made him a poet was urging his countrymen to rise up. And rise up they did. In late 1641, riots in London drove the King out of the city. The English Civil War began the following August. That same month, Milton had the shock of his life.

The poet had received from his father an income that included various debts, on which he received interest. In summer 1642, Milton visited one of his debtors, Richard Powell, at home in Oxfordshire. He returned to London, a month later, with a wife: Powell's seventeen-year-old daughter Mary. After a month of marriage, she left London to visit her family. She promised to return but didn't. Milton sent several letters and she didn't respond. He sent a servant and the servant was rudely turned away. The Civil War made travel difficult, but this did not disguise the fact that he had been abandoned. What had gone wrong? We know little about Mary: Milton's voluminous writings leave no grain of her voice, her thoughts, her interests. She had a large family, who were Royalist in politics and traditional in religion. It's little surprise she didn't take to life in the city with an older, puritanical scholar. One contemporary account says she didn't like listening to her husband beating his students – a detail that shivers on the page.[11] It's extraordinary that anyone imagined the marriage would work, but economic necessity sometimes produces romantic illusions. For his part, Milton must have been naive. After so short a period in the paradise of marriage, he had been cast out. How he reacted would make him notorious.

Less than a year after Mary left, Milton published a substantial new treatise. He had turned his experience of marriage into a campaign. The treatise, entitled *The Doctrine and Discipline of Divorce*, argued for reforming English divorce law. Even though Henry VIII had made England Protestant in order to annul a childless marriage, divorce was unobtainable for all but the wealthiest and most powerful people. But the 1640s was a time of radical change, and Milton set his mind to it. The problem was that he had to go not only against the common law but against the very words of Jesus, who had condemned divorce: 'whosoever shall put away his wife, saving for the cause of fornication, causeth her to commit adultery: and whosoever shall marry her that is divorced committeth adultery' (Matthew 5:32). Milton argued that something else was more fundamental to Christianity than even Jesus's words. Scripture, he said, should be interpreted according to the most important commandment: to love (Romans 13:8). Marriage should be about love, two souls linked in the delight of conversation, rather than simply sexual reproduction. Being confined in an incompatible marriage, Milton said, was like being 'a living soule bound to a dead corpse'. With this, he entered the limelight – and for all the wrong reasons.

During the English Civil War, people started challenging religious authority, demanding their own say in how to worship and what to believe. It wasn't only Royalists who were threatened by this. The increasingly conservative Presbyterian faction in Parliament viciously attacked religious radicals, and this now included Milton. His enemies called him a libertine, a divorcer, and a wife-beater. He was summoned before Parliament to answer for his views, and once again experience led to a piece of radical political thinking. He wrote a pamphlet called *Areopagitica* (1644) attacking censorship and defending the freedom of expression. 'A good book', Milton writes, 'is the precious life-blood of a master-spirit.'[12] Bad books and wrong ideas are also necessary, for how do we know what to believe unless we can test our ideas? Untested virtue is not virtue at all but 'an excrementall whitenesse'.[13] With Mary's departure, Milton had come to believe that experience was better than untested innocence, a belief that would later structure his epic.

By the summer of 1645, the King's cause was waning, and this had an unexpected impact on Milton's life. One day he was visiting elderly relatives, and 'on a sudden he was surprised to see one whom he thought to have never seen more, making Submission and begging Pardon on her Knees before him'.[14] Mary had returned. It's not clear how this was stage-managed, nor whether Milton had done anything to bring it about, though he seems to have been putting financial pressure on the Powell family.[15] Whatever led Mary to seek him out, they lived as man and wife from then on. Less than a year later, she gave birth to a daughter, Anne. In the summer of 1646, the King surrendered and, for the next two years, the two sides tried to negotiate a new political settlement. The Presbyterians wanted peace, while the Independents – a faction that included Milton and the ruthless army general, Oliver Cromwell – were pushing for more extensive reforms. Then there were the radicals in the army, known as the Levellers, who called for votes for all men. This came to a head in the Putney Debates of 1647, where the army debated these issues. Ultimately, the Levellers were sidelined by the leaders of the army, but the debates led to a crucial turn away from negotiation. There was now talk of a future without a king. Some said the land could be cleansed only by his death. Finally, the King was put on trial. On 30 January 1649, he was led to the scaffold. The stroke that cleaved his head from his neck was met with a groan from the crowd.[16] A week later, England was declared a Republic.

Soon after, Milton was given a role in the new government as Secretary of Foreign Tongues, writing and translating diplomatic correspondence. He also became a member of the Council of State, the executive body governing England, and was tasked with deciding which books should be censored. He put his beliefs into practice, permitting the first English translation of the Qur'an, among other non-Christian books. Most importantly, the new government asked him to defend the execution of the King and champion the cause of democracy. He wrote an important treatise, *The Tenure of Kings and Magistrates*, which argued that it was just to depose a king who had become a tyrant. Milton had become a propagandist for the new regime, and this spawned many enemies. Royalist writers poured torrents of ink into efforts to spoil his reputation, calling him a monster, a sodomite, a prostitute, and a mushroom. When he went blind, in 1652, they said it was a divine punishment. This period also saw another kind of loss. His wife, Mary, died in childbirth and, six weeks later, his son, John, died too. The poet was now the widowed father of three daughters: Anne, Mary, and Deborah. Several years later he married again, and happily, but his wife, Katherine, died after they had had only two years together. In sonnets written in the wake of these events, he describes a world made dark by loss.[17]

Milton's commitment was undiminished, even as the Republic ran into difficulties. Parliament needed to call an election, but they feared that the electorate would vote for candidates who would call for the restoration of the monarchy. They had come to a standstill. On 20 April 1653, Oliver Cromwell interrupted a debate. He stepped into the middle aisle of the chamber, crying out: 'You are no Parliament, I say you are no Parliament; I will put an end to your Sitting.'[18] He called a troop of musketeers into the chamber: they cleared out the MPs and locked the doors. After that, Cromwell briefly considered taking the crown: England still lacked the stability that monarchy offered. But his conscience – and his outraged army comrades – prevented him. Cromwell hand-picked a new Parliament, composed mostly of Independents, army officers, and Fifth Monarchists, religious radicals who believed that Christ's return was imminent. This belief didn't make them easy to negotiate with, and within a year Cromwell dissolved Parliament a second time, establishing himself as Lord Protector, the sole leader of England, Scotland, and Wales. This was far from the republic that Milton wanted, but he maintained that it was 'the rule of the man most fit to rule'.[19] At least Cromwell wanted to ensure religious tolerance for all Protestants. To Milton, he was better than the alternatives.

The Protectorate lasted until shortly after Cromwell's death in 1658. On his deathbed, he nominated his eldest son, Richard, as his successor. Richard was not the man most fit to rule. He failed to reconcile the various factions and England's future was once again uncertain. Around that time, a friend suggested to Milton that he write a history of the English Civil War. Milton replied: 'What we need is not one who can compile a history of our troubles but one who can happily end them.'[20]

John Milton as a political saint. Engraving by Giovanni Battista Cipriani (1760), made for the radical agitator Thomas Hollis, and based on an image made during the poet's lifetime.

In April 1660, Prince Charles, the dead King's son, was invited to restore the monarchy. That same month, Milton wrote a pamphlet, *The readie and easie way to establish a free Commonwealth*, desperately trying to convince his nation not to restore the monarchy, but it was too late. Shortly after that, he went into hiding.

King Charles II returned to England in May 1660 to almost universal jubilation, with church bells ringing throughout the land, bonfires burning, and fountains running with wine. He officially forgave those who fought against his father, but he made an exception for the regicides: the men who had signed the King's death warrant. Those regicides who were still alive were hunted down, arrested, and brought to trial. Those who had died were exhumed, and their remains were hanged, drawn, and quartered. Parliament decided to punish twenty men who were not regicides, and someone proposed Milton. Eventually, however, his friends in Parliament prevailed. (Touchingly, one of them was the Royalist poet William Davenant, whose life Milton had saved under the previous regime.) Milton avoided punishment but he continued to fear retribution. Two of his books were burnt by order of the state. He was imprisoned and released only after paying a large fine. It was then, as a blind man, twice widowed, in a state where the fight for liberty had been lost, that he returned to his abandoned epic.

In his final years, Milton lived a mostly quiet life in London. He was goaded in print by vengeful Royalists but unable to respond and thereby, in doing so, draw dangerous attention to himself. This meant he had to focus on writings that would find readers beyond his own political camp. Most importantly, it allowed time to write poetry. In *Paradise Lost*, Milton describes composing the poem thanks to 'nightly visitation' by his muse.[21] He would hold the poem in his mind until morning, when one of the young men who served as his secretaries was there to write it down. Milton referred to this, rather disgustingly, as being 'milked'. Composing this ten-thousand-word epic poem while being unable to see it on the page was an extraordinary feat of mental gymnastics and it came at a significant personal cost.

In those years, Milton forced his daughters, Mary and Deborah, to read to him (the eldest, Anne, was excused because of a speech impediment).[22] They apparently read to him in languages including Hebrew, Syriac, Greek, Latin, Italian, Spanish, and French, which they could pronounce but not understand.[23] This was the invisible labour behind *Paradise Lost*, and eventually, it became intolerable for them. In 1662, Milton's daughters got their revenge. They conspired with a maidservant to sell their blind father's books.[24] When he found out, their relationship began to disintegrate. Soon after, he married for a third time, and his daughters didn't like their new stepmother. Eventually, he arranged for them to be sent away – to work for other families. While Milton was finishing his great epic, his family was falling apart.

When the plague came to London, in 1665, Milton rented a cottage in the village of Chalfont St Giles. That summer, he finished *Paradise Lost*. It was first published in 1667, and then again in July 1674, reorganised from ten books to twelve. This would be its final form, for Milton died that November and was buried in the church of St Giles. After his death, *Paradise Lost* did become the enduring monument that the young poet had hoped to create, although its afterlife was wildly different from anything he could have expected. What was it about the poem that made this possible?

In the opening lines of *Paradise Lost*, the poet implores his muse to guide his writing. Milton believed that *Paradise Lost* was inspired by a divine spirit. But if repeating Christian truths were all this poem did, it would hardly have had such a deep influence among so many non-Christian readers. There is in *Paradise Lost* something that has granted it a long afterlife in the modern world. The end of the invocation hints at it. Milton says to his muse:

> What in me is dark
> Illumine, what is low raise and support,
> That to the height of this great argument
> I may assert the eternal providence
> And justify the ways of God to men. (I:22–6)

Consider the phrase: 'What in me is dark / Illumine'. The way it's split across two lines creates a moment of suspense. We might wonder: what in him *is* dark? This could refer to the poet's capacity for sin. Milton could be asking his muse to expose his sins and, in doing so, redeem them. But darkness in this poem isn't necessarily a bad thing. Later in *Paradise Lost*, Milton refers to God's 'Dark Materials' (II:916). This inner darkness could also be divine.

In the English Renaissance, some works of literature were referred to as dark writing. Edmund Spenser said that his epic poem, *The Faerie Queene* (1590), made use of a 'dark conceite'.[25] He was talking about allegory, a kind of fiction that signifies some other meaning, often a spiritual or political one. Allegories were written darkly, requiring the reader to think carefully about what they might signify. Dark writing could also refer more generally to the ambiguities of poetic language. In his famous *Defense of Poesy* (1595), Philip Sidney wrote 'there are many mysteries contained in poetry, which of purpose were written darkly, lest by profane wits it should be abused'.[26] This intentionally obscure way of writing means that superficial readers ('profane wits') will not be able to gain easy access to its truth. It could also be prophetic: someone uttering dark words would not necessarily know what they had said, and it would remain for others to decipher them. Because *Paradise Lost* was divinely inspired, it gave voice to something that the poet wasn't fully in control of, which might only be understood by his readers. Its poetic darkness would prove crucial to its enduring life.

Paradise Lost went out into a world that was undergoing a transformation. The culture of humanism – reading classical texts to discover knowledge – gradually gave way to a culture of experimentation and observation. Across Europe, scientists were trying to defend knowledge from the wars of religion of the sixteenth and early-seventeenth centuries. The findings of Copernicus, Galileo, and Kepler reshaped visions of the universe. Founded in 1660, the Royal Society of London for Improving Natural Knowledge promoted a newly codified method of producing scientific truths, and the discoveries of Boyle, Hooke, and Newton transformed the understanding of matter. There was an increasing confidence that nature could be manipulated, made more plentiful and accommodating. Rejecting an unchanging, traditional society, philosophers – during what we now know as the Enlightenment – insisted that society could be improved in infinite ways. With its emphasis on freedom, political revolution, and scientific discovery, *Paradise Lost* was well suited to the Enlightenment but it also spoke to the other side of the times.

Milton's epic followed the fortunes of empire. In 1600, England was still a relative backwater on the edge of the Continent, its language rarely spoken outside its borders. It had colonised Ireland, Wales, and small patches of North America, but little more. Then, during the seventeenth century, it gained territory across the Caribbean, most importantly the sugar colonies of Barbados and Jamaica, and began to claim a larger share in global trade. The Royal Africa Company, founded in 1660, secured England's share in the Atlantic slave trade, and the East India Company established lucrative monopolies on trade with Asia. By the time of Milton's death, England was a superpower to rival the gold-rich empires of Spain and Portugal. Epic had been important to other empires, so England had to have its own epic poet.[27] It couldn't be Shakespeare, who never wrote an epic, and no one else in the seventeenth century had written anything close to *Paradise Lost*, so it had to be the more controversial Milton.[28] His poem may not have been openly imperialistic, but its influence was carried by the ships taking England's language, religion, and politics across the globe.

In the eighteenth century, *Paradise Lost* became a classic. Many of the most influential writers wrestled with its influence. This was a bit like Peter Pan trying to stick down his own shadow: Milton had done so much to define success that a writer had to be like him and not like him at the same time. The critic Joseph Addison said: 'Our language sunk under him', as if Milton were a monster dragged on to a boat that proved too small to bear it.[29] Towards the end of the century, however, something more extraordinary happened. *Paradise Lost* was taken up by people participating in revolutions in America and France. If at first those revolutions appeared to be faithful to the aims of the English Republic, they soon went further, demanding rights for the working classes, for women, for slaves. As those revolutions changed their societies, *Paradise Lost* mutated. It mirrored the new contradictions of the times. Women read Milton as both an antagonist and a spur to gender equality. Scientists thought about his account of Creation as they came up with groundbreaking theories. Satanist priests fell under the sway of a Christian poem.

Some modern critics claimed that epic poetry had become impossible as the stability of modern nation states made the heroic action that epic depended on increasingly outmoded.[30] But countless modern readers, especially those living in proximity to revolutionary change, used Milton's poem to recognise something epic in their own lives. And in return, they gave it new life.

★

For a long time, I was afraid of Milton. As an undergraduate, I had to read *Paradise Lost* and write an essay about it in the space of a week. I left it too late, which meant I had to read the entire poem – all 10,565 lines of it – in a single day. I should say that my eyes passed over it because I hardly read it at all. I was left only with the impression that the ending was the most beautiful piece of writing I had ever read. I remained intrigued by Milton and his part in the revolutionary Civil War, and some years later, I decided to write a chapter of my PhD about him. But I soon found that I couldn't bring myself to take on *Paradise Lost* and the mountain of criticism devoted to it. Milton, with his inexhaustible lust for learning, had defeated me.

Then, in 2018, I was teaching in a prison in New Jersey. It was a class for incarcerated students working towards their BA. I was there as a volunteer, while in the penultimate year of my PhD. In the first session, I gave the students one of Shakespeare's sonnets. When we came to discuss it, I mentioned metre, the system of rhythm used in traditional English poetry. Several students said they wanted to learn more about metre. I wasn't sure why: maybe they believed it would be necessary to get a good grade, or maybe they were just curious about this unfamiliar system of rhythm. The next week, I brought in some examples of metrical poetry, including the opening lines of *Paradise Lost:*

> Of man's first disobedience, and the fruit
> Of that forbidden tree, whose mortal taste
> Brought death into the world, and all our woe (I:1–3)

I wrote the first two lines on the blackboard and explained how its metre, known as iambic pentameter, alternates between unstressed and stressed syllables, with five stresses (or beats) in each line. I wrote a mark above each one:

/ / / / /
Of man's first dis-o-be-dience, and the fruit
/ / / / /
Of that for-bi-dden tree, whose mor-tal taste

I asked the class to read it aloud with me, and together we emphasised the stressed syllables like a tuneless choir. I had no idea what they might make of this rather abstract exercise, but as soon as I had finished explaining it, a student – I will call him Mark – put his hand up. The first line is disobedient, he said simply. I asked him to explain. To follow the metre, Mark continued, the reader must choose whether to confine 'dis-o-be-dience' to four syllables or else say 'dis-o-be-di-*ence*' and in doing so disrupt the order of the line.

It was a brilliant insight. Freedom is not only a theme of *Paradise Lost*, Milton tells us, it is embedded in the very experience of reading it. In a 'Note on the Verse', which acts as a brief introduction to *Paradise Lost*, he explains why he decided to write in unrhymed iambic pentameter. He says rhyme is a kind of 'bondage', a trivial sing-song effect that restricts what the poet can say. Besides, Milton says, many of the best poems – the epics of Homer and Virgil – didn't rhyme. Because of this, his decision to write unrhyming iambic pentameter, also known as 'blank verse', was restoring an 'ancient liberty' to poetry.[31] The fact that Mark had seen this, in the smallest fragment of *Paradise Lost*, made me think about Milton's poem in a new way.

It was only when I had to teach *Paradise Lost* that I read it properly. It was an undergraduate seminar at Princeton and the students were not only English majors, but also students majoring in computer science, economics, and maths. Now that I had to help others to understand it, I found the poem easier to understand. I was struck by the pleasure my students received from *Paradise Lost*, and I found it easier to enjoy myself. That year, Milton's visions of Hell, Heaven, and Eden began to invade my imagination. When the pandemic broke out, I had moved back to England, having finished my PhD. The one temporary job I had lined up quickly evaporated, so I was unemployed. One thing I knew how to do was teach *Paradise Lost*. Thinking of how much my students had seemed to enjoy it, I decided to run an online seminar – which I advertised to friends and acquaintances. Enough people wanted to take it that I ended up teaching *Paradise Lost* five days per week, for the next three months. By the time the seminar had finished, the poem had suffused my whole world. I noticed its influence everywhere: in the novels I was reading and the films I watched. I found out about Malcolm X's interpretation and learnt how Milton had influenced the American

Founding Fathers. I realised that Mark's brilliant response to it wasn't an anomaly. This poem could still speak vividly to contemporary readers.

Because of his role as a champion of Parliament in the English Civil War, sometimes claimed to be the first modern revolution, Milton has been a cornerstone of the Western political tradition, and his epic tells a story about the crises and contradictions of that tradition. One book could never hope to follow the spores of its influence everywhere in the world that it has migrated. Instead, I focus on twelve readers (or groups of readers):

Thomas Jefferson (1743–1826): polymath, lawyer, politician, and second President of the USA

William Wordsworth (1770–1850) and Dorothy Wordsworth (1771–1855): siblings, poets, and leading exponents of the English Romantic movement

Baron Vastey (1781?–1820): anti-colonial philosopher and secretary to Henri Christophe, the first King of post-revolutionary Haiti

George Eliot (1819–80): Victorian novelist, translator, and critic

James Redpath (1833–91): radical abolitionist, journalist, and proprietor of the *Weekly Anglo-African*

The Mistick Krewe of Comus (founded 1856): a secret carnival society in New Orleans

Virginia Woolf (1882–1941): modernist novelist and critic

Hannah Arendt (1906–75): German philosopher, Jewish refugee activist, and Cold War liberal

Malcolm X (1925–65): American Muslim minister and Black nationalist leader

C. L. R. James (1901–89): Trinidad-born historian and Trotskyist agitator

Jordan Peterson (1962–): Canadian psychologist, professor, and internet celebrity

The students in my class at a New Jersey prison, 2018–19

Each chapter looks at one of these encounters, describing how *Paradise Lost* illuminated their world. We also follow the poem's story, exploring some of its most important, beautiful, and disturbing passages, so that someone who hasn't read *Paradise Lost* can understand.

The story begins with the American, French, and Haitian revolutions, then goes on to consider other political transformations, including the American Civil War, the women's movement, and the Cold War. It also considers revolutions that were primarily cultural, including Romantic poetry, New Orleans' Mardi Gras, and modernism. Some of the readers are radicals but others are conservative, liberal, and ambivalent. *Paradise Lost* encourages some of them to revolutionary acts, but it discourages others. These encounters are as varied as the readers themselves, but one thing is consistent: they use Milton's epic to grasp something about their world. In telling their stories, this book describes how literature has played a part in the long struggle born of the belief that the fundamental human condition is one of freedom.

1. Thomas Jefferson Isolates Himself

It begins in darkness with a creature in excruciating pain. We don't know who it is, or where it is languishing, not yet fully conscious. At this point, all the reader knows is that we are in a place that is deep and dark. Like the creature, waking without memory, the reader needs to know what has happened.

> Him the almighty power
> Hurled headlong flaming from th' ethereal sky (I:44–5)

For now, the creature is only called 'he'. He has been condemned to a cruel punishment by an 'Almighty Power'. Looking around him, the creature sees:

> A dungeon horrible, on all sides round
> As one great furnace flamed, yet from those flames
> No light, but rather darkness visible (I:61–3)

The creature is bound in chains, scalded by an intense heat. He sees his second-in-command lying nearby, and it's only now that we are told the name of this poem's protagonist. It's not the name he had in Heaven but one he took on after raising a rebellion against God, a name that comes from the Hebrew word for 'adversary': Satan.

Paradise Lost begins in this peculiar state of anonymity. The delay in naming Satan means we know his punishment before his crime. The poem invites us to empathise with what he is feeling before we judge him. Satan recognises his second-in-command, Beelzebub, beside him. This sight causes Satan to utter a speech of tragic grandeur:

> Oh how fallen! how changed
> From him, who in the happy realms of light
> Clothed with transcendent brightness didst outshine
> Myriads though bright (I:84–7)

Satan remembers Beelzebub in Heaven, fighting 'Myriads' of good angels, and outshining all of them. Now he is ruined, and Satan acknowledges it is his fault. But soon he turns to strategy. Satan tells Beelzebub that their fallenness is a change in appearance only. He calls his enemy a tyrant and declares that their rebellion had 'shook his throne' (I:105).

Anyone who knows anything about the life of John Milton will recognise that this plot recalls the revolutionary Civil War that shook the English King's throne in the 1640s and succeeded in toppling him. The earliest readers of *Paradise Lost* noticed that the devils loomed curiously large in it. In 1670, an Anglican priest called John Beale remarked that it contained 'long blasphemies of devils'.[1] The disapproving Beale put this down to Milton's own radicalism. For when Satan speaks, what comes out of his mouth are arguments similar to those that Milton had made in his own career as a propagandist for the English Republic. This similarity means that Satan makes a special demand on the reader: *Sympathise with me*. This is one reason Milton's poem has so persistently appeared in later revolutionary moments. When, in the 1770s, a rebellion broke out in England's North American colonies, some remarked that the rebels resembled Milton's Satan. But the American Revolution brought *Paradise Lost* to life in a new way because the revolutionaries themselves were reading it.

Thomas Jefferson was born on his family's plantation in Virginia in 1743. His father died when he was fourteen, expressing a final wish that his son receive a classical education. The boy was sent to study with the classicist James Maury, who may have advised that he begin keeping a commonplace book.[2] This was a time-honoured practice for ambitious readers, marking out passages that seemed useful or beautiful. Jefferson's commonplace book includes passages from philosophy, history, and poetry, in ancient Greek, Latin, and English. There are forty-seven passages from Milton, more than any other English poet, and Jefferson would carry them in his memory for the rest of his life.

Jefferson wasn't unique in his devotion to Milton. In the eighteenth century, an age of neoclassical tastes, Milton's ability to imitate ancient poetry was revered, and critics gilded his poetry with superlatives:

it was the most beautiful, noblest, sublimest. According to one critic, 'Milton occupied a place, not only in English literature but in the thought and life of Englishmen of all classes, which no poet has held since and none is likely to hold again.'[3] *Paradise Lost* was used to teach children grammar and young men public speaking, as an advice manual for married couples and priests. For some readers, it was not only a guide to the Bible, but a substitute for it, and details that Milton had invented were sometimes even mistaken for the real thing. In an increasingly secular society, where scripture was reduced to the status of human literature and literature was raised to the status of inspired scripture, *Paradise Lost* managed to be both. But not everyone was able to forget Milton's disturbing politics. The philosopher Edmund Burke described Milton's poem as 'dark, uncertain, confused, terrible, and sublime to the last degree'.[4] The sublime, an aesthetic caused by encounters with things that are vast, terrifying and unknowable, was associated with periods of political turbulence.

When Milton died, his cause was at its lowest ebb. If England was anything to go by, modern republics simply didn't work. A decade later, however, this changed. The new English King, James II, threatened to return England to Catholicism. So a group of elite Protestants invited the Dutch Prince, William of Orange, to take the throne. The Glorious Revolution of 1688 established a new balance of power between King and Parliament, paving the way for England's current constitutional monarchy. The critic William Hazlitt wished Milton had been alive to see the moment when the King's power was curbed for good, assuming he would have approved.[5] In the years after 1688, the English ruling class split into two factions and Milton's reception was no less divided. The conservative Tories denounced him as a 'king-killer', whereas the liberal Whigs were quietly influenced by his writings on liberty, but didn't want to be openly associated with him.[6] Others venerated Milton precisely for his radical politics. In London, a mysterious Calves' Head Club convened to celebrate King Charles I's death day. They were said to feast on calves' heads, swearing an oath on a copy of Milton's works.[7] One of the most important readers of Milton was the Irish freethinker John Toland. After being exiled from Ireland for writing a book against the sacraments, Toland moved to London. There, he produced an edition of Milton's political writings, and wrote a biography to remind the English that their great poet had been a radical. These efforts were crucial to ensuring that the radical Milton arrived in America.

Milton had been read in England's North American colonies during his lifetime. His friend Roger Williams became the founder of Rhode Island, where he implemented some of the reforms that Milton had championed. In Puritan Massachusetts, the witch-hunter Cotton Mather owned Milton's books. In the eighteenth century, it was less his religious views and more his political republicanism that meant Milton weighed down the desks of America's future revolutionaries. The passages from *Paradise Lost* that Jefferson copied into his commonplace book reflect both a personal and a political interest. In the early 1760s, Jefferson was recovering from the deaths of his father and his sister, and he copied passages about death and grief. In 1762, he was courting Rebecca Burwell, and his commonplace book also includes passages about romance and gender, including a penetrating question by Milton's Adam: 'Among Unequals what Society / Can sort, what Harmony or true Delight?' (II:383–4) If Adam and Eve are not equals, how can they be true companions? This question would later prove to be grimly significant for Jefferson.

But Jefferson's main interest was in the demonic. In 1762, he wrote a letter full of references to the Devil. While he was staying at his sister's house, rats had eaten some of Jefferson's valuable possessions, and a leak in the roof had destroyed a picture of his beloved Rebecca Burwell. Incensed, he wrote to a friend: 'I am sure if there is such a thing as a devil in this world, he must have been here last night and have had some hand in contriving what happened to me.'[8] The word 'if' is significant. Like other freethinkers, Jefferson was sceptical of the existence of the Devil: a few years later, at a meeting of American legislators, someone proposed an Act of Parliament against Devils, and it was laughed out of the room.[9] Satan was not necessarily real, but he would still prove influential.

Jefferson's commonplace book shows a marked interest in Satan. Of the twenty-nine passages from *Paradise Lost*, eleven are about him. Jefferson copied down this passage from Satan's first speech:

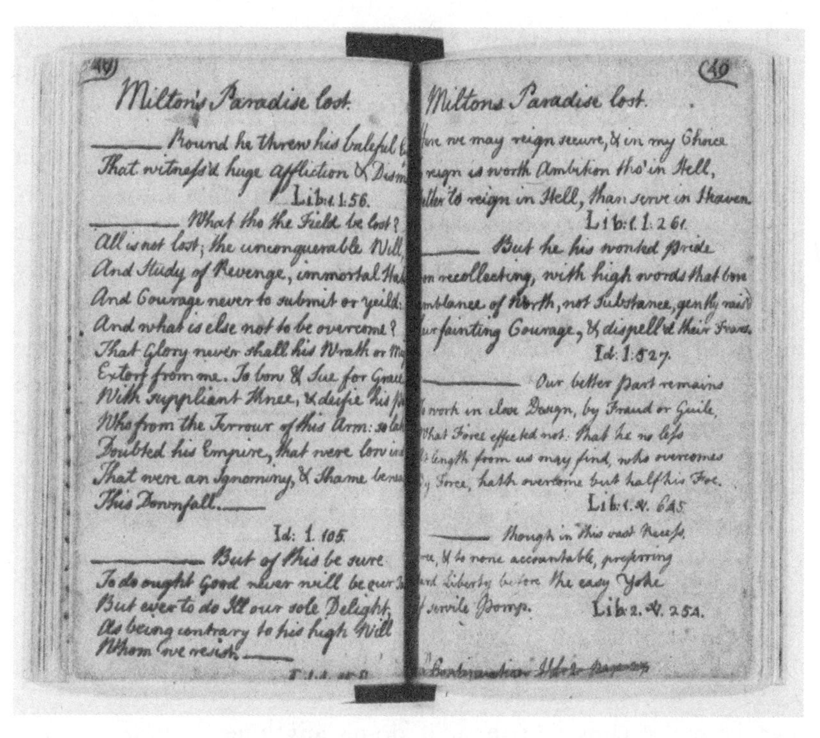

Milton's Paradise lost.

——— Round he threw his baleful
That witness'd huge affliction & Dism
Lib. 1:56.
——— What tho the Field be lost?
All is not lost; the unconquerable Will,
And Study of Revenge, immortal Hat
And Courage never to submit or yeild:
And what is else not to be overcome?
That Glory never shall his Wrath or M
Extort from me. To bow & Sue for Grac
With suppliant Knee, & deifie his
Who from the Terrour of this Arm: so la
Doubted his Empire, that were low in
That were an Ignominy, & Shame bene
This Downfall. ———
Id: 1. 105.
——— But of this be sure
To do ought Good never will be our
But ever to do Ill our sole Delight,
As being contrary to his high Will
Whom we resist. ———

Miltons Paradise lost.

ere we may reign secure, & in my Choice
reign is worth Ambition tho' in Hell,
tter to reign in Hell, than serve in Heaven.
Lib. 1. l. 261.
——— But he his wonted Pride
recollecting, with high words that bore
mblance of Worth, not Substance, gently rais'd
ur fainting Courage, & dispell'd their Fears.
Id. 1:527.
——— Our better part remains
work in close Design, by Fraud or Guile,
What Force effected not: that he no less
length from us may find, who overcomes
y Force, hath overcome but half his Foe.
Lib. 1. v. 645
——— though in this vast Recess,
e, & to none accountable, preferring
d Liberty before the easy Yoke
servile Pomp. Lib. 2. v. 254.

Passages from *Paradise Lost* copied out by Thomas Jefferson in his commonplace book (*c.* 1756–62).

> What though the field be lost?
> All is not lost; the unconquerable will,
> And study of revenge, immortal hate,
> And courage never to submit or yield:
> And what is else not to be overcome? (I:105–9)

It is a statement of absolute undying determination, and it's easy to see why an ambitious young man would find it useful. You might notice that 'immortal hate' sounds less healthy, but overlooking little details like that, it would be easy to be seduced by these sublime speeches. But what did Jefferson see in these lines? The early 1760s was a time of defiance, when laws passed by the British Parliament were increasingly unwelcome in Virginia. Did Jefferson intuit that Satan's enemy, the distant tyrant, bore some resemblance to the King of Britain? Or did he simply admire Satan's deathless commitment? Later events would make the connection between Milton's Hell and America unavoidable.

Jefferson wasn't the only young American reading *Paradise Lost* in those years. Two other men who would later number among America's most famous revolutionaries were also admirers of Milton. Like Jefferson, Benjamin Franklin and John Adams read Milton not only as a great poet but as the champion of a republican tradition stretching back to Ancient Greece and Rome, revived in Renaissance Florence and revolutionary England, which they would bring back to life in America.[10] A legal student in Massachusetts daydreaming about his future, Adams marvelled at Milton in his diary:

> A hazy, dull Day. Reading Milton. That mans Soul, it seems to me, was distended as wide as Creation. His Powr over the human mind was absolute and unlimited. His Genius was great beyond Conception, and his Learning without Bounds. I can only gaze at him with astonishment, without comprehending the vast Compass of his Capacity.[11]

The young Adams despaired of doing anything of note himself, lamenting that his mind was 'in as great Confusion, and wild disorder, as Miltons Chaos'.[12] Several years later, he was impressed by a young woman who wanted to talk about Milton and other literary authors.[13] Not too impressed, fortunately, so he could marry Abigail Smith, who became his guide and confidante, and shared his habit of seeing the world through *Paradise Lost*.

In the early 1760s, Benjamin Franklin was visiting the Royal Society in Piccadilly, London. A printer, scientist, and inventor, Franklin's experiments had made him famous across Europe and he had recently been elected a member of the prestigious society. One day, Franklin noticed Thomas Hollis, a wealthy merchant, looking at him across the room. Hollis was too shy to approach the great American scientist, but he later sent Franklin a copy of Toland's *Life of Milton* as well as expensive folios of Milton's works.[14] These were not innocent gifts: Hollis was a radical trying to foment a republican revolution by writing, editing, funding, and distributing books. In the 1750s, he had realised that America was more fertile ground for his efforts than

Britain, and he started to build relationships with the men capable of reforming the colony.

Franklin didn't need to be encouraged: as a young man, he had written out his own private liturgy, and it included a prayer said by Milton's Adam and Eve; as a printer, he had typeset, published, funded, bought, and sold editions of Milton; after Milton was accused of plagiarism, Franklin was relieved to see 'our great Poet vindicated'.[15] In 1759, he had a copy of Milton by his bed. Nevertheless, Hollis was clearly on the right track. In 1764, Harvard's library was destroyed in a fire, so he sent boxes of books in a ship across the Atlantic, hoping to inspire young republicans in New England. That same year, he defended Milton against a Royalist critic, who claimed *Paradise Lost* was an expression of remorse for the English Civil War.[16] After Hollis's death, his adoptive son, Thomas Brand Hollis, continued his work. The two men appear in a painting by Canaletto: the older man resplendent in a bright yellow coat, the younger man caught in his shadow. They hoped their flood of books would help prepare America for revolution, and they were right.

In the 1760s, as tensions mounted between the British Parliament and its American colonies, Jefferson was studying law and reading prodigiously. While the law gave him 'a view of the dark side of humanity', he said that poetry allowed him 'to qualify it with a gaze on the bright side'.[17] But *Paradise Lost* did both, expressing his highest aspirations and darkest secrets. In 1764, he bought a gilt edition of Milton's works for £1, part of a collection lost when in 1770 his family home burnt down. By then, construction had already begun on Monticello, the neoclassical villa on a mountain in Virginia. It was designed by Jefferson and its location is said to have been inspired by Milton's mountain-top Paradise.[18] After joining the Virginia legislature in 1769, Jefferson remained obsessed with poetry. In 1770, he began to court Martha Wayles Skelton, writing letters to her in the 'Miltonic style', according to a friend who had read one.[19] The letters were destroyed, so we don't know what that sounded like, but Jefferson may have drawn on the deeply romantic passages in *Paradise Lost*, such as one where Eve tells Adam: 'With thee conversing I forget all time' (IV:639). They were married on New Year's Day 1772.

Jefferson's home, Monticello, in the Piedmont region of Virginia. He is said to have been inspired by Milton to situate it on a mountaintop.

At the outbreak of war with Britain and the thirteen American colonies, in April 1775, references to Milton in American political writings begin to sprout like mushrooms after rainfall. In early 1776, a pamphlet called *Common Sense* was published in Philadelphia. Written by a recent migrant from Kent, Thomas Paine, it rallied Americans to the cause of independence. Paine condemned the possibility of peace with a quotation from *Paradise Lost:* 'never can true reconcilement grow where wounds of deadly hate have pierced so deep'.[20] Milton's authority seemed to confirm that there could be no peace between Britain and America. What Paine doesn't mention is that these words come from one of Milton's devils. An iconoclast at heart, he likely didn't care.

Several months later, as delegates from the thirteen colonies met at the Second Congressional Congress to discuss the war, an anonymous pamphlet called *Thoughts on Government* was published. It outlined the basis for a republican constitution. Even while it did so, its author complained that the English held republicans like Milton in such contempt that 'No small fortitude is necessary to confess that one has read them.'[21] For this reason, he wished to remain anonymous. Soon, however, his identity became known: it was the delegate from Massachusetts, John Adams. One evening after that, Paine visited Adam's apartment to discuss their different visions of the American republic. Adams told Paine he didn't approve of his iconoclastic use of Bible quotations in *Common Sense*; 'he laughed, and said he had taken his Ideas in that part from Milton'.[22] Paine had used Milton to put scripture at the service of revolution. By 1776, Milton had become American.

The Continental Congress eventually agreed that reconciliation with Britain was impossible. In June 1776, they tasked Thomas Jefferson with writing the document that would announce their independence. The thirty-three-year-old Jefferson was chosen because he represented Virginia, the most populous colony, and because – in the words of John Adams – 'you can write ten times better than I can'.[23] To do this, Jefferson retreated to the parlour of a house in Philadelphia where, for seventeen days, he composed a document of just over a thousand words. He showed a draft to Franklin and Adams. Then, they presented it to the Congress, who debated it word by word, and finally voted to approve it. It became official on 4 July: 'The unanimous Declaration of the thirteen united States of America'. This being done, a new nation was created.

The Declaration was designed to easily gain the assent of the Congress and it succeeded by articulating thoughts that the majority of free American men would agree with. It opens by setting out the principles on which the colonies were seeking independence from Britain. Jefferson presented them as a statement of the obvious:

> We hold these truths to be self-evident, that all men are created equal, that they are endowed by their Creator with certain unalienable Rights, that among these are Life, Liberty and the pursuit of Happiness.[24]

In fact, these truths were by no means 'self-evident'. (The philosopher David Hume, for one, rejected the belief that rights could be natural.) Jefferson later claimed that he didn't consider other writers when preparing the Declaration because he didn't want to be either too original or too derivative.[25] But as he isolated himself, voices flooded in: not only those of living Americans but also those of the dead. Jefferson later admitted that the Declaration drew on 'Aristotle, Cicero, Locke, Sidney Etc' – both ancient and modern theorists of republican government. But its famous opening words come closest to a pamphlet by Milton.

The Tenure of Kings and Magistrates is Milton's most radical political tract. It argues for the right of a people to overthrow their king, an argument founded on the idea that all men enjoy natural rights. Like Jefferson, Milton claims that this is common sense. He writes: 'No man who knows aught [anything] can be so stupid to deny that all men naturally were born free, being the image and resemblance of God himself.'[26] These are strikingly similar to Jefferson's words: 'We hold these truths to be self-evident, that all men are born equal.' An earlier version of Jefferson's statement is even closer: 'We hold these truths to be *sacred and undeniable*.' (It's thought to have been changed by Franklin, who told Jefferson to leave God out of it.) Was Jefferson, when he wrote the opening to the Declaration of Independence, intentionally echoing Milton's king-killing treatise? We don't know if Jefferson read *The Tenure of Kings and Magistrates*. If he did, he might have wanted to avoid mentioning it, since he wasn't proposing to kill the King of England, only to secede from his realm.

Yet Jefferson was certainly influenced by Milton's political writings. Just a year after the Declaration, Jefferson read two of Milton's political pamphlets, *Of Reformation in England* (1641) and *The Reason of Church-Government* (1642), in Toland's 1698 edition. At that time, Jefferson was drafting a 'Statute for Religious Freedom' for the constitution of Virginia. It was an important attempt to establish a clear separation between church and state, as well as a fulfilment of independent America's distinction from Britain, where the monarchy and national church were intertwined. Jefferson wanted the United States to tolerate different forms of worship, rather than imposing a state religion on its citizens. He wrote that truth 'is the proper and sufficient antagonist to error, and has nothing to fear from the conflict'.[27] This is a close echo of an image of truth as a female warrior in Milton's pamphlet on freedom of the press, *Areopagitica*, and Jefferson's proposal to separate church and state was also close to Milton's own thinking. Jefferson must have seen himself in the young Milton – he was virtually the same age as the poet had been at the outset of the English Civil War – as he shaped the new American Republic.

In the 1780s, as the American ambassador in Paris, Jefferson returned to Milton. After a debate about poetry with the marquis de Chastellux, he wrote an essay, 'Thoughts on English Prosody'. Jefferson quotes Milton more than any other poet, repeating Milton's claim that unrhyming poetry is 'unfettered', meaning free to express itself more fully.[28] Later in the essay, Jefferson accuses Milton of 'servile' plagiarisms – for using whole sentences from the Book of Genesis.[29] But even this criticism follows Milton's insistence – in the 'Note on the Verse' – that poetry is a matter of liberty or bondage. Jefferson accepted Milton's argument that *Paradise Lost* was, in every unrhymed line, an expression of freedom. It seems likely that Milton's epic, as much if not more than his political prose, helped to make the need for revolution self-evident, forging associations between ideas and feelings, lending the high dignity of epic to the love of freedom and the hatred of tyranny. But it was a complicated legacy. For the first character in *Paradise Lost* to voice these revolutionary sentiments, and the one to do so most forcefully, is Satan.

Even as he lies on the burning lake in Hell, Satan refers dismissively to his enemy, the one who 'Sole reigning holds the tyranny of heaven' (I:124). This is a shocking blasphemy. You'd expect that from Satan, but what's more surprising is the fact that he sounds like Milton, inveighing against Charles I. It was traditional for Christian poets to use Hell as an opportunity for score-settling: Dante humbly put fewer of his personal enemies in Hell than his mediaeval predecessors.[30] In *Paradise Lost*, we have the exact opposite: Satan and the devils resemble Milton's former comrades. This is why Satan's speech against God comes close to Jefferson's words castigating the British tyrant. This similarity wasn't lost on Jefferson's enemies in Britain, who wrote satires in which they cast the American revolutionaries as devils in Hell.[31] But did Jefferson ever see himself in Milton's fiend? There's a reason to believe so, but it's personal rather than political.

As Jefferson isolated himself to write the Declaration, the person who brought him tea was Robert Hemings. The fourteen-year-old Hemings also helped the Founding Father to dress, shaved him, and served him at table.[32] He was Jefferson's relative by marriage, being the son of Jefferson's father-in-law, as well as his property. Jefferson's relationship to slavery is complicated: he included a sentence against the slave trade in the Declaration, which was taken out by the pro-slavery Georgian delegates. But Jefferson was a slave owner, the largest in his county, and abolishing the slave trade would actually have made his own slaves more valuable. However, he later drafted other laws that would gradually abolish slavery in large parts of America. In *Notes on Virginia* (1781–5), Jefferson attacks slavery as a corrupting influence on white people. He calls it 'tyranny' and says that it would take a miracle for a man to 'retain his manners and morals undepraved by such circumstances'.[33] He was speaking from personal experience.

During his presidency, Jefferson was accused of fathering children with one of his slaves: Robert's sister, Sally. The president's accuser was an unscrupulous journalist and the intention was clearly blackmail, so the rumours were treated with suspicion. But the truth descended among Sally Hemings's children, and DNA evidence has confirmed that Jefferson was the father of at least one of her children.[34] In 1783, the fourteen-year-old Sally had accompanied Jefferson's daughter to visit him in Paris, and it's thought to have been there that their relationship became sexual. Little more is known about it. We don't know what Sally Hemings thought of Jefferson, but other enslaved girls described their predatory masters as satanic tyrants.[35] Their relationship surely involved an act of 'tyranny', something that Jefferson himself recognised. As Milton asked, in the passage Jefferson copied into his commonplace book: what society can exist between people who are not equals? Some critics have suggested that Jefferson saw himself in Milton's Satan, with his declarations of independence in Hell.[36] But Satan – a revolutionary who turns out to be

Satan on the Burning Lake. Mezzotint engraving by John Martin (1825).

a tyrant – might have made Jefferson think of the contradiction between his public character and his private conscience. Milton's hypocritical Satan may have been a mirror.

Contradictions like these were not unusual among the champions of Western democracy. The valorisation of freedom as the central political value was born in ancient Greece, when the free condition of citizens was distinguished from that of the slaves they owned.[37] It was commonly said that English air was 'too pure for the slave to breathe', and this was enshrined in law in the famous Mansfield judgement of 1772, but slaves were still held on ships in English ports, fugitives transported back to the colonies, and auctions held on English soil, as the trade in human lives made the nation rich.[38] What was new in the seventeenth and eighteenth centuries was the claim that all men were equal, that freedom was their natural right. People who supported those claims had to explain why those same rights were denied to slaves. Some did so by way of racism, the doctrine of might is right, or the ideology that slavery was a benevolent institution. Others were unable to ignore the contradiction, and abolitionist organisations were established in Britain and America in the 1770s and 1780s. Meanwhile, uprisings by enslaved people showed that slavery was intolerable, inspiring fear and guilt in the colonial powers. The uprisings also changed the way people saw *Paradise Lost*.

Jamaica, July 1776

In Hanover Parish, a boy was found to have removed the bullets from his master's pistol, replacing them with balls of cotton covered in oil. Nearby, another plantation owner found black sand in his gun. He asked a neighbour to help investigate. They called for refreshments, and the man carrying the punch accidentally hit the bowl on the marble edge of a counter. The bowl broke, revealing, at the bottom, the unmistakable silt of arsenic. These incidents were taken as the signs of an impending uprising. There had been uprisings throughout the eighteenth century in the Caribbean, but this one was entangled with the American Revolution. For months, slave owners in Jamaica had debated the war between Britain and its American colonies. Over dinner, they had praised the revolution, spluttering about the tyrannical control that Britain wielded over its colonies. Behind the back of each diner stood a silent man, ready to serve but also able to understand. Then, on 3 July, the British regiment had joined a convoy bound for New England. It was the third regiment to leave the island that year, and the enslaved population were watching. Across the parish, hushed conversations were happening. On 6 August, the Governor of Jamaica reported 'we are now in the most imminent danger'.[39] The conspiracy seemed to have spread across forty estates, uniting field and household slaves, mixed-race 'Creoles', and maroons (former slaves living in autonomous communities). They intended, it was said, to wipe out all the white people on the island. Eventually, the uprising was suppressed but the news travelled.

The following year, Samuel Johnson was at a dinner in Oxford. He was a literary giant, as the compositor of the great English dictionary, but he was no establishment man. He grew up in modest circumstances in a provincial town and dropped out of university due to lack of funds, and he was not interested in kowtowing to professors. At dinner, Johnson proposed a toast: 'to the next insurrection of the negroes in the West Indies'.[40] If this was intended to shock his hosts, he was entirely sincere. He had long been a supporter of slave insurrections. One reason for this was Francis Barber, his manservant and intimate companion.[41] Barber had been a slave in Jamaica, so may have told his employer about the degradations slavery involved. Johnson remarked that slave owners would go to Hell, where they would find a climate similar to Jamaica's.[42] Johnson pointed out that many of the Americans making a fuss about liberty were also slave owners, and he believed that this same hypocrisy had wormed its way into *Paradise Lost*.

At that time, Johnson was working on a monumental series of fifty-two biographies, *Lives of the Most Eminent English Poets* (1779–81). This included an iconoclastic life of Milton, which shudders at the poet's 'puritanical savageness'.[43] Johnson sees *Paradise Lost* as a duty, declaring that 'No one ever wished it longer.'[44] But his deepest criticism is the same one he made of the American Revolution: 'they who most loudly clamour for liberty do not most liberally grant it'. Despite his concern with liberty, Milton had been guilty of a 'Turkish contempt of women'.[45] Despite this, Johnson admires Milton's accomplishments. He says that Milton succeeded in making Satan 'speak as a rebel, without any such expressions as might taint the reader's imagination'. Johnson didn't see Satan's speeches as blasphemies, but he certainly didn't sympathise with Milton's chief devil. There's no sign that Johnson made a connection between Satan and the West Indian slaves, but ten years later, a writer with more intimate knowledge of slavery would do exactly that.

Olaudah Equiano was the most famous African man in eighteenth-century England. He was an early champion of the abolitionist movement and wrote a celebrated autobiography, *The Interesting Narrative of the Life of Olaudah Equiano*.[46] The book describes his capture as a child in West Africa, being transported to America in the hold of a slave ship, his later career as a sailor, and how he arduously purchased his own freedom. Later, he settled in England, married, and converted to Christianity. In the book, published in 1789,

Equiano recalls approaching the Caribbean island of Montserrat. Dwindling sugar production had led the plantation owners to neglect it: provisions had become scarce, and discipline by the Irish overseers increasingly violent. (This led to an uprising on St Patrick's Day four years later.) Equiano had heard of the horrors of Montserrat, and as the ship approached, his terror mounted. Unable to describe it, he inserts these lines:

> Regions of sorrow, doleful shades, where peace
> And rest can rarely dwell. Hope never comes
> That comes to all, but torture without end
> Still urges . . . [47]

These unattributed lines come from Book I of *Paradise Lost*, and the dark ecology of Milton's poem gives words for the Hell of slavery.[48] Equiano alludes to Milton three more times, but without ever mentioning him by name. Did Equiano see a connection between Caribbean slavery and Milton's fallen angels? Like them, African slaves had been exiled from their home and cast into a terrible dungeon. But Equiano surely would not have compared African slaves to devils.[49] This, perhaps, is one reason Equiano doesn't mention the source of these lines. Whatever the intention, this ambiguous moment invites us to recognise something about *Paradise Lost* that many readers, before and since, have overlooked: the fallen angels are slaves.

We learn this when Beelzebub replies to Satan's first speech. Beelzebub is far less confident about their capacity to resist. He's willing to accept that God is all-powerful and wonders why God hasn't just killed them, why he has sent them to Hell.

> That we may so suffice his vengeful ire,
> Or do him mightier service as his thralls,
> By right of war, whate'er his business be
> Here in the heart of hell to work in fire,
> Or do his errands in the gloomy deep (I:148–52)

Having lost the War in Heaven, Beelzebub says, they are now God's 'thralls' – his slaves. In the ancient world, people became slaves by fighting on the losing side in a war, and being saved from death: this is known as 'war slavery'.[50] As God's slaves, Beelzebub wonders what labour they will have to do for God: his phrase 'work in fire' evokes the gold mines of Spanish America, or the hot fields of Jamaica and Barbados.

It is a testament to how vividly *Paradise Lost* spoke to readers that Thomas Jefferson, a slave owner, and Olaudah Equiano, a former slave, were both drawn to Satan's speeches. In a letter written in 1825, a year before his death, Jefferson quoted Satan's first dauntless speech, the same lines he had written in his commonplace book: 'All is not lost . . .'[51] But this quotation, like Equiano's use of Milton, betrays no sympathy for Milton's devils. There is no evidence that either man sympathised with Satan. Eighteenth-century readers didn't want to do that – at least not yet. Jefferson died, like a good patriot, on 4 July 1826, exactly fifty years after the Declaration of Independence. At his death, vast debts, incurred by his grand building projects, meant that 130 of his slaves were sold at the auction block into the merciless Southern slave market. In the decades after that, Jefferson's contradictions would come back to haunt America. Before that, Milton's revolutionary spirit migrated to France.

2. Dorothy Wordsworth Brings Her Brother an Apple

London, 1790

At around 8 a.m. on 4 August, two workmen disappeared into a hole near the altar of St Giles, Cripplegate. Down in the hole, the men pulled an old box into the daylight. Other men peered over their shoulders. The box had been sealed with lead but part of it had corroded, leaving a gap at one end. A pawnbroker called Laming then put an exploratory hand inside. Another man tried to pull the lead covering aside but it wouldn't give. They sent one of the workmen to fetch a mallet and chisel. He cut the box open, revealing the head and torso of what had once been a man, wrapped in a burial shroud. By this point, the air must have been thick with dust. Not just ordinary dust but the dust of the dead, that getting into your mouth, tells you: *I am what you one day will be*. Under the shroud, the corpse was well preserved, its ribcage still intact. One man tried to lift the cloth. Under his touch, the ribcage collapsed. Human form disintegrating into matter. The shock must have hit the men in their stomachs, jolting them out of their curiosity. They descended into a possessive frenzy, tearing the body of John Milton to pieces.

In 1674, Milton had been buried next to his father. After the church underwent alterations, the exact location of their coffins had been forgotten, but some parishioners had heard rumours from their grandparents. Then, in 1790, the church was undergoing repairs, so the vestry clerk and churchwarden decided to see for themselves if the rumoured location was true. On 3 August, they directed the workmen to dig, and in the chalky soil beneath the church floor, they found a wooden coffin and a leaden one. After washing them, they found that neither coffin bore an inscription: both were clearly old. Confident they had found what they were looking for, the men retired to Fountain's pub, where they got merry and started to boast about their discovery. Other drinkers expressed an interest in seeing the great poet's coffin, so they decided to meet again the next day.

We don't know what the men who gathered in St Giles church the following morning thought of Milton's poetry or his politics. The pub landlord Fountain pulled at the poet's teeth. When they didn't come out, someone else knocked them out with a stone. Laming took up the poet's entire lower jaw with his hands. He lifted the skull and saw underneath it hair combed and tied back. The coffin had been washed the previous day so the hair was wet and rotting. Word travelled, and crowds flocked to the church. The parish gravedigger let them in for a sixpence each as the day grew dark, striking a tinder-box to light the remains. People who didn't want to pay started climbing through the windows.

London was scandalised by the news. There were reports that the whole parish had been afflicted by a strange dental illness. One of the grave robbers felt himself grasped by a cold hand. The poet William Cowper cursed those who committed 'indecencies' against the divine poet.[1] Some insisted that the corpse wasn't Milton's, but a woman's. Three days later, a lawyer called Philip Neve visited the church. An amateur critic, who had written a book about Milton, he was appalled to hear what had happened. The tomb had now been shut up, but Neve interviewed the perpetrators, and later published his findings.[2] The indignant lawyer recovered some hair, a piece of skin, and a rib. He hoped to be able to reassemble the body, but by then it was too late. There was a flourishing black market in Milton's body. Several thousand people believed themselves to be in possession of his teeth.

The frenzy of the tomb robbers suggests that what happened was far from rational. During the early days of the Restoration, Milton had feared being torn apart by a Royalist mob, comparing himself to the ancient poet Orpheus, who was ripped to shreds by the Maenads, female followers of Dionysus. Now it had happened, not because of his radical politics but because of his fame as a poet. The poet Horace wrote of the *disjecta membra poetae*, 'the limbs of a dismembered poet', meaning the circulation of lines and phrases removed from their original context.[3] This was not necessarily a bad thing: when the poet's identity was still recognisable in a fragment of their work, it was a sign of their enduring reputation. Likewise, the dismemberment of Milton's corpse was the expression of reverence: his name was highly valuable and ordinary Londoners craved these fungible tokens. The breaking of his body – part eucharist, part riot – marks the beginning of a new age, in which the revolutionary poet was both a divinity and a scapegoat, who was torn apart because he had never died.

London in 1790 was gripped with the terror and exhilaration of revolutions, first in America and then in France. Milton was no less present in France than he had been in America. *Paradise Lost* had been translated into French in 1729, and the radical *philosophes* who challenged religious doctrine, paving the way for the French Revolution, saw him as a predecessor. Pierre Bayle described him as an enemy of kings, Voltaire put him on a par with Homer, and Rousseau called him 'the divine Milton'. Milton's political writings were summoned in the early days of the Revolution. In 1789, after social unrest, the King called a great assembly, the Estates General, where the people's representatives would meet with the nobles and the clergy to decide the future of the nation. One man dominated the proceedings: 'His immense mass of hair, his lion-like head, stamped with extreme ugliness, were astounding, almost frightful; nobody could take their eyes off him.'[4] This was Honoré Gabriel Riqueti, the comte de Mirabeau – the people's representative from Marseilles. Mirabeau had spent several years in England, where he was introduced to Milton's work. Now he saw France facing the same dilemma that England had in the 1640s: tyranny or liberty. Mirabeau translated two of Milton's pamphlets, and the first appeared on the eve of the Estates General: *Sur la liberté de la presse, imité de l'Anglois, de Milton.*[5] The second, published in 1792 after Mirabeau's death, was part of *Tenure of Kings and Magistrates*, but Milton's king-killing tract proved too radical and was suppressed by Mirabeau's friends. That year, the radical Jacobin club in Paris commissioned busts of eight 'friends of liberty', and Milton was one of them.[6] The English writer Helen Maria Williams – who attended debates at the Jacobin Club – recalled that the poet's name 're-echoed through the hall'.[7] If many readers in the eighteenth century had been content to see him as a poet, his politics had become unignorable.

The French Revolutionaries didn't only transform ideas about society. 'They found despotism in heaven', writes the historian Jules Michelet, so the traditional Christian God had to be overthrown.[8] The French Revolution had unsettled Christian myths – and *Paradise Lost* with them. Likewise, in England, radicals began to reimagine *Paradise Lost* in their own wild ways.

No one had a more involved relationship with Milton than the poet-printer William Blake. A friend visiting Blake at home in Lambeth discovered him and his wife Catherine naked in their summer house. The friend, aptly called Thomas Butts, reported that Blake said: 'Come in! It's only Adam and Eve, you know!'[9] The poet and his wife were acting out *Paradise Lost*. Blake later wrote a poem, entitled 'Milton' (1810), about a dream vision in which Milton emerged out of his foot. But it is in a book of heretical paradoxes, *The Marriage of Heaven and Hell* (1792), that Blake says something about *Paradise Lost* that has become the most famous modern interpretation of Milton:

> The reason Milton wrote in fetters when he wrote of Angels & God, and at liberty when of Devils & Hell, is because he was a true Poet and of the Devils party without knowing it.[10]

Milton unconsciously preferred Satan to God, Blake says, and this is why the most memorable parts of his poem are those devoted to Hell. In making this claim, Blake uses an image of slavery: fetters are shackles worn on one's feet. This is a reference to Milton's claim that rhyme is bondage, but in 1792, it would have called to mind the slaves fettered on British ships and British plantations in the Caribbean.[11] Blake's claim is an extraordinary one: Milton's mind was shackled when he wrote of God, but when he wrote about Satan, he achieved true freedom. In their uprisings, enslaved people had shown again and again that they would seek freedom at the greatest personal cost. It now seemed to abolitionists like Blake that slaves were the only people who were truly free.[12] This is why, to write his greatest poetry, Milton had to identify with God's slave, Satan. Reimagining Milton became part of a new poetic revolution in England, the leaders of which were Dorothy Wordsworth and her brother William.

★

Dorothy Wordsworth was born in 1771 in the Lake District, north-western England. After a happy early childhood, the death of her mother caused her to be separated from her three brothers. While they were sent to school, she was raised by relatives. She missed her older brother, William, most of all. Born a year apart, the two had a deep connection. While he studied at Cambridge, she helped raise her relatives' children. Despite this isolation, Dorothy developed an appreciation of great literature – her library included Homer, Shakespeare, and Milton – as well as a mature prose style. William recognised this, and one of his earliest poems, 'An Evening Walk', completed at the age of twenty-two, was dedicated to his 'sole sister'. In 1794, Dorothy went to stay with her brother at a friend's home in Dorset, and from then on, they were inseparable. Their relationship was the defining event of her life, the most important influence on his poetry, and it has long raised questions about incestuous desire.[13] It also meant that *Paradise Lost* took on a special significance.

William, who was setting out to become a great English poet, saw Milton as his most significant predecessor.[14] As a Cambridge student, he went to a gathering in the room at Christ's College where the temperate Milton had lodged as a student. William got drunker than ever before or after, then ran back to attend the compulsory evening church service at his own college, and inwardly pledged never again to dishonour his pure vocation.[15] In the summer of 1790, William visited France, intending to walk across the Alps. The day after he arrived was the anniversary of Bastille Day, a public holiday known as the Feast of the Federation, when the French King publicly acknowledged the people's representatives in the National Assembly. As an Englishman, William was welcomed, since many assumed that what was happening in France was going to be a constitutional revolution like England's Glorious Revolution of 1688. William later wrote of the breathless optimism of those times: 'Bliss was it in that dawn to be alive, / But to be young was very heaven!'[16] After graduating, he returned to France. He travelled to Orléans, intending to improve his French. There he had a relationship with a French Royalist, Annette Vallon, and she became pregnant. Wordsworth was still convinced that a revolution could bring an end to poverty. But

A miniature of Dorothy Wordsworth as a young woman by an unknown artist (early 1800s?). Given as a gift to her niece Dora, it remains in the possession of the Wordsworth family.

it was at that point the revolution turned to terror, with massacres throughout France. He left before Annette gave birth.

Back in England, William kept faith with the Revolution. He hoped to return to France, but they were now at war with Britain, making it all but impossible. In 1797, he and Dorothy went to stay in rural Somerset. Coleridge went to meet them, and it was there that they became 'three persons and one soul'.[17] Their bohemian way of life alarmed the locals, who believed they were radicals preparing for a French invasion. A government spy was sent to follow them, and recorded their eccentric habits: like the impressionist painters, who took their canvases out to paint *en plein air*, the three friends took their notepads out on their walks to record their impressions. Their poetry was effusive, sincere, and, when compared to the highly varnished work of their contemporaries, provocatively plain. At its most extreme, it looked like this:

> The cock is crowing,
> The stream is flowing,
> The small birds twitter,
> The lake doth glitter,
> The green field sleeps in the sun.[18]

This poem, which William apparently wrote in the fields, shows a reader how to look at the world as if for the first time, to see it without the opiate of habit. When published, it would earn him almost universal scorn.[19] Byron called the poem 'namby pamby'.[20] It may have seemed controversially new but William was also imitating Adam and Eve in *Paradise Lost*, who praise God in spontaneous effusions of blank verse.

Wordsworth and Coleridge wanted to revive the spirit of Milton's poetic revolution, liberating poetry from the constraints of custom. In 1798, they published *Lyrical Ballads*, a co-written volume. In its famous preface, Wordsworth proposes to abolish the artificial language and abstract concerns of eighteenth-century poetry, which were associated with the absolutist English monarchy. Instead, poets should fill their poems with 'the real language of men in a state of vivid sensation'.[21] Claims like this earned Wordsworth a reputation as a poetic Jacobin. But as the French Revolution foundered, he became less convinced by political violence. He came to believe that poetry could help to bring about a slower renovation of the human spirit, gradually changing the moral habits of its readers and then society itself. It would do so by taking 'effusions' of passionate words and giving them lasting form. William often used Dorothy to do this: his poem 'Lines Written a Few Miles above Tintern Abbey' describes visiting a landscape he had seen five years before, only this time, accompanied by Dorothy. He now sees it through her 'wild eyes'.[22] It was in Somerset that Dorothy started to keep a journal, documenting their daily activities and her own impressions of nature. This was something that she did for William, and possibly at his request. Her journals were a resource for his poetry: it was in those private pages that she recorded the daffodils which he turned into his famous poem. But Dorothy also made of her daily writings a private artwork, and one in which she, too, would imitate Milton.

In 1799, as Napoleon Bonaparte launched a coup in France, William and Dorothy returned to the Lake District. Prodigious walkers, they travelled there from County Durham, crossing the spine of England by foot. In a quiet part of the Lake District, they established their home. That corner of rural England became the resting place of Romantic poetry. It was where the Wordsworths' poetic revolution was preserved and where it faded away.

Thursday 6 May 1802 was a busy day at Dove Cottage, a small, whitewashed house in the village of Grasmere where Dorothy and William lived. In the morning, he was working in the garden, which runs up the steep hill behind the cottage. He was constructing a bower: a small, open timber hut adorned with climbing plants. At one o'clock, Dorothy came up to give him an apple. She sat on a seat he had constructed and preserved the moment in her journal, the phrases strung across by dashes, quick and vigorous, like the brush-strokes in an impressionist painting:

> The small Birds are singing – Lambs bleating, Cuckow calling – The Thrush sings by Fits, Thomas Ashburner's axe is going quietly (without passion) in the orchard – Hens are cackling, Flies humming, the women talking together at their doors – Plumb & pear trees are in Blossom, apple trees greenish – the opposite woods green, the crows are cawing. We have heard Ravens. The Ash Trees are in blossom, Birds flying all about us.[23]

Like Milton's Paradise, no violence is present in the garden: even their neighbour's axe is gentle. But this is a Paradise where time has entered. She adds: 'The primroses are passing their prime.' Even in early summer, there is the unmistakable sign of death.

William and Dorothy had been reading *Paradise Lost* together. In February 1802, she wrote in her journal: 'After tea I read aloud the 11th Book of Paradise Lost we were much impressed & also melted into tears.'[24] That spring, the influence of Milton's Eden streamed through their writings and daily doings. But it was Milton's Adam and Eve that shaped their life together.

In 1802, the influence of Milton's Eden streamed through their writings and daily doings. Inspired by Milton's poem, they play-acted as Adam and Eve. William and Dorothy's imitation of Milton's first couple was not unique – Blake did so with his wife in their summer house – but with them it carried the perfume of incest. Adam and Eve are not only husband and wife but also, in a sense, brother and sister. It might have been what led William to build a bower: it is where Adam and Eve sleep. This Paradise was threatened: later that year, William was to marry their friend Mary Hutchinson. Dorothy no doubt feared being replaced in his affections. Is that what she thought about, that afternoon, as she brought him an apple, thinking of Milton's Eve bringing Adam the apple and him deciding to Fall with her out of love? She recorded the Edenic moment in her journal: stealing the final months together before their life was changed for ever. That spring, her last alone with him, she wrote her most sumptuous prose.

William was married that October. On the morning of the ceremony, he and Dorothy said an emotional farewell, which she later recorded in her diary.

> I gave him the wedding ring – with how deep a blessing! I took it from my forefinger where I had worn it the whole of the night before – he slipped it again onto my finger and blessed me fervently.[25]

She couldn't bear to attend the ceremony. Marriage interrupted the fantasies that they had played out with the help of *Paradise Lost*. But they continued to live together. William's poetic ambitions were now supported by both his wife and his sister. Meanwhile, Dorothy continued to make her own wild observations in journals and letters.[26] In the years to come, when they received news from France – where Napoleon was accumulating power – they couldn't help but think of Milton's poem. For as we read on, Satan's character shifts like the many-coloured scales of a snake in the grass.

★

Dove Cottage in Grasmere, the home of Dorothy and William Wordsworth from 1799 to 1808.

Satan and Beelzebub lie on the burning lake. Angels are shapeshifters, but they don't seem to be able to morph out of their chains. As they talk, they hold their heads above the surface of the water, like two lizards in a jacuzzi. Satan's body is now described for the first time, and it's horrific:

> With head uplift above the wave, and eyes
> That sparkling blazed, his other parts besides
> Prone on the flood, extended long and large (I:193–5)

The phrase 'other parts' carries a hint of innuendo, as if inviting us to imagine Satan's genitals, bobbing up at the surface. Here, his angelic form has been reduced to a disgusting formlessness. After Satan's first dauntless speech, Milton has told us he is 'racked with deep despair' (I:126). He is like a spy in a radical movement, outwardly brave but secretly fearful.

Then, of a sudden, the two fallen angels rear up from their flaccid state. How is that possible? Milton has told us they were bound by 'adamantine chains' (I:48). In a cinema adaptation, Satan's ballooning biceps might strain against his bonds until they snap into fragments. He doesn't receive that satisfaction here. Instead, Milton gives us a mini sermon, telling us it was God who magicked away the chains so that he could 'Heap on himself damnation' (I:215) like a tourist at a bottomless buffet. Milton says Satan's evil is going to bring about goodness. He just doesn't know it yet, as he flies across the lake, the wind in his still-angelic hair. We are probably supposed to laugh at his pride, not realising he's the plaything of an all-powerful God. But a radical reader might view these invitations to mockery as a tyrant's propaganda. Empires tend to ridicule those who resist them. If Satan were the butt of every joke, *Paradise Lost* would be boring. Thankfully, whenever he appears ridiculous, Satan comes out with a line of immortal revolutionary grandeur.

The fallen angels reach land. Satan inspects his new home. Aristotle said the heroes of tragedies should fall from high places, and these angels have fallen from the highest place to the lowest, making this quantitatively speaking the most tragic event imaginable. Like a tech CEO contemplating child labourers in a mineral mine, Satan looks at the scene with feeling but soon he finds a way to accept it:

> Farewell happy fields
> Where joy for ever dwells: hail horrors, hail
> Infernal world, and thou profoundest Hell
> Receive thy new possessor (I:249–52)

Satan has an impressive ability to accept his lot. This could be a mindfulness technique for the twenty-first century as you scroll through the news: twenty 'hail horrors' every morning. As one forsaken by God, condemned to an existence of toil and suffering, without hope of redemption, Satan's condition has evoked sympathy in many modern readers because it is their own.

Satan seeks to reassure Beelzebub, telling him they will make a new home in Hell. He alchemises reasons to turn despair into hope:

> The mind is its own place, and in itself
> Can make a heaven of hell, a hell of heaven. (I:254–5)

Is this true? Can you really enjoy inner bliss in the midst of physical suffering? Satan sounds like one of the ancient Stoic philosophers, who claimed a man could burn alive without suffering if he had cultivated the correct attitude of indifference to the external world. Like many Christians, Milton thought Stoicism was nonsense, since it denied the God-given passions. But this statement is a powerful one. The Stoic philosopher Epictetus was a slave, and for many oppressed people, the idea of inner freedom has been preliminary to the belief in the revolutionary possibility of full freedom in this world. Satan's words are clothed in republican grandeur and they require a forensic attention from the reader. Can we trust what he says? Even his most famous line turns out to contain a seed of doubt:

> Here we may reign secure, and in my choice
> To reign is worth ambition though in hell.
> Better to reign in hell, than serve in heaven. (I:261–3)

The final word gives the line the possibility of an unstressed syllable at the end – '**Heav**-en'. This would break the metre, pulling the rug from under Satan's highfalutin' claim. But it would be a mistake to think of this as grounds for ridicule, for even his ruin is heroic.

Satan staggers across the burning ground, using a spear tall as a Norwegian pine as a crutch. He calls out to his army, who are lying stupefied on the lake: 'Awake, arise, or be for ever fall'n!' (I:330). Milton likes to use 'or' in misleading ways, to pose false dilemmas, and here the rebel angels appear to have a choice but in fact they are damned whatever they do. This command has an immediate effect. Up they spring and begin to move zombie-like across the lake. It is the kind of speech that human politicians can only dream of, rousing the masses with machine-like efficiency. As they move towards him across the black landscape, we are introduced to the twelve principal fallen angels: Moloch, Chemos, Baalim, Ashtaroth, Astarte, Thammuz, Dagon, Rimmon, Osiris, Isis, Horus, and Belial. Their original names have been erased from memory, so Milton calls them by the names they later take on as pagan gods. Thammuz, for example, is a god in Assyria, before being renamed Adonis and worshipped by women in ancient Israel by a love cult denounced by the prophet Ezekiel. Milton flexes his considerable learning while showing how pagan gods cause immorality. Milton must have felt a lot like the blind Ezekiel in the 1660s when he composed his prophetic poem amid the hedonism of Restoration London. As Satan watches his followers gather, his heart soars. Milton tells us that they are an army greater than all those, 'baptiz'd or infidel' (I:582), who fought in the Crusades. Comparing the Devil's followers to the Christian crusaders is surely one reason why Malcolm X saw *Paradise Lost* as a critique of white supremacy. But when he describes the demonic masses, Milton seems to get carried away.

As he faces his troops, Satan is no longer revolting but actually very sexy. His face, scarred by thunder and anxiety, is ruined but still beautifully proportioned, like a grizzled Hollywood star. Milton compares the radiant Satan to a solar eclipse:

> As when the sun new risen
> Looks through the horizontal misty air
> Shorn of his beams, or from behind the moon
> In dim eclipse disastrous twilight sheds
> On half the nations, and with fear of change
> Perplexes monarchs. (I:594–9)

Eclipses are bad omens – one was said to have foreshadowed the murder of the tyrant Julius Caesar – and this passage almost made the King's censor stop the poem from being published. William Wordsworth found this metaphor so sublime it made him feel faint. If you aren't seduced by this poetry, you aren't reading it right. Satan now tells them he has a plan. In Heaven, he says, there was a rumour (Heaven, naturally, is a place of thrilling gossip) that God planned to create a new world. They will go to that world and get their revenge. But first they must debate how to do it. The fallen angels mine the earth of Hell for ore with which to make a grand building: this is Pandaemonium, a name Milton coined, meaning 'place of all the devils'.

They all convene in the great chamber. Satan presides over it on a huge, bejewelled throne. He calls the fallen angels, who have squished themselves into particles to enter the chamber, 'deities of Heav'n' (II:11). If you want to dominate people, it's a good idea to flatter them. Then he opens the floor.

The first to speak is Moloch. Even if we can't beat God, he says, we should get our revenge through total war. At the end of his wooden speech, Moloch frowns at the audience, as if to frighten them into agreement.

The next speaker is Belial. God is omnipotent, the slippery Belial says, so open war is futile. We should just stay here. We are already better off than when we were chained to the burning lake. Things might continue to improve, he says optimistically.

Like Belial, Mammon wants to stay put. He doesn't want to return to Heaven and submit to 'Forced hallelujahs' (II:243). Instead, they should make do with Hell, seeking 'Hard liberty before the easy yoke / Of servile pomp' (II:256–7). This sounds just like Milton, who had argued for republican austerity against monarchic luxury. Hard work will make Hell more accommodating, Mammon says. He's noticed that there are gold and jewels in the burning soil. The mass of devils begin murmuring, as if nearly convinced.

This is where the mask of democracy begins to slip. Someone rises to disagree with Mammon. At first, it's not clear who. The new speaker looks like an old senator, wise and responsible. The chamber is as still as a summer night. This is Beelzebub, but he is standing to propose someone else's argument. Like a politician bent by the interest of corporate lobbyists, the individual conscience on which democracy depends has been perverted. Beelzebub rejects Mammon's argument: this is 'our dungeon', he says, not some place we can just redecorate. It is intolerable to remain under the power of a distant tyrant. We must resist, Beelzebub says, only not openly. We must go up to the world and tempt its inhabitants to join them in Hell, forcing God to 'abolish his own works' (II:370). Who could come up with this evil other than Satan?

The devils are thrilled, their eyes sparkling as they vote yes. Satan's plan having been confirmed, Beelzebub asks who among them is willing to cross the 'dark, unbottomed, infinite abyss' (II:405). The quest to defeat a faraway monster is part of many heroic stories. Here, the monster is space itself. In the seventeenth century, the ancient idea of an infinite universe had been revived, and the philosopher Blaise Pascal said 'the eternal silence of these infinite spaces terrifies me'. No one answers Beelzebub's challenge. Finally, Satan rises to accept it. He will make the journey alone, he says, and govern Hell as its sole ruler. Then he ends the debate before anyone can object. It should be clear by now that Hell is a mere parody of democracy.

By 1802, it was clear that Napoleon had not come to save the French Revolution. Like Satan, he had morphed from a champion of republican liberty to a tyrant. As he followed these developments, William Wordsworth tried to write his own epic. Coleridge had sketched out a plan: it should be three times the length of *Paradise Lost*, it should sing of why the French Revolution failed, and it should lay the groundwork for a future renovation of the human spirit. This was an insane ambition and William would spend the rest of his life trying to accomplish it. When he was struggling to do so, he distracted himself with short poems. But here, too, he was following in Milton's footsteps.

On 21 May 1802, Dorothy read him Milton's sonnets. Written in turbulent moments, they depart from the lover's angst of Shakespeare's sonnets and focus instead on liberty. William knew them by heart but hearing them read aloud fired his imagination. He wrote three sonnets that afternoon, the first in a sequence of 'Sonnets Dedicated to Liberty'. One of them begins:

> Milton! Thou should'st be living at this hour:
> England hath need of thee: she is a fen
> Of stagnant waters . . .[27]

William summons the poet like the ageing hero of an action movie, back for one more job: to restore true political liberty to England, where economic self-interest ruled the day. As Napoleon betrayed the Revolution, William sought to revive Milton's spirit in his own poetry.

In the summer of 1802, peace between Britain and France allowed William and Dorothy to travel to Calais to see Annette and meet his daughter Caroline. There, they saw first-hand the effects of Napoleon's rule. William remarked on the cynical indifference of the French people, so unlike the 'festivals of liberty' that he had witnessed in the early days of the Revolution. Liberty had become a hollow word. Another sonnet marks William's return to English ground, the former Jacobin sounding a note of unmistakable patriotism. He now saw England as the final bastion of liberty. This change of heart is described in his long poem, *The Prelude*. Wordsworth finished a draft of it in 1805, although it wasn't published until his death. *The Prelude* is a quite different epic to *Paradise Lost* – a story of the development of his mind during his childhood, education, and travels in France; of his early optimism about revolution, growing disillusionment, and hope for some future renovation of the spirit. *The Prelude* is one of the great long poems in English: a virtuosic performance in blank verse and a reflection on the failed revolution. But if it is his *Paradise Lost*, it sounds a very different political note.

When Wordsworth looks back at the early days of the French Revolution, his language is haunted by Milton's language. He describes the people thronging home from the 1790 Festival of the Federation as a swarm of bees: we might detect an echo of Milton's devils as bees entering Pandaemonium. Many believed the Festival of the Federation to be the culmination of the Revolution, but it proved to be only the beginning, and the echo of *Paradise Lost* hints that the French crowds later became demonic. When he recalls the Great Terror of 1792, William describes the followers of Maximilien Robespierre, who carried out the massacres, as 'elate and jocund'.[28] These are words that Milton uses to describe Eve, drunk on her new-found power after eating the apple. Echoing Milton's Eve turns the Great Terror into a repetition of the Fall. When he describes the fall of Robespierre, Wordsworth once again summons Milton's devils. He was staying in a small village in the Lake District when he heard that 'this foul tribe of Moloch was o'erthrown'. Stunned by the news, Wordsworth turns to look at the sunlit English hills, and sees them as a 'crown of burning seraphs'– language that recalls Milton's descriptions of God.[29] By 1805, when Wordsworth wrote these lines, his hopes had turned towards the individual encounter with nature.

Wordsworth also mines his own similarities to Satan. In one passage from *The Prelude*, describing his childhood, Wordsworth remembers waiting with his brother for some horses to take them from their boarding school back home for the Christmas holiday. Their father was meant to send the horses, but they didn't arrive. Impatient, William had climbed a nearby hill to look for them:

> Thither I repaired,
> Scout-like, and gained the summit; 'twas a day
> Tempestuous, dark, and wild, and on the grass
> I sate half-sheltered by a naked wall.[30]

He takes this metaphor from *Paradise Lost*, where Milton compares Satan approaching the world to an army scout, creeping over a hill to spy an enemy city (III:543–51). Eventually, the horses arrived. But then, ten days after the boys' return home, their father had died.

> The event,
> With all the sorrow that it brought, appeared
> A chastisement; and when I called to mind
> That day so lately past, when from the crag
> I looked in such anxiety of hope;
> With trite reflections of morality,
> Yet in the deepest passion, I bowed low
> To God who thus corrected my desires.[31]

Wordsworth sees his father's death as a punishment for his 'trite reflections of morality', an obscure phrase that seems to refer to his cursing his father for neglecting him. But once he is older, that painful recollection comes to seem a precious lesson. Wordsworth doesn't identify with Satan, as Blake did, in order to suggest that Milton's revolutionary Devil was sympathetic. Instead, he compares himself with Satan in order to explore his impulses to a tyrannical pride, something he also saw in those who led the revolution astray. Milton's language provides a deep structure for Wordsworth's poem, showing how the French Revolution had become a lost Paradise.

This is where Wordsworth and his predecessor part ways: Milton never entirely lost faith in revolution. One reason for Wordsworth's increasing conservativism was financial. Having grown up in relative poverty, and earned little money from his writings, he suddenly came into an inheritance. His father had been owed money by his aristocratic employer, Lord Lowther, and it had never been paid. Then, in 1802, Lowther's son finally settled the debt. Wordsworth still believed in the power of poetry to change hearts and minds, but he became more cautious. By 1805, he was writing patriotic poetry about Britain's victory in the Battle of Trafalgar. By 1815, he saw Napoleon's defeat at Waterloo as an act of divine providence. Another reason for this change of heart was the savage criticism of his work. The critic Francis Jeffrey, in the *Edinburgh Review*, attacked him with unremitting viciousness. William had called himself a 'simple water drinking bard', claiming continuity with Milton's austerity, and Jeffrey attacked this pretentiousness.[32] Criticism made him haughty: 'Mr Wordsworth is never interrupted,' Wordsworth's wife, Mary, told the young poet John Keats at a dinner in 1817. The following year, Keats tried to visit Wordsworth at home in Grasmere and was horrified to discover that he was out campaigning for Lord Lowther's Tory candidate, who was being challenged by an abolitionist. Either Wordsworth's groundedness in his community had led him to accept aristocracy as a fact of life, or he had been bought off.

By then, Milton's radical legacy had passed down to a younger generation: Percy Shelley and Lord Byron. Byron's criticisms of Wordsworth were even more damning than those of Jeffrey, because he used comic rhymes:

> Thou shalt believe in Milton, Dryden, Pope;
> Thou shalt not set up Wordsworth, Coleridge, Southey;
> Because the first is crazed beyond all hope,
> The second drunk, the third so quaint and mouthy . . .[33]

Byron and Shelley claimed inheritance from Milton, embracing Satan as a hero, whom they far preferred to Milton's God. This caused Wordsworth's friend Robert Southey, the Poet Laureate, to call them 'the Satanic school'. It was a term the young poets embraced: Byron invented brooding heroes, whose psychological complexity and anti-establishment views were indebted to Milton's Satan. In 1812, Shelley wrote his own *Declaration of Rights*, calling for the revolutionary rights against oppressive laws. It ends with Satan's line: 'Arise awake or be forever fallen!' A box of the pamphlet was confiscated by customs in Ireland, so Shelley sent copies to a friend in Sussex, to the consternation of the local authorities.[34] But it was Shelley's nineteen-year-old wife who produced the most extraordinary work inspired by *Paradise Lost*.

After abandoning his first wife, Percy Shelley eloped with Mary Godwin, the daughter of two radical writers: Mary Wollstonecraft and William Godwin. In 1817, the newly married couple travelled to Lake Geneva, where Lord Byron had rented a villa. Byron had renamed it Villa Diodati, because of its connection with the Diodati family – friends of Milton, who the poet was rumoured to have visited in the villa on his way home from Italy. That summer, a volcano in Indonesia caused the weather to turn bad, and the Shelleys spent several days sheltering from rain at Villa Diodati. One evening, Byron said: 'We will each write a ghost story.'[35] The men soon started to compose their stories, but Mary remained uninspired. Each morning, they would ask her if she had anything, and she would say no. Finally, one night, she was visited by a series of images. This was the embryo of *Frankenstein*.

Milton's epic infuses Shelley's novel. She had read *Paradise Lost* in 1815, and again in 1816, and earlier in 1817, her husband had read it aloud to her. When *Frankenstein* was published, Mary gave it an epigraph from *Paradise Lost*: lines in which Adam reproaches his creator for giving him the freedom to disobey him.

The monster created by Dr Frankenstein is both Adam and Satan: he comes to bitterly resent his own creation, and when Dr Frankenstein refuses his request for a mate, the monster vows to destroy his creator. But *Frankenstein* is not only a story influenced by Milton, it's also one in which the monster actually reads *Paradise Lost*:

> It moved every feeling of wonder and awe, that the picture of an omnipotent God warring with his creatures was capable of exciting. I often referred the several situations, as their similarity struck me, to my own.[36]

Frankenstein's monster, like so many other readers, finds *Paradise Lost* to be a commentary on his own existence.

The next year, Percy wrote a mock treatise 'On the Devil and

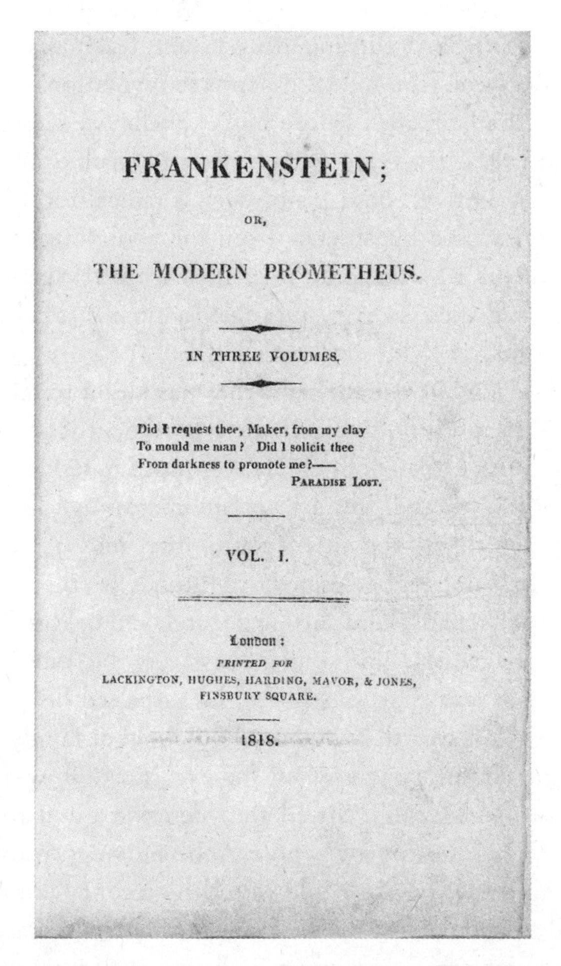

FRANKENSTEIN;

OR,

THE MODERN PROMETHEUS.

IN THREE VOLUMES.

Did I request thee, Maker, from my clay
To mould me man? Did I solicit thee
From darkness to promote me?—
PARADISE LOST.

VOL. I.

London:
PRINTED FOR
LACKINGTON, HUGHES, HARDING, MAVOR, & JONES,
FINSBURY SQUARE.

1818.

Mary Shelley, the title page to the first edition of *Frankenstein*, with its epigraph from a speech by Milton's Adam.

Devils', in which he claimed that 'The Devil owes everything to Milton.' Where earlier poets had represented a cloven-hoofed beast, Milton made the Devil sublime. Percy reused that material for his 'Defence of Poetry' (1821), an essay that ends with the famous statement: 'Poets are the unacknowledged legislators of the World.' These words are perhaps most true of Milton: his poetry moved readers to revolutionary acts by describing a Satan whose speeches unmask God's tyranny. This is the most famous political legacy of *Paradise Lost* but the poem also contains a more subtle political training: showing Satan turning into a tyrant, teaching the reader to distinguish between true and false claims to revolutionary freedom.

Wordsworth's heirs died before him – Shelley and Keats in 1821, and Byron in 1824. By 1830, when his poetic revolution was beginning to gain followers, he had not been a radical for a long time. Wordsworth excused his absence from the abolitionist movement, claiming that the rural location prevented his participation, but he increasingly disdained the rash, misguided actions that radical politics sometimes involves.[37] He had relinquished not only his belief in violent revolution but also the hope that was meant to take its place. The Lake District was not somewhere to lay the seeds of a new revolution, but a refuge from politics. He continued to fashion himself as a second Milton, though this act became increasingly hollow. One cruel story, which has the air of plausibility, tells of Wordsworth being shown a watch that belonged to Milton, with the poet's initials engraved on it.[38] He took out his own watch and held it up, waiting for someone to remark how similar they were. No one saying anything, he put it away. In some ways, he surpassed his predecessor. Like Milton, Wordsworth had a busy household of family members, who copied out his poems when his eyes hurt. It was far more harmonious than Milton's: their letters describe a unit that seemed to read and feel as one, organic whole. At his most egotistical, Wordsworth believed that poetry could effect the reconciliation between the individual and nature. But he knew his happiness was grounded in others, particularly the people in his home, and his writing returns again and again to his sister and 'dear friend'.

Dorothy spent the final decades of her life physically infirm but still, quietly, filling her journals with vigorous, proto-modernist writings. When *The Prelude* was finally published, after William's death in 1850, it seemed a criticism of revolutions rather than the work of someone disillusioned but still, at heart, hopeful. Wordsworth did arguably become the next great English poet after Milton, though one more ambivalent about revolutions. But by then, Milton's legacy had been taken up by readers beyond European seas.

3. Baron Vastey Fires Back

Satan flies out of Hell, and Milton compares him to a fleet of ships in the Indian Ocean, which, when seen from the coast of Bengal, appear to hang in the clouds. Like the merchants buying spices to season European tables, whose voyages will help to birth modern capitalism, Satan is on his way to do a trade that will spoil the world.

But now he encounters something horrifying. The Gates of Hell are guarded by two figures. One is half-woman, half-serpent. Around her waist is a band of hounds; they periodically burrow into her womb and then burst out of it – a shocking image. The other shape is terrifyingly formless, distinguished only by his accessories: a spear and a crown. We don't know what he is, and neither does Satan. In mutual fear, Satan and the male shape begin to fight.

The female figure quickly puts herself between them. 'O Father,' she cries, 'what intends thy hand . . . Against thy only son?' (II:727–8) Satan is stunned. His memory still imperfect after his fall, he doesn't recognise either of them. Now she says, with wounded dignity:

> Hast thou forgot me then, and do I seem
> Now in thine eye so foul, once deemed so fair . . . ? (II:747–8)

When Satan first conceived of his rebellion against God, she says, she was born out of his head. She now tells him her name: Sin. Her story is one of incestuous abuse: falling in love with his own image, Satan had made her pregnant. She then gave birth to a child: Death. These are the only allegorical figures in *Paradise Lost*. They are meant to illustrate the Christian theory of sin: having conceived a sinful thought, the sinner is tempted by that thought, falls in love with sin, which then causes death. Satan persuades them to let him pass, arguing that his journey will benefit them too, letting them come up into a fresh world and feed on its creatures. This vision, enchanting to Sin and Death, should make you shudder. Sin opens the gates, like Pandora, letting trouble into our world.

Outside Hell is Chaos. It is everything that is not part of the created universe. Satan catches sight of Heaven, and beneath it, he sees his destination:

> fast by hanging in a golden chain
> This pendent world, in bigness as a star
> Of smallest magnitude close by the moon. (II:1051–3)

The world is connected to Heaven by a golden chain, like a pendant, a gift from God to humankind. It is a gift we see through the eyes of one who can't appreciate it, only ruin it. That is Satan's purpose, as he wings his way towards the world, which means towards *us*. As he does so, we see a side of him that is not sublime but shallow and familiar. It was this Satan, a sneak and a thief, that a Haitian writer thought of as he watched the nations of Europe desperately trying to save slavery.

It rises huge above the plains, brooding on the mountain's spine. Walls of stone tower a hundred feet above the mountain's tip, plunging down in steep slopes to the east and west. Slit windows look suspiciously across the valley. On its ramparts are cannons captured from the armies of the most powerful empires in the world, pointing out at the horizon. This fortress was once the largest in the Americas, a symbol of liberty and a formidable presence on the island.[1] Known as the Citadelle Henri, it was built by the man who became the first king of post-revolutionary Haiti.

In 1791, enslaved people in Haiti, then a French colony called Saint-Domingue, rose up against their masters. Buoyed by the French Revolution, and the power vacuum it had created, the slaves started to demand their own rights. The sugar island was the most lucrative colony in the Western world, and the imperial powers of Europe didn't give it up willingly. The rebels fought off the French, British and Spanish armies – an extraordinary feat. The de facto leader of the rebellion, a former slave called Toussaint Louverture, believed it was impossible to maintain their independence unless they had the support of the French, so he kept them on his side without giving up control of the island. He did this by arguing that the slave uprising was the fulfilment of the values of the French Revolution. In the early days of the uprising, a slave owner had returned to the blackened ruins of his plantation to find that the one building left standing was his library.[2] It had been used as an office by the local leader of the uprising. All of the slave owner's books had been burnt, but on his desk, he found one volume, Abbé Raynal's *Philosophical History of the Two Indies*, a book that criticised the violence perpetrated by European powers in the Americas and Asia. It had been left open at a page that prophesied the coming of a 'new Spartacus', who would lead the slaves to freedom and carry out terrible reprisals against their former torturers.[3] The leader who had done this was Louverture. He had inserted himself into Raynal's prophecy, announcing himself as that Spartacus. This episode indicates what one historian calls Louverture's 'epic faith in the written word', how he used the European revolutionary tradition to emancipate Haiti.[4] Long ignored by Western historians, the Haitian Revolution transformed the Age of Revolutions, demonstrating that enslaved people were capable of liberty no less than European citizens.[5]

Many Europeans were horrified to see their speeches about liberty being taken so literally by the slaves. Fearing that their own colonies would imitate the rebellion, Britain invaded Haiti and waged five years of fruitless war. It was an eighteenth-century Vietnam: Britain lost 13,000 men. In 1798, they negotiated a humiliating peace with Louverture. This brought a brief respite for Haiti. But Napoleon could not tolerate their independence. In late 1801, the Peace of Amiens made the Atlantic safe for French ships, and Napoleon turned his sights to France's former colony. In November that year, he sent a navy to extinguish the rebellion. For months, the French ships were trapped in the port by heavy winds, but eventually they sailed. When they appeared on his horizon, Louverture said darkly: 'All of France has come to Saint-Domingue.' They had come to restore slavery. In June 1802, the Haitian leader was ambushed and captured. A month later, he was in France, where he was transported to a castle prison in the Jura mountains. In Britain, Louverture's capture was almost universally denounced: France was their enemy, so it was convenient to support the slave uprising. Even the Tory magazine the *Anti-Jacobin* said there was no doubt who was 'the hero, and who the demon'. When William and Dorothy Wordsworth visited France in August 1802, they followed the news about Louverture's capture. Having lost his belief in class struggle, William was now focused on wars of national liberation. The news inspired him to write another Miltonic sonnet: 'To Toussaint Louverture'. Even as he expresses solidarity with the Haitian Revolution, Wordsworth's sonnet contains a creeping uncertainty about revolutionary leaders, which enters through an echo of *Paradise Lost*.

'Toussaint, the most unhappy Man of Men!' Wordsworth begins. Extraordinarily, this anticipates the Haitian leader's own memoir – published fifty years later – in which he calls himself '*le plus malheureux des hommes*' (the most unhappy of men).[6] Not knowing where Louverture is imprisoned, Wordsworth wonders if he can hear nature from his cell. This would be some consolation, Wordsworth says, because the very elements are on his side. The sonnet gathers to a conclusion that is unmatched in its grandeur by any other short poem I know:

> Thou hast left behind
> Powers that will work for thee; air, earth, and skies;
> There's not a breathing of the common wind
> That will forget thee; thou hast great allies;
> Thy friends are exultations, agonies,
> And love, and man's unconquerable mind.[7]

These lines echo Louverture's own words: he had told his followers that 'freedom is a right given by nature' and claimed a special affinity with the elements, to explain his extraordinary stamina and ability to escape certain death many times.[8] The penultimate word, however, is not Louverture's but Satan's.

Wordsworth's phrase 'unconquerable mind' plucks its adjective from *Paradise Lost*. It comes at the moment of deepest despair , when Satan announces that an 'unconquerable will' (I:106) will drive their resistance. This is fitting for Louverture's situation, but superimposing Satan on to the Haitian leader makes for a suspicious kind of praise. There may have been a grain of truth in the comparison, since Satan is a freedom fighter who turns into a dictator, and the end of Toussaint's tenure had involved an ever-stricter leadership. But the comparison also indicates a pessimism about revolutions. The comparison makes Milton's Satan look like an anti-imperialist revolutionary but also insinuates in the Haitian leader a hint of the demonic.

Two months after Wordsworth's sonnet was published, Louverture died in a freezing prison cell, intentionally neglected by his captors. In Haiti, the struggle continued, now led by Louverture's former second-in-command, Jean-Jacques Dessalines. After the French were finally defeated, in November 1803, Dessalines established a new state. There were massacres of white colonists, which were eagerly reported in Europe as evidence of the barbarity of the revolution. As he prepared to proclaim independence, Dessalines was presented with a declaration written by an elderly aide, who was an admirer of Jefferson. He read it to his leader and other aides on 31 December 1804. But the document lacked 'fury and vengeance', and Dessalines's young secretary Boisrond-Tonnerre declared that it would be better written on the skin of a White person.[9] Dessalines approved this sentiment and overnight, Boisrond-Tonnerre rewrote the declaration. He read it to Dessalines on 1 January 1804, the day that Haiti was reborn.

'Citizens', the Haitian Declaration of Independence proclaims, 'it's not enough to have expelled from your country the barbarians that have bloodied it for two centuries.'[10] Liberty had to be preserved, and the effects of imperialism utterly uprooted: 'We must, with one last act of national authority, forever assure the empire of liberty in the country of our birth.'[11] However, the proclamation didn't mention the rights to be enjoyed by the Haitian people: all power would reside with Dessalines, who signed the document alone. Haiti was only the second independent state in the Americas, after the United States, and it was the first state to permanently abolish slavery. The new liberty would require them to uproot all vestiges of European imperialism. Dessalines informed President Jefferson that they had thrown off 'the yoke of tyranny', but Jefferson refused to acknowledge it.[12] Their path would be different from that of the white republics. Instead of imitating the principles of the French or American Revolutions, they would follow the example of the Taino people, the indigenous inhabitants of the island, who chose to die rather than suffer the loss of their liberty. The new state would take its name from its indigenous, Taino name: Ayiti or Haiti. In restoring its indigenous name, and rooting out the European influence, Dessalines declared: 'I have avenged America.'[13]

In 1805, after Napoleon crowned himself Emperor, Dessalines followed suit. This did not last long: the following year, the Emperor of Haiti was murdered and the young state split in two. The ghosts of colonialism had not been exorcised, but neither had the hope for liberty. Where Wordsworth had seen a hint of Milton's Satan in Toussaint, a Haitian writer would turn the accusation around.

Five miles behind Citadelle Henri lies the palace of Sans Souci. It was built for the new King of northern Haiti, Henri Christophe. Born enslaved in the English colony of Grenada, Christophe had won his freedom fighting for the French army in the American Revolution. He worked as a cook in Saint-Domingue and then rose to be an important general in Louverture's army. After the assassination of Dessalines, he became President of northern Haiti. Then, in 1811, he had himself proclaimed King. That same year, work began on Sans Souci. It was the grandest palace in the Caribbean. Meaning 'without worry', its name was inspired either by Frederick the Great's palace at Potsdam or a maroon leader called Sans Souci who had been killed by Christophe in an internecine struggle.[14] These two very different possibilities are a testament to Christophe's contradictory ambitions: to realise European liberty in a Black state.

Designed in the neoclassical style, and surrounded by ornamental gardens, Sans Souci was decorated by the same retailers London patronised by the Prince of Wales. When the King couldn't get the wallpaper he wanted, he had gold doubloons hammered into the walls.[15] At the same time, he established an ambitious education system. Like Toussaint before him, Christophe believed Haiti's independence was reliant on its exports, and he went about trying to raise production levels. He introduced measures that coerced former slaves back to the plantations they had fled during the Revolution. To create a society where everyone was free, the King commanded an army of labourers

Sans Souci, Pleasure Palace of King Henry Christophe of Haiti (1836). Engraving by Carl Ritter, who visited the island before the palace was destroyed in an earthquake

with strict military discipline.[16] It was these unfree labourers who built the new symbols of liberty, the Citadelle and Sans Souci. This is not the only paradox of Christophe's kingdom. After Dessalines's death, the southern part of Haiti had become a republic. Alexandre Pétion, the leader of the south, was rumoured to be conspiring with France, willing to pay reparations to Haiti's former colonists in return for their support against their northern enemies. Christophe, who was resolutely against reparations, attempted to forge diplomatic links with France's enemy Britain. Haiti's former colonists were still threatening to reconquer Haiti and regain possession of their old plantations. So Christophe was justified in claiming that his despotic rule was the final bastion of Black liberty.

When Christophe was attacked, it was the job of Jean Louis, baron de Vastey (pronounced Va-tay), the King's secretary, to defend him.

Vastey was born in Ennery, northern Haiti, in 1781. He was the son of a white plantation owner and his mixed-race wife, a relative of the novelist Alexandre Dumas. This meant, in the all-important racial classifications of the time, that Vastey was a *gen de couleur* – a free person of colour. He was wealthy but denied the social privileges reserved for white people. As the historian Marlene Daut notes, many of the most basic facts about Vastey's identity are still unknown: no picture of him survives, and even his first name has been the subject of debate.[17] He seems to have been educated in France but later returned to Haiti. Vastey himself said that he joined Toussaint's army at the age of fifteen, but it's also possible that he was forced to fight in the French army against the revolution.[18] This uncertainty might stem from Vastey's own wish to suppress his former complicity with slavery.[19] But it's also a sign of the bitter times he lived through. His enemies spread vicious rumours about him, one of them claiming that, while living in France, he took part in the Great Terror.[20] We know little about Vastey's experience of the Haitian Revolution. In 1804, he was working as a secretary in Dessalines's government alongside Boisrond-Tonnerre. When Christophe was crowned in 1811, in a lavish ceremony, Vastey was made a baron in the new aristocracy. He received a coat of arms – a quill – that reflected his role as the defender of his King.

The Haitian Revolution didn't only take place in the plantations, woods, and seas of Haiti, but also in the books and newspapers crossing the Atlantic. Haitian writers radicalised the Atlantic republican tradition, and Vastey was one of the non-white authors who used that tradition to argue that colonialism and slavery had made the freedom-loving states of Europe into tyrannies. In 1814, Vastey published a treatise called *The Colonial System Unveiled.* The book catalogues the mutilations, rapes, and murders perpetrated by overseers and plantation owners. In its opening, Vastey proposes to interview the dead:

> I shall consult the shades of the dead, those unfortunate compatriots of mine you threw alive into a fiery furnace; those you ordered be put on a spit, roasted, impaled, or subjected to a thousand other forms of torture invented by the powers of hell![21]

In exhaustive detail, Vastey's book shows colonialism to be anything but an enlightened regime: a mediocre experiment to see how much human life could be degraded and exploited.

Vastey speaks from familiarity with the barbaric system. He describes a plantation owner from Marmelade, who wants to throw an infant, whose constitution seems too weak to be useful to him, into a lime kiln. The slave owner's daughter, whom Vastey names as Élisabeth Mimi, begs him to let her raise the child. The slave owner relents, but only when he is convinced that it will not cost him anything. Vastey then says:

> *Laurent*, which is the name of that child, is now forty-five years old, the father of a large family, an excellent plantation manager, a steadfast tiller of the Haytian soil. Mimi, virtuous and good, you are no longer with us![22]

Although he doesn't acknowledge it, Vastey is writing about his own family: his grandfather was the cruel slave owner and his mother the virtuous intercessor. He clearly knew Laurent personally. Instances of mercy are scarce in the book, which shows slavery to be a system maintained by lazy, cruel farmers of human life. On a plantation in Les Cayes, a labourer accidentally caught her arm in the sugar mill, and the overseer had to cut off her arm to prevent the rest of her body from being caught in the machine. When the overseer told his mistress, Madame Langlois, she replied: 'Gracious me, that wouldn't have been such a disaster when all's said and done, if it weren't that her body might have spoiled my cane-juice.'[23] After that, Vastey stops, saying that a full account of the viciousness of colonialism would require many volumes.

Vastey's writings are a singular account of this modern evil and Haiti's unprecedented attempt to overthrow it. At this time, literature was viewed – by both Haitians and their enemies – as a crucial indicator of the capacity for self-government. In 1774, the French writer Abbé Raynal had claimed that the New World had not produced a single great poet.[24] An indignant Thomas Jefferson had replied, in his *Notes on Virginia*, that only when America had 'existed as a people as long as the Greeks did before they produced a Homer, the Romans a Virgil, the French a Racine and Voltaire, the English a Shakespeare and Milton' – i.e. many centuries – would this insult be fair.[25] In the same work, Jefferson claimed that Black people were incapable of literary genius. This provoked a response by an eminent French abolitionist, Abbé Henri Grégoire. In his response, *De la littérature des nègres* (1808), Grégoire celebrated Haiti as an example of Black genius and compared Haiti's critics to Satan looking in at Paradise, poised to invade and spoil it.[26] Vastey must have been following this exchange, because he borrowed Grégoire's Milton analogy in his most admired work.

In 1815, an ex-colonist called Mazères published a pamphlet arguing that Haitians should 'reunite' with France to save themselves from the 'barbaric' Henri Christophe.[27] It fell to Vastey to respond. In a pamphlet entitled *Reflexions on the Blacks and Whites* (1817), Vastey identifies his opponent as a former plantation owner from the Quartier Morin, responsible for atrocities.[28] Rather than recounting those atrocities, Vastey calls the authorities of the Enlightenment to a defence of Haiti. Perhaps misleadingly, given his likely education in France, Vastey describes himself as 'an islander, who has had no instruction but his books'.[29] Whatever the truth, his books provide extensive support. His opponent had tried to recruit the great French political theorist Montesquieu to attack Black sovereignty, so Vastey points out that the 'immortal Montesquieu' had himself argued that slavery is inexcusable.[30] Vastey's library must also have included *Paradise Lost*, because he compares his enemies to Milton's devils:

> their pride is untameable! like the infernal spirits in their horrible assemblies, such as the immortal Milton has described them after their fall, the ex-colonists, though vanquished, thunderstruck, and precipitated into the abyss, still struggle by every method their villainy can suggest to recover the empire of which a just and retributive God has for ever deprived them.[31]

It's a perfect analogy, since Milton compares Satan to European ships, crossing oceans to satisfy their appetites for sugar, tobacco, and spice. Like Milton's devils, Haiti's former colonists are plotting their revenge even after being defeated and cast out of Haiti. Unlike Wordsworth,

Vastey doesn't see a hint of Satan in the Haitian revolutionaries. Instead, he sees the colonists as the embodiment of evil, and he calls Mazères the 'Beelzebub colonist'.[32] Vastey hadn't just copied the reference from Grégoire; he had also gone back to the source, using *Paradise Lost* to describe Haiti assaulted by devils. These allusions, brief as they are, help to cast Haiti's struggle as an epic.

There was no epic poem of the Haitian Revolution. *L'Haitiade*, a set of neoclassical songs thought to have been co-written by Louverture's son Isaac, was only published in 1878. Its preface admits it isn't on a par with *Paradise Lost*.[33] Instead, Haiti's epics have been written by historians: most famously, C. L. R. James's *Black Jacobins: Toussaint Louverture and the San Domingo Revolution* (1936), a militant call for postcolonial revolutions, and more recently Laurent Dubois's *Avengers of the New World: The Story of the Haitian Revolution* (2004). Vastey became the first Haitian historian of the revolution when his *Essay on the Causes of the Revolution and Civil Wars of Hayti* appeared in 1819, and the book has a distinctly epic tenor. Vastey defends King Henri Christophe, arguing that it would be an error to imagine that 'liberty flourishes more in republics than in monarchies'.[34] Pointing out that the southern republic was conspiring with the French, who sought to restore slavery, Vastey shows that kingdoms may be freer than democracies. He compares Christophe to Oliver Cromwell, 'who sought to attain the chief power, but never desired to reduce their country beneath a foreign yoke'.[35] The King, whose enemies had called him a tyrant, was in fact the best defender of liberty. Vastey sounds an even more epic note in *Reflexions on the Blacks and Whites*, when he declares:

> Hail to thee, happy land! Land of my choice! Hail to thee, Hayti, my country! Sole asylum of liberty where the black man can lift his head to behold and participate in the bounties dispensed by the universal Father of Man.[36]

Given the two explicit allusions to Milton in the same text, it's possible that this is an intentional echo of Satan's words: 'hail horrors, hail / Infernal world, and thou profoundest Hell' (I:250–1). If this was deliberate, Vastey was once again turning Milton's poem against European imperialism, to declare that, once home to all the horrors of slavery, Haiti had become a haven of liberty. If the echo was unintentional, we must still determine why it is Satan's words that come so close to those of later freedom fighters, rather than those of the poem's good characters. We can only answer this after meeting Milton's God.

As Satan flies to Eden, God is looking down through the cataract of stars. He knows what is going to happen: the humans will disobey him and eat the fruit. His omniscience is a problem both for the plot and for Milton's theology: why wouldn't God just stop Satan? Even more strange, when God describes his newborn humans, he sounds irritable:

> *Ingrate*, he had of me
> All he could have; I made him just and right,
> Sufficient to have stood, though free to fall. (III:97–9)

Many readers find it difficult to like this intemperate God. The critic William Empson even compared Milton's deity to Stalin.[37] Is the poet failing in his ambition 'to justify the ways of God to men' (I:26)? He seems fixed, unmoving, like the carved wooden statues that Portuguese merchants bought in West Africa in the sixteenth century and called *fetiço*, believing that they had bought the very things that local people worshipped as gods. During the English Civil War, Parliament's soldiers tore down painted wooden statues from cathedrals, wishing to rid England of the same error of mistaking mere things for God. But the God of *Paradise Lost* seems just that: wooden.

How can we make sense of this? God could have decreed that they would automatically resist temptation, but he decided not to. Instead, he decreed that man should be free to obey or disobey him. God, definitely a cat person, says he wouldn't be able to enjoy love if it were compulsory. But how can our freedom be reconciled with his omnipotence? Here, Milton is wading into the major Protestant debate of his century. The sixteenth-century theologian John Calvin maintained that God, before the creation of the world, decided who was saved (the elect) and who was not (the reprobate). This means that good works have no effect on salvation. In the 1590s, a Dutch follower of Calvin called Arminius had questioned this. How could automatic damnation be compatible with God's goodness? he wondered. Over the

God in Heaven looks down on Satan. Engraving by John Baptist Medina for the 1688 edition of *Paradise Lost*.

next two decades, Arminius and his followers began to attack Calvin's theory. This controversy split the Dutch Church, and soon migrated to England. Milton came to adopt an Arminian position. He believed that humans had free will to accept or reject grace. This is why Milton's God is so defensive: he doesn't want to be mistaken for a Calvinist. 'If I foreknew', God says of the human disobedience that is still to come, 'Foreknowledge had no influence on their fault' (III:117–18). Adam and Eve had free will and they chose to disobey him. This is Milton's attempt to clear God of all responsibility for the Fall, but it may not be entirely convincing. Why couldn't God just keep the humans in Eden like pets? Milton does answer this, and we'll return to it. For now, God seems like King Herod in a nativity play, demanding blood.

After God finishes speaking, something strange happens. God replies to God. The deity of *Paradise Lost* is split into two: Father and Son. At some point, Milton became a heretic, departing from the orthodox ideas about the Trinity. He now believed that the Father came *before* the Son, rather than being 'co-eternal' with him, as any orthodox Christian should believe. The Son we meet in *Paradise Lost* isn't called Christ, since he isn't the human version (yet). He encourages his father to be merciful, pointing out that punishing the humans for something that wasn't entirely their fault is inconsistent with God's infinite goodness. What's more, it would make Satan's revenge successful, causing the abolition of God's creation, which God would never do.

God the Father responds gratefully, calling the Son his 'chief delight' (III:168). God the Father says he will offer grace to all. Some will receive 'peculiar grace' (III:183), while the rest have enough to find their way up the thorny path to Heaven. But he wants something to compensate for the disobedience of Adam and Eve: 'rigid satisfaction, death for death' (III:212). Like Hell, Heaven needs its champion. The angels are cowardly silent. Then the Son steps up.

> Behold me then, me for him, life for life
> I offer, on me let thine anger fall. (III:236–7)

The Son will die for humans. Like Satan, who earns his evil throne by courage, the Son merits his eminence in Heaven by this act. If you're not moved by this sacrifice, you're missing out. People who find Milton's God unsympathetic rarely have much to say about the Son. What could be more moving than to lay down one's life for another? The angels rejoice, casting their flower garlands into the air like happy graduates. The Son has tempered the Father's rage, helping him to make the right decision. As we have already noted, Milton's household was nothing like this. But he wrote into his poem a picture of merciful fatherhood. The fact that it is a fantasy may be why it isn't the most convincing part. The revolutionary Satan was a far more powerful character, and this is why so many readers were drawn to it.

The Citadelle, northern Haiti (*c.* 1963). Built by an army of labourers under the supervision of Henri Christophe, from 1805 to 1820, it was never actually used in Haiti's defence.

Vastey's haven didn't last for long. In 1820, a coup led King Christophe to commit suicide. The coup was led by the republicans from the south, with the help of the French. Vastey was killed soon after that, and his body was thrown into a well. But even his death remains a mystery: one traveller claimed to have met Vastey in 1828, happily retired and living in Cape Haitien.[38] Whatever the truth, Haiti was plunged into another cycle of violence. Some years later, an earthquake left the palace of Sans Souci in ruins. Conservative commentators took the violence of post-revolutionary Haiti as proof that a free Black state was a foolish dream – Wordsworth may have been thinking of it when he said he no longer supported immediate abolition because it could lead to 'worse evils'.[39] But Vastey's works survived as proof that self-government was preferable to the evils of colonialism.

In 1817, a man tried to smuggle *Reflexions on the Blacks and Whites* into Jamaica, and it was confiscated by the fearful British authorities.[40] But his pamphlets were soon circulating in America, where they influenced abolitionists in the decades leading up to the American Civil War.[41] Vastey wasn't the first Enlightenment writer to oppose colonialism, but writing emerging from the first successful revolution against slavery was important. Like the captured cannons on the top of the Citadelle, he had turned European thought – and Milton with it – against European imperialism.

4. George Eliot Sees Her First Man

Having crossed Chaos, and plunged into the created universe, passing other worlds without so much as a glance, Satan lands on a mountain near Eden. There, he bursts into a soliloquy, a dramatic form in which a character speaks to themself. This soliloquy is thought to have been one of the first parts of the poem that Milton wrote, as early as 1640, when he still thought it was going to be a play. Satan is disturbed by doubt. He regrets his rebellion against God and admits that he can't make a Heaven of Hell, as he claimed earlier. He now says: 'Which way I fly is hell; myself am hell' (IV:75). But he's too proud to repent. He re-dedicates himself to evil and flies on.

In the land of Eden is an enclosure protected by steep slopes on every side, covered in thorns: this is Paradise. At the top of the slope are tall trees, and behind those, a high, green wall. As he approaches it, Satan is caught in the sweet breeze flowing out from the Garden.

> So lovely seemed
> That landscape: and of pure now purer air
> Meets his approach (IV:152–4)

It feels as though it is happening in real time: 'of pure *now purer* air'. Once again Milton compares Satan to a merchant ship: one approaching the coast of Mozambique, where the wind blows perfumed airs from the shore across the bows, and the sailors pause their journey to enjoy a foretaste of the commodity they are there to buy. As his pleasure subsides, Satan remembers his mission. He approaches the wall and 'At one slight bound high over leaped all bound' (IV:181). What was the point in the high wall, if Satan – the one creature it was designed to keep out – could just hop over? It's difficult to shake the thought that the architect has not done his job properly. How could God let this evil spirit prey on his newborn babes?

Inside the Garden, trees bear fruit of edible gold, and 'odorous gums and balm' (IV:248). A fountain irrigates the Garden with meandering streams whose beds are pearls and golden sand. Happy, natural excess. Lions fool around with goats. Milton creates images of bliss through inversions of grammar and of reality, as when he says: 'And without thorn the rose' (IV:256). Eden is the origin of all myths: the Golden Age, the Elysian Fields, the Hesperian Gardens. 'If true,' Milton says, 'here only' (IV:251). Of all the beauty in Paradise, the best is last to be created. They are standing in the garden, like characters in a video game waiting to begin.

> The fiend
> Saw undelighted all delight, all kind
> Of living creatures new to sight and strange:
> Two of far nobler shape erect and tall,
> Godlike erect (IV:285–9)

They are perfect but different: Adam has 'hyacinthine locks' (IV:301) that fall to his shoulders in tight curls, and Eve has 'wanton ringlets' (IV:306) that fall to her waist, covering her genitals. Adam's hair expresses his natural self-discipline, Eve's 'implied subjection' (IV: 307–8), meaning that it required restraint. The hierarchy between them is as absolute as that between human and God, and Milton formulates this in a cold, clear way: 'He for God only, she for God in him' (IV:299). One eighteenth-century editor assumed Milton had meant to say: 'she for God *and* him' rather than this patriarchal formulation.[1] From now on, the story is going to be as much about Adam and Eve as it is about Satan, and Milton's vision of the first humans will be no less polarising.

Eve leans against her husband, innocently exposing her breasts. Watching this, Satan explodes:

> Sight hateful, sight tormenting! Thus these two
> Imparadised in one another's arms
> The happier Eden (IV:505–7)

I love that adjective: *Imparadised*. As a way of voyeuristically picturing them in each other's arms, it's perfect. Other people's relationships often look more perfect than they are, and Satan doesn't realise that theirs is already fraught with insecurities. Even as Milton describes his patriarchal Eden, he shows its difficulties.

Adam and Eve have been born as adults. Eve talks about her birth, and it is full of ambivalence. One day, she awoke on a bed of flowers, uncertain where she was. She came across a body of water and lay on the bank, inclining forward to look in:

> A shape within the watery gleam appeared
> Bending to look on me: I started back,
> It started back, but pleased I soon returned,
> Pleased it returned as soon with answering looks
> Of sympathy and love (IV:461–5)

Notice how Milton uses the line break as a kind of mirror: 'I started back, / It started back'. Nowhere is poetry so close to Disney animation. Like Narcissus, Eve is captivated by the image. Then a voice in her head tells her it is her own reflection. The voice guides her away from the lake, and, like a contestant on a reality show, towards a creature who is to be her mate. But she notices that he is less beautiful than the image in the water. Even though he's the only other person in the world, she isn't interested. She starts to run away and he follows, crying that he has given his rib for her to be born. She is part of his soul, he says. She hesitates. He seizes her hand, and she is tamed.

In the late-eighteenth and early-nineteenth centuries, rising literacy rates meant that more women read *Paradise Lost* and left a record of what they thought of it. Many were devoted to it: Anne Yearsley, a Bristolian woman known as the milkwoman poet, was well acquainted with it.[2] The poet Anna Seward claimed she could recite passages when she was three years old.[3] A tailor's widow in London boasted that her admiration for Milton was one of the things that had attracted her late husband.[4] There's no way to generalise about women's interpretations of Milton but they did lead the charge in thinking about how his personal life related to his work, and whether *Paradise Lost* invented a new theory of patriarchy or helped in its undoing.

The most important writer to do so was the revolutionary proto-feminist writer Mary Wollstonecraft. In her first published work, *Thoughts on the Education of Daughters* (1787), Wollstonecraft declares she is 'sick of hearing of the sublimity of Milton'.[5] She then clarifies that she means hearing about Milton, and other great poets, from people 'who could not enter into the spirit of those authors, or understand them'.[6] She recommended adventurous reading, rejecting received opinions and going back to the source. This was Milton's spirit, too. Writing about him was a family trade for Wollstonecraft: in 1797, she married William Godwin, whose radical treatise *An Enquiry Concerning Political Justice* (1793) helped to popularise the radical revaluation of Satan. The same year that they married, Wollstonecraft died in childbirth. Her daughter Mary survived, and would later write her Miltonic novel *Frankenstein*. But Wollstonecraft anticipated both of them in her radical examination of *Paradise Lost*.

In 1792, Wollstonecraft wrote her most important work, *A Vindication of the Rights of Woman*, which demanded for women the rights that the French Revolution had demanded for all men. The pamphlet contains a searing analysis of Milton – this might be surprising had we not already seen other writers using him to make political arguments throughout this period. Wollstonecraft claims that the poet makes Eve, 'our frail mother', little more than a doll for Adam's desires.[7] In this, she says, he was like 'Mahometans' in believing women don't have a soul – this isn't true of Muslims, but it carries the force of her accusation against Milton's patriarchal Eden.[8] Great men are often misled by their desires, Wollstonecraft adds charitably. In other ways she recognises that Milton agrees with her own assessment of women's mental capacities. For Eve is made to be not only Adam's companion but also his equal, created so that he could experience a rational companionship that depends on equality. Wollstonecraft saw Milton's spirit as divided for and against women. By the time her *Vindication* was influencing the women's suffrage movement in the United States, formed in Seneca Falls in 1848, her double-edged judgement of Milton had been taken up by another important writer.

Coventry, England, July 1848

Ralph Waldo Emerson was in England when he met a provincial woman who gave him a start. The towering figure of American letters, he had led a group of young New England men and women away from institutional religion. Inspired by Milton, Romantic poetry, German philosophy, and Eastern religion, the Transcendentalists discovered God in nature and in their own minds. They had captured imaginations on both sides of the Atlantic, and Emerson's lectures in England were wildly popular. It was a time of radical change, with street-fighting in Paris and Chartist gatherings on the commons outside English cities. Emerson was in his forties, willowy in stature, and unsophisticated (he said) as 'plain old Adam'.[9] But he was a force of American optimism and open-heartedness. In July, Emerson stayed at a house in Coventry belonging to a wealthy bohemian that was a stopping point for writers, reformers, and anyone who was a little bit 'cracked'.[10] One of the other guests was the twenty-eight-year-old Mary Ann Evans, whose voice revealed her West Midlands upbringing. As he listened to her, Emerson was taken aback. Evans's intelligence didn't belong to this provincial scene. Emerson wanted to know what she had been reading. He said she was a 'calm, serious soul'.[11] For her part, less than composed, Evans wrote to a friend: 'I have met Ralph Waldo Emerson, – the first man I have seen.'[12] If she was play-acting as Eve seeing Adam for the first time, this was the opposite of their unhappy first encounter in *Paradise Lost*: a moment of pure desire for a man who was her equal. George Eliot – for it was she who Emerson met that day – would go on to use Milton's life as the material for a horror story.

Mary Ann Evans was born in 1819 in Nuneaton, Warwickshire, the rural heartland of England. Evans's father was the estate manager for a wealthy aristocrat, whose estate included a coal mine. The Industrial Revolution had sent canals and railways across the English countryside, and the future novelist and her brother fished in the canal and heard industrial machinery as they lay in bed at night.[13] Evans was sent to a local boarding school, where she became evangelical. Her faith was soon outstripped by her reason: she learnt Latin, Greek, Italian, French, and German, and read voraciously. In 1839, she wrote: 'My mind presents just such an assemblage of disjoined specimens of history, ancient and modern; scraps of poetry picked up from Shakespeare, Cowper, Wordsworth, and Milton.'[14] In this she was no different from many other young Victorian men and women, except that her ambitious reading was only just beginning. Reading loosened her religious certainties, a process accelerated by meeting the bohemian Charles Bray in 1842, at whose house she met Emerson and other freethinkers. She read writers questioning the foundations of Christian belief, and she started translating David Strauss's *Life of Jesus*, which controversially treated him as a historical figure rather than God. In 1849, Evans moved to London, changing her name to the more sophisticated Marian. She lodged with the publisher John Chapman and became somehow entangled in his marital drama. She escaped and Chapman only coaxed her back with the offer to help him revive the *Westminster Review*, once England's pre-eminent intellectual publication, which he had just bought. And it was Chapman, in 1851, who introduced her to George Henry Lewes in a foreign-language bookshop in London's Burlington Arcade.

Lewes was a critic, novelist, and social scientist, but, at first, Evans didn't think much of him. She didn't write glowingly of him as she had of Emerson. She called him 'Mirabeau in miniature', referring to the smallpox marks on his face, shared by the comte de Mirabeau (who translated Milton in the early days of the French Revolution). An acquaintance unkindly described Lewes as 'the ugliest man in London'. But his appearance wasn't the reason for Evans's lack of interest. She had recently been rejected by his friend, the psychologist Herbert Spencer, and she didn't expect to fall in love a second time – certainly not so soon.[15] The following year, she met Lewes again, and after that he became a familiar presence in her letters. The serious Marian had written him off for his ironic attitude, but she came to see it as a mask for a deep thinker.[16] By 1853, they were in a relationship. But there was a problem: Lewes was married. His wife, Agnes, was having an affair with his friend Thornton Hunt. Inspired by the bohemian life of Percy Shelley, Hunt kept a house in London where

George Henry Lewes (1870s). A *carte de visite*, a cheap photographic print, designed to be exchanged with friends.

lovers came and went. Agnes came and eventually didn't leave again. Lewes had separated from her but they couldn't get a divorce – divorce was expensive, difficult, and entailed a reputation-destroying accusation. The freethinking Evans decided she didn't mind that he was married, and the couple eloped to Germany. When they returned, they confirmed the suspicions of their friends that they were living in an illegal relationship. Some thought her monstrous, others insane.[17] Her brother stopped speaking to her, as did some of her closest friends. Respectable women wouldn't call on her. The scandal gave her an unwelcome connection to Milton.

In 1855, Evans and Lewes moved to suburban Richmond upon Thames to insulate themselves against society's scorn. Their companionship was deep and mutually sustaining. She is said to have read everything, and what she didn't read, he read.[18] One day, she reviewed a new biography of Milton. 'The principal phases and incidents of Milton's life are familiar to us all', she writes, as if embarrassed for him and for herself.[19] She discusses his unhappy marriage with an evident understanding: 'tender pity might be had of those who have unwarily, in a thing never practised before, made themselves the bondmen of a luckless and helpless matrimony'.[20] Since people aren't allowed to rehearse marriage, the law shouldn't punish them for not getting it right the first time. She was thinking not only of Milton but also of Lewes. Two centuries after Milton's campaign for divorce reform, the law in Britain still made divorce difficult. Eliot's review refers to an ongoing campaign by Caroline Norton, who had left her abusive husband, been prosecuted for adultery, and denied a divorce. In 1857, a bill would be passed, permitting men to divorce on the basis of adultery alone. But for women, adultery had to be coupled with some more serious wrong. In writing the review, Evans must have felt discomfort about her own case, as a woman living with a married man. She made it clear that such cases deserved not only pity but new laws. Milton's life had clearly made an impression. That same year, she wrote in a letter about her husband's health: 'I have just been reading that Milton suffered from indigestion, quite an affecting fact to me.'[21] Why was it so affecting? Perhaps because she continued to associate Milton with Lewes: not only for his unfortunate marriage but also because she thought of Milton as a husband.

Evans nursed a desire to write fiction, and Lewes encouraged her to try: they needed the money. When she finished writing her first story, they read it together and wept at the ending. It was good. Published under a man's name – George Eliot – her first novel, *Adam Bede* (1859), was an immediate hit. As Eliot's fame grew, she and Lewes moved to a larger house, where they hosted more, receiving luminaries including Emerson. Even though her marriage status had made her a pariah, Eliot described Victorian society in her novels with a generosity of spirit that had not been extended to her. By this time, she was not exactly a radical, but her early scepticism survives in her subtle understanding of character.[22] Like Wordsworth, she had come to see the impediments to progress as inevitable, especially in rural England. Her novels would dramatise a conflict between reformers, who wanted to change the world but didn't entirely live in it, and those rooted in the world who couldn't accept change. But Eliot's unusual marital situation was both her connection to Milton and the source of an enduring radical charge in her work.

With their demonic seducers, unsuspecting heroines, and regency Edens, the novels of the eighteenth and nineteenth centuries everywhere show the influence of *Paradise Lost*. Henry Makepeace Thackeray dropped echoes of it into his sprawling social satire, *Vanity Fair*. In *Jane Eyre*, Charlotte Brontë used echoes of Milton's threatened Paradise to describe the vulnerability of a governess in Thornfield Hall, where her employer, Mr Rochester, spies on her in the garden. Readers would have been as unsurprised to see Milton's lines as references to the Bible. *Paradise Lost* was not only a wellspring of influence but also a measure of ambition. For Eliot, as for Wordsworth, Milton's epic was something to read when preparing to write a career-defining work. She and Lewes were in the habit of reading aloud to each other in the evenings. In 1870, they read *Paradise Lost*, and it found its way into the story she was writing.

'Miss Brooke' was about a young woman living in the provinces whose marriage goes terribly wrong. Eventually, Eliot decided to fold it with another story she had been writing and together they became a novel, *Middlemarch: A Study of Provincial Life* (1871–2). Despite its modest subtitle, it is an ambitious work. In the book's 'Prelude', Eliot talks of how spirited young women could find 'no epic life' in her society. Epics sent their protagonists far beyond the domestic sphere, on paths more adventurous even than Eliot's own unusual life. Instead, *Middlemarch* displaces the wish for heroic action into domestic, middle-class, provincial Britain. As she wrote her novel, Milton was in her mind. In 1872, while writing its final part, Eliot wrote to a friend:

> Glad you are reading my demigod Milton! We also are rather old-fashioned in our light reading just now; for I have rejected Heyse's German stories, brand new, in favour of dear old Johnson's 'Lives of the Poets,' which I read aloud in my old age with a delicious revival of girlish impressions.[23]

George Eliot in 1865, when she had published four novels but not yet started work on *Middlemarch*. Drawing by Frederick William Burton.

What were those 'girlish impressions'? Was Milton her girlhood crush? Did she, years before meeting Emerson, 'the first man I saw', fantasise about Milton as a husband? This is the first time we have encountered someone with a crush on the poet. References to and echoes of *Paradise Lost* litter most of Eliot's seven novels, but in *Middlemarch* this unusual erotic view of Milton is held up to scrutiny.

Dorothea Brooke, the protagonist of *Middlemarch*, is a young woman of great vitality. Framed by tightly braided hair, her face glows with interest in the world. She hopes for a marriage of minds, but this proves difficult in the provincial town of Middlemarch. One man who might have been her match, the ambitious doctor Tertius Lydgate, falls for a materialistic young belle. The one man who shows interest is the bluff Tory baronet, Sir James Chettam. Her frustrated desire is expressed via a fantasy of marrying a long-dead writer:

> She felt sure that she would have accepted the judicious Hooker, if she had been born in time to save him from that wretched mistake he made in matrimony; or John Milton when his blindness had come on; or any of the other great men whose habits it would have been glorious piety to endure, but an amiable handsome baronet, who said 'Exactly' to her remarks even when she expressed uncertainty—how could he affect her as a lover?[24]

It's understandable to admire Milton for his poetry, but to imagine marrying him is questionable. The other writer she mentions – the seventeenth-century Archbishop Richard Hooker – was also the victim of a bad marriage. Given her tastes, it's little surprise that Dorothea falls for the elderly, learned priest Edward Casaubon. He seems to be exactly what she is looking for: a fatherly, learned scholar, who might need her help with his work. If Dorothea proves useful, he might even bother to educate her.

Dorothea sees her suitor through the rose-tinted spectacles of *Paradise Lost*. She had read it, as George Eliot had, as a young woman of marrying age. When Casaubon explains the nature of his research, Dorothea compares him to Milton's 'affable archangel'.[25] She is thinking of the archangel Raphael, who gently educates Adam and Eve in Milton's Eden. When Dorothea's sister and uncle speak unkindly of Casaubon, the narrator cautions us not to jump to conclusions:

> I am not sure that the greatest man of his age, if ever that solitary superlative existed, could escape these unfavourable reflections of himself in various small mirrors; and even Milton, looking for his portrait in a spoon, must submit to have the facial angle of a bumpkin.[26]

Milton here is 'the greatest man of his age', and a byword for physical attractiveness. In a world where women were denied the opportunity to *be* Milton, it's no surprise that Dorothea's goal is to marry someone like him. But the poet didn't educate his wives, and nor would Casaubon. He turns out to be the last thing Dorothea needs.

'I live too much with the dead,' Casaubon says in a moment of self-awareness. He's writing a book called *The Key to All Mythologies*, which proposes to discover the true origins of all pagan myths in

Christian scripture. This theory is curiously similar to the idea in Book I of *Paradise Lost*, that the fallen angels have an afterlife as devils in pagan society. If Casaubon was unconsciously reproducing Milton's poetic idea as a serious theological hypothesis, it's no wonder that he lives with an increasing dread that his labours have been in vain. His ambitious project is misguided, impossible, and he will never finish it. Once they are married, Dorothea urges him to publish his research, and he becomes enraged. Perhaps you know someone who has made a book the secret destiny of their soul and then has never written it. Casaubon is the most extreme version of these people. Everyone in Middlemarch except for Dorothea can see the truth. Her sister, Celia, compares Casaubon to a 'death's head moth'. Celia thinks of his fruitless learning as a kind of 'damp', fearing it will spread to her sister like furniture in an abandoned house. Casaubon's nephew, Will Ladislaw, calls the marriage a 'virgin-sacrifice'. A brief reference to galvanism – the science of electrocution, used in *Frankenstein* to animate the patchwork of corpses that make up the monster – suggests that Eliot might have been thinking of Mary Shelley's novel. Like Frankenstein's unhappy monster, who longs for a female version of himself, the only marriage Dorothea can imagine turns out to be a gross mismatch.

Now disillusioned, Dorothea compares Casaubon to Milton once again. Now the comparison is less favourable: 'Dorothea had thought that she could have been patient with John Milton, but she had never imagined him behaving in this way'.[27] She comes to see that, in her husband, the living spirit of religion has become deadening. To use Milton's unforgettable metaphor, Dorothea is 'a living soule bound to a dead corps'. Casaubon limps on, alive enough only to oppress his wife. She insists that she wants to be useful, even if she can't be stimulated.

> 'Could I not be preparing myself now to be more useful?' said Dorothea to him, one morning, early in the time of courtship; 'Could I not learn to read Latin and Greek aloud to you, as Milton's daughters did to their father, without understanding what they read?'

Her husband replies:

> 'I fear that would be wearisome to you,' said Mr Casaubon, smiling; 'And, indeed, if I remember rightly, the young women you have mentioned regarded that exercise in unknown tongues as a ground for rebellion against the poet.'[28]

One of the extraordinary things about *Middlemarch* is the empathy Eliot extends to characters who in another novel would be mere villains. Casaubon's experience of marriage is tragic – his young wife proves to be a torture to him. Later, when Casaubon becomes conscious of his imminent death, and the waste of his life's work, Eliot's writing is devastating. Here, even the most unlikable man deserves pity. And it falls to Casaubon to make the criticism of Milton that Eliot didn't make anywhere else: that the poet drove his daughters away with intolerable demands. It might have seemed ungrateful for Eliot to criticise Milton for the things that a million other men had done to their wives and daughters. He did at least write a masterpiece – unlike Casaubon. But Eliot's criticism of her 'demigod' is there, in Dorothea's abject wish to be used and in Casaubon's smiling refusal.

The first half of *Middlemarch* is a horror story about the waste of women's potential. For Eliot, Milton represented not only the heights of achievement but also the way that men have prevented women from flourishing. There *were* women who lived heroic lives, even in the provinces: I don't know if Eliot knew how much Dorothy Wordsworth's quick-eyed observations informed William's poetry, which Eliot loved. But she did know how often men stood in front of them. Later in the novel, Dorothea's uncle mentions offhand that Casaubon's spirited young nephew, Will Ladislaw, might make a good secretary 'like Hobbes, Milton, Swift – that sort of man.'[29] This is a hint of her future happiness.

The sky over Eden now glows with stars. The creatures are asleep, except the nightingale: 'She all night long her amorous descant sung' (IV:603). The word 'am-or-ous' contains an extra, unstressed syllable, which makes it sound like a cascade of words: 'AM-or-ous

DES-cant'. Adam tells Eve that the next day they must begin to prune and shape the garden. Incapable of innuendo, Adam says 'More hands' (IV:629) are needed to carry out the task. It is their job to mate. Eve replies: 'Unargued I obey' (IV:636). If this sounds disturbingly robotic, she launches into a speech that is a perfect Renaissance love poem:

> With thee conversing I forget all time
> All seasons and their change, all please alike (IV:639–40)

It is an acknowledged experience of romantic love to lose consciousness of time. This is what Satan means when he says their relationship is the 'happier Eden' (IV:507): it is without time, without regret about the past or anxiety about the future. Eve's speech echoes Milton's argument, in his writings on divorce, that conversation is the main pleasure of marriage. Without Adam, she continues, Paradise would not be Paradise:

> Nor grateful evening mild, nor silent night
> With this her solemn bird, nor walk by moon,
> Or glittering starlight without thee is sweet (IV:654–6)

She now asks a strange question: who are the stars for, if they still shine while we are asleep? This signals a burgeoning curiosity about the world around her: Adam will try to contain it, but he will fail, and it will bring about their downfall.

The married couple retire to a bower embroidered with flowers, a sacred place where no insect dare enter. Inside, Eve decorates the bed with petals, and a heavenly choir provides the soundtrack. Adam and Eve pray to God, asking him to help them populate the Earth. Then Milton describes the first sex in history:

> Straight side by side were laid, nor turned I ween
> Adam from his fair spouse, nor Eve the rites
> Mysterious of connubial love refused (IV:741–3)

'Ween' is one of the least erotic verbs in English: it means speculate, something that Milton does only very coyly, saying that the two humans did not turn away from each other. These negative statements – 'nor turned I ween . . . nor Eve . . . refused' – offer a kind of linguistic bower for the sexual act. Other Christian writers claimed that Adam and Eve did not have sex in Eden: Milton attacks them as 'hypocrites' (IV:744). Sex is holy, he insists, when done with the right heart. This is the moment of greatest happiness and it is all too brief. For here is Satan, 'Squat like a toad, close at the ear of Eve' (IV:800). That is where he is discovered by the archangel Uriel and a squad of God's policemen. What was he whispering in the ear of the sleeping Eve? And what, if anything, did she hear? We won't find out until the next chapter. Now Satan flees, but before long he will return.

The scenes between Adam and Eve describe marriage tenderly, showing its bliss but also its difficulties. In this, Milton anticipated Eliot's own portrait of marriage. In the moving 'Finale' of *Middlemarch*, after telling us about Dorothea's new marriage, Eliot's story converges with Milton's poem:

> Marriage, which has been the bourne of so many narratives, is still a great beginning, as it was to Adam and Eve, who kept their honeymoon in Eden, but had their first little one among the thorns and thistles of the wilderness. It is still the beginning of the home epic – the gradual conquest or irremediable loss of that complete union which makes the advancing years a climax, and age the harvest of sweet memories in common.[30]

Middlemarch shows that marriage is not a happy ending, as it is in Shakespeare's comedies, and thousands of eighteenth-century novels. Marriage is, instead, the beginning of another epic. This is one way in which George Eliot's epic novel imitated *Paradise Lost*, which ends when Adam and Eve's marriage is still only just beginning. But here she doesn't name Milton, perhaps because in her treatment of marriage, she had outdone him.

Eliot's relationship with Lewes followed the traditional gender hierarchy in many ways: he held the purse strings, and kept her protected from the world, perhaps too strictly.[31] We can only speculate, since they maintained a conventional Victorian privacy. But it's clear that, with him, she found happiness. Late in life, a reader asked her if Casaubon was based on Lewes. Eliot replied that Casaubon was partly based on herself: she, too, lived 'too much with the dead'.[32] How else

After their first night in Eden, Adam gently wakes Eve, who has had a bad dream. Engraving by Gustave Doré (1866).

would she have written so intimately of Casaubon, if his monstrosity had not also been, to some extent, her own? Happily, Eliot had a life partner who was quite the same way inclined: Lewes was writing a huge tome about psychology, and the couple jokingly referred to it as the *Key to all Psychologies*. There is a kind of necrophilia in anyone who spends too much time reading old books, and they were alert to that. Milton may have been a girlish crush, but as a mature writer, Eliot came to see him as a cautionary tale. Incompatibility turns marriage into a living death, and even necrophiliacs need more than that.

George Eliot was no revolutionary. She had limited interest in the women's movement, although she did make a contribution to Girton, the first women's college at Cambridge. If her writing was radical, it was in the generosity with which it treated individuals who had been ostracised by a society for desires that were blameless and sincere. Her novels were a crucial tonic to Victorian prudishness, and Victorian readers loved them, even the Queen. Lewes died in 1878, and after a period of intense mourning, Eliot suddenly married. Her husband was the forty-year-old John Cross, a devoted follower and close friend. Marriage brought her new respectability, and a letter of congratulation from her estranged brother. When Eliot died, in 1880, it was deemed that she could not be buried among the poets in Westminster Abbey because of her unorthodox relationship history. But the deadening moral conservativism of Victorian society did not stem the growing consciousness that expanding education and ambitious writers helped create.

5. James Redpath Tries to Start an Insurrection

Adam rises before the dawn. The ground is dewy with pearls. He is perfectly rested but turns to find Eve sleeping fitfully. He whispers that they must rise and make the most of the day. She opens her eyes and clings to him. In the night, she says, she was woken by a voice that sounded like his. The voice told her to rise and enjoy the night's cool tranquillity. 'I rose as at thy call but found thee not' (V:48). She began to walk the dark paths of the garden, under a pregnant moon. The voice led her to the Tree of Knowledge: the one from which they are forbidden to eat. Next to the tree, she saw a creature. Unlike Adam, this creature is immediately alluring: an angel with 'dewy locks' (V:56). Before her eyes, the heavenly creature had spoken to the tree, asking why its fruit was forbidden. What's wrong with knowledge? the angel had asked. Why would God put the tree here, if it were not good? She watched in silent horror as 'He plucked, he tasted; me damp horror chilled' (V:65). He offered her the forbidden fruit; suddenly they flew up into the air, and just as suddenly the creature was gone.

Adam listens in dismay. His wife has an erotic dream about someone else on their wedding night. She's not responsible for her dreams, but it's impossible for him not to feel betrayed. Still, he wants to comfort her. At night, he tells her, reason retires and fantasy takes its place, carrying out its own 'wild work' (V:112), creating mad shapes out of experience. Adam then says that evil thoughts can enter our mind without causing a stain: Eve is still innocent.

> So cheered he his fair spouse, and she was cheered,
> But silently a gentle tear let fall
> From either eye, and wiped them with her hair (V:129–31)

Adam sees these tears as signs of her remorse, and he kisses her cheeks. But we might also wonder if Eve's tears are the sign of something unconsoled in her: an intuition that this creature will return to tempt her again, or that an unacceptable desire now lingers in her.

Adam and Eve then praise God for his creation. God is listening, and he turns to the archangel Raphael, instructing him to go down to Eden and warn them about Satan. He doesn't do this to protect the humans but so they can't blame him for their eventual Fall – once again, God comes across as legalistic and unlikable. Raphael flies down to Eden, appearing to the humans like a moon swimming into the telescope of Galileo, a ship sailing from world to world, a phoenix being born in fire. The humans guess that this apparition is coming to tell them something. Adam asks Eve to prepare some food, as he goes out to greet their guest. They sit to eat a meal of nuts and berries:

> Meanwhile at table Eve
> Ministered naked, and their flowing cups
> With pleasant liquors crowned: oh innocence
> Deserving Paradise! (V:443–6)

If picturing Eve as a naked waitress seems pornographic, Milton adds that the angels could look at her without lust or jealousy. Unlike the fallen human reader.

The angel then tells Adam about death, which will be painless, an effortless transition to Heaven. If you are obedient, Raphael adds.

With the quickness of a clever child, Adam asks: what do you mean 'if'? How could we disobey our Maker? Eve is silent, but she's listening.

You have been made free to choose obedience, Raphael says. Others have disobeyed, and they have fallen from Heaven. Adam is curious to hear more. So Raphael promises to tell of the civil war in Heaven. This will be the main action in *Paradise Lost* – an epic within an epic.

Boston, Massachusetts, 1853

On 27 January, a man known as 'the golden trumpet of abolition' gave a speech to the American Anti-Slavery Society. Wendell Phillips was a Harvard-educated lawyer who had converted to the cause of anti-slavery after witnessing a pro-slavery mob rampaging through the streets of Boston, and he soon became a popular speaker on the abolitionist circuit. In the 1850s, abolitionism was still a fringe position, even in Massachusetts, which was the birthplace of the white abolition movement. It was a time of caution in the federal government. The US Senate had recently passed the Great Compromise of 1850, which abolished slavery in some states but preserved it in others. Bundled into the Compromise was the Fugitive Slave Act, which required that slaves who escaped to the North be returned to their Southern masters. No place in the United States was now safe for fugitive slaves. The senator for Massachusetts, Daniel Webster, had controversially supported the measure. The abolitionists never forgave him for this act of realpolitik, and that was what Phillips was there to talk about.

Phillips was speaking at the Melodeon Hall in downtown Boston, where the highlights that year included a troupe of acting monkeys and a conjurer known as the 'great wizard of the north'. His speech that night was both serious and theatrical. Where the cautious churches failed to support abolition, Phillips declared, the theatres were ready for it. The American public was open to abolition, even as their cowardly political representatives delayed. Referring to the 'moderates', and their attempts to appease the Southern Slave Power, Phillips compared the US Senate to 'that other Capitol'.[1] He was talking about Hell, and its Parliament, Pandaemonium. As a younger man, Phillips had read Milton devotedly and had followed in the poet's footsteps on a trip to Florence. Now he was using Milton's work to paint the US Senate as a chamber of demons. Working the crowd to his conclusion, Phillips declared: 'our friends go down there, and must be dwarfed into pigmies!'[2] The Northern politicians, sacrificing their moral principles for a seat at the table, are like devils squeezing themselves into atoms to enter the chamber. If Milton's Hell is a parody of democracy, some human assemblies are no better.

The abolitionist struggle was born from the contradictions of American independence. The US Constitution, signed in 1787, had established a lasting unity between the states. It didn't mention the word 'slavery', neither outlawing the practice nor explicitly approving it. But Jefferson's declaration had opened with a claim about equality that was incompatible with its existence. Most of the Northern states quickly abolished slavery, but the Southern economy remained dependent on it. The politics of the early 1800s, when the United States was expanding west, involved a careful balancing act: every time a new slave state was created, a new free state would be created. This balance lasted for a surprisingly long time: more than fifty years. But the abolitionist movement was growing. At first, their strategy was to demonise slavery, and this frequently involved *Paradise Lost*.

Abolitionists had long seen Milton as an ally. In his triumphant book *The History of the Rise, Progress, and Accomplishment of the Abolition of the African Slave-trade by the British Parliament* (published in 1808), the English abolitionist Thomas Clarkson writes: 'Several of our old English writers, though they have not mentioned the African Slave-trade, or the slavery consequent upon it, in their respective works, have yet given their testimony.'[3] And one of those writers is 'our great Milton'. Clarkson was the most effective campaigner for the abolitionist cause, from its beginnings in 1787 to the British Parliament's abolition of the slave trade in 1807 and then of slavery itself in 1833. The pragmatic Clarkson didn't worry himself with the details: in fact, Milton said little about the possession of humans as property and cared most about the idea that monarchy made Protestant citizens into 'political slaves'. In the 1830s, American abolitionists would resurrect the same wishful image of an abolitionist Milton.

The most influential abolitionist in the United States was William Lloyd Garrison. The Massachusetts-born printer launched his career with an incendiary speech on 4 July 1829. Instead of celebrating America's independence, Garrison announced that it was sleepwalking towards an uprising that would be worse than the Haitian Revolution, an event regarded with horror by many white Americans. Garrison rejected gradual emancipation and opposed the American Colonization Society, which proposed to ship slaves to American colonies in Africa. His chosen method was 'moral suasion': persuading his fellow Americans that slavery was evil. This made him notorious, especially in the slave states. Maryland imprisoned Garrison, and fined him, and Georgia put $5,000 on his head.[4]

Undaunted, he compared the 'ridicule and abuse' he faced to that which Milton had suffered in the 1640s, declaring: 'It is honorable to be in the company of JOHN MILTON.'[5] But the poet had an even more important role to play. In 1831, Garrison launched a newspaper, the *Liberator*. In its pages, 'Pandaemonium' became shorthand for slavery, pouring moral scorn on the Southern Slave Power.[6] Garrison wasn't interested in identifying with Satan, like an introspective Romantic poet; instead he used Milton to identify the workings of the Devil in America.

The passing of the Fugitive Slave Act in 1850 led to frustration with Garrison's methods. Whereas Garrison believed the US Constitution was fundamentally pro-slavery, and said the free states should secede from the Union, others disagreed. These abolitionists did not want to secede; they wanted to rid the Union of slavery, by violence if necessary. The most famous was former slave Frederick Douglass, a charismatic speaker and the author of three memoirs. In the second of these, *My Bondage and My Freedom* (1855), he describes how he emancipated himself mentally while still enslaved after physically standing up to a violent overseer. In Douglass's lecture 'Self-Made Men' (1856), he recognises a similar quality in Milton: 'Vast acquirements and splendid achievements stand to the credit of men of feeble frames and slender constitutions,' Douglass says: 'Milton was blind.'[7] Men and women who were physically weak could still be effective in the struggle for liberty, he insisted: 'those men were more to the world than a thousand Sampsons'.[8] By 'self-made', Douglass wasn't talking about money-making but a freedom of the mind – one achieved by violence, if necessary.

One of the most radical abolitionists was the heavy-drinking, idealistic, and energetic journalist James Redpath. Born in England, Redpath migrated to America in the late 1840s. At that time, he was 'an abolitionist, but a very mild one'.[9] At the age of nineteen, he became a journalist for the *New York Tribune*, which was run by the famous anti-slavery editor Horace Greeley. As a junior reporter, one of his jobs was to reprint accounts of Southern slavery in a column entitled 'The Facts of Slavery'. In 1854, inspired by Harriet Beecher Stowe's bestselling anti-slavery novel *Uncle Tom's Cabin*, Redpath travelled to the American South to observe slavery for himself. He wanted to ask enslaved people if any of them supported slavery. He visited plantations after dark, sometimes sleeping in slaves' cabins and departing before dawn. His reports circulated widely in Northern papers, and were later published as a book, *The Roving Editor, Or Talks with Slaves in the Southern States* (1859). Redpath was not interested in recycling sensational accounts of violence: instead, he created a unique record of the political beliefs of enslaved people. The experience made him an 'ultra abolitionist'.[10] He now believed the only solution was a violent one.

In 1855, Redpath travelled to Kansas, which was then embroiled in a Border War between pro- and anti-slavery militias. He was there not only as a reporter but also as a militant. Redpath sought out the secret encampment of John Brown, a zealous abolitionist who had travelled to Kansas with his sons to fight tooth and nail against the pro-slavery militias. He became one of Brown's key supporters, and may have encouraged him to the most radical act of the decade. In October 1859, with twenty-one volunteers, Brown attempted to seize an arms depot at Harpers Ferry in Virginia, hoping he could precipitate a general uprising across the South. The raid was under-resourced, badly planned, and quickly put down. Brown was seized and his supporters went into hiding. That same year, as the insurrectionist leader was tried for treason, Redpath wrote *The Public Life of Captain John Brown* (1859), a resounding endorsement of his insurrectionary methods. Herman Melville later called Brown 'the meteor of the war', because, less than two years after Harpers Ferry, the Civil War broke out. Once again, Milton was present at this revolutionary moment, this time not as a republican theorist or a Puritan moralist but as a preacher of insurrection.

In 1850s New York, a Black vanguard had prepared to fight a war against slavery, with Milton at their fingertips. The *Anglo-African Magazine*, a pioneering literary publication founded by Thomas Hamilton, was established with the goal of promoting the education of Black people as a means to political power. In its pages, one writer quoted one of Satan's adamantine phrases: 'To be weak is to be miserable.'[11] To crush slavery, they would need Black schools and Black

James Redpath as an abolitionist reporter in the Kansas Border War, holding a rifle and a copy of the *New York Tribune* (*c.*1856).

magazines. The *Anglo-American* set new standards for publishing, including in its pages eminent Black writers including Frederick Douglass, Martin Delany, James McCune Smith, and Frances Ellen Watkins Harper.[12] Hamilton also set up a weekly newspaper, the *Weekly Anglo-African*, which distinguished itself from other Black periodicals by reporting both on Southern slavery and life in the North, where Black people were still not accorded full citizenship. Founded in 1859, it had followed the deteriorating relations between North and South. Then, in the early morning of Friday 12 April 1861, the Confederate battery on the southern side of Charleston Harbour had started firing at Fort Sumter, the Union outpost on the northern side. 'The War Commenced' – announced the *New York Times* the next morning, as the bombardment continued.[13] Soon after that, a journalist started to write an editorial for the *Weekly Anglo-African*.

The unsigned editorial appeared in the newspaper the following Saturday, 20 April. Its title announced its militant message: 'Close Up! Steady!' These are instructions that a drill sergeant would bark at troops in a parade, ordering them to catch up with those marching ahead. The editorial, however, begins on a different note:

> One of the finest passages in Milton's 'Paradise Lost' is that in which he describes the grief of the fallen archangel, Satan, at the discovery of the sad plight of his associates and his evocation of the stricken host from the stupor in which they had lain entranced. It is a sublime effort of inventive genius.[14]

The writer is thinking of Satan's speech in Book I of *Paradise Lost*, when he rouses his stupefied followers from the burning lake. Readers of the *Weekly Anglo-African* were well prepared to recognise this. In the 1830s, New York's Black vanguard had gathered in educational societies to discuss poetry and politics.[15] In 1839, Charles L. Reason – later the first Black college professor – gave a talk to New York's Phoenixonian Society, which considered the merits of Milton and Wordsworth, to his listeners' 'universal satisfaction'.[16] At the Institute for Colored Youth in Philadelphia, students read Milton in the Junior Class.[17] *Paradise Lost* was required reading for the future leaders of the Black community.

Confident of its readers' familiarity, the *Weekly Anglo-African* editorial then compares the scene from Milton's Hell with the condition of Black Americans:

> the poet's conception is more than realized in the prostrate condition of those immortal beings to whom the Almighty has given skins of ebon hue [i.e. Black Americans]. If the contemplation of the contrast between the former beatitude and present misery of his guilty followers could melt the soul of the archfiend, with what commiseration must pure intelligences [i.e. angels] have viewed our ruin, and wondered why God's justice was so long delayed?[18]

Given that Satan wept to see the other fallen angels brought down to Hell, what would God's angels think of Black people's treatment in America? Why had they been denied justice for so long? Then the editorial comes to its point: 'God's time is come, and the batteries of Charleston harbor thunder forth to us his call: "Awake! Arise!" '[19] They will revive the spirit of 1776, it continues, only this time making sure the new revolution would benefit Black people. If this seems as clear as day, in April 1861 Black Americans were not at all certain how they could fight against slavery.

At the beginning of the American Civil War, Black men were not permitted to fight in the Northern army. Thanks to the deep-seated prejudices of the time, white politicians doubted that they were capable of fighting, and they were not even permitted to drill.[20] In May, an informal regiment of Black men marched up Broadway in New York, and they were forcibly dispersed. In July, the governor of New York refused a fully equipped Black regiment.[21] Both sides insisted that the Civil War was not about freeing the slaves: the South was fighting for states' rights, the North was preserving the Union. Because of this, there were disagreements in New York's Black community about what they could do to help the Southern slaves: whether to lobby to fight in the Union army, organise slave conspiracies, or simply wait. In May 1861, Thomas Hamilton chaired a lively debate on the issue that was attended by many eminent Black New Yorkers. But the author of the *Weekly Anglo-African* editorial was not Hamilton, who had sold the newspaper one month earlier. The 16 March issue had announced that the new editor was George Lawrence, someone 'long and favorably known to this community'.[22] Lawrence was the son of a prominent Black preacher, whose first published work was a poem about a slave uprising.[23] The new editor of the *Weekly Anglo-African* was at ease in the insurrectionary mode. But it may not have been Lawrence who wrote the editorial.

The new owner of the *Weekly Anglo-African* was James Redpath. After John Brown's execution, the energetic young journalist had become sidetracked. In 1859, a lecture on Toussaint Louverture by Wendell Phillips had piqued Redpath's curiosity and he had visited Haiti. He fantasised about becoming a 'philanthropic pirate', using the seas to liberate the Southern slaves.[24] Soon, however, he was entangled in a new scheme. Between the time that Redpath's ship left New York and arrived at Cape Haitien, there was a coup in Haiti, and

The Attack on Fort Sumter, 12 April 1861. Contemporary engraving by Albert Bobbett.

Nicholas Geffrard had been installed as President. In Haiti, Redpath had an interview with the island's new leader. The Haitian countryside had been underpopulated since the Revolution, and Geffrard wanted to persuade Black Americans to help stimulate its cotton industry by attracting skilled emigrants. Several hundred free Black people had emigrated there from Louisiana.[25] In 1860, Redpath visited Haiti again and had another interview with the president, who was wearing a 'blue velvet smoking cap, with rich embroidery'.[26] Geffrard asked if he was on the run from the US government – this was just after Harpers Ferry – but Redpath assured him that they were no longer trying to arrest him. Still, at that moment, it was not clear where the next insurrection would come from. Brown had failed and civil war seemed implausible. It was at that moment that Redpath became the General Agent of the Haitian Emigration Bureau, at a generous salary of $3,000 per year. This was why Redpath bought the *Weekly Anglo-African* some months later: he wanted to promote the controversial cause of emigration.

Having bought New York's eminent Black periodical, Redpath

moved its printing to Boston, where he could oversee it, while Lawrence remained in New York. Redpath sent his former colleague, a white journalist called Richard Hinton, to work alongside his editor. This arrangement didn't last long. In mid-May, Redpath wrote a haughty letter to Hinton: 'I am the leader of the Haytien emigration movement, & the editor consequently of the organ of it.'[27] A week later, Redpath fired Hinton, declaring: 'I must be free to work out my own destiny.'[28] That same month, Redpath reassured Lawrence of his editorial freedom: 'Pray remember this – that you will give free expression to your own thought, not asking whether it agrees with mine or not.'[29] Despite this, Redpath seems to have maintained a tight control of the editorial direction. Under his ownership, the *Weekly Anglo-African* had abandoned its impartiality and had become an organ of the Haitian Emigration Bureau. This was the main reason for Redpath's choice of editor: Lawrence was the New York agent of the bureau.

The takeover of the *Weekly Anglo-African* by Redpath – who was not only white but also an emigrationist – was divisive. Many Black Americans opposed the emigration movement, believing they should stay in the United States and demand full citizenship. However, the Fugitive Slave Act of 1850 had raised the issue again – if fugitive slaves weren't safe in the North, some thought, maybe they should leave America? Some eminent writers supported the idea. But for many Black people, the idea of emigrationism remained out of the question. Subscribers to the *Weekly Anglo-African* resented the fact that a white man had taken over an important forum for debate among the Black community and put it to the service of such a contentious project. On 17 May, a group of Black men arranged a meeting in Boston to organise their opposition to Redpath. They sent their resolutions to the leading abolitionist newspapers:

> Resolved, That we firmly, flatly, uncompromisingly oppose, condemn and denounce as unfair and unjust, as unwise and as unchristian, the fleeing, colonizing efforts urged by James Redpath, the white, seconded by George Lawrence, Jr., the black, who is employed by him.

> Resolved . . . we do declare that he [Redpath] is not justified in the deceptive policy of placing at the head of the paper, like the figure-head of a ship, the name of George Lawrence, Jr., a colored man.[30]

The anti-emigration men asked Garrison's opinion: he said that he didn't oppose 'voluntary emigration'.[31] Quoting a line from *Paradise Lost* – 'The world was all before them' – Garrison said that he wanted Black people to be free to go wherever in the world they wished but he didn't want to encourage racist whites to believe 'they can be effectually "got rid of"'.[32] Emigration was not the solution, Garrison said, for the thousandth time. It was abolition without delay.

Until so recently, Redpath had been of the same mind. He believed in immediate abolition, going beyond Garrison in his belief in violent means. Encouraging Black Americans to emigrate to Haiti did not, in Redpath's mind, inhibit the abolition movement. But a white man leading this controversial project was bound to generate resistance. As Garrison pointed out, Redpath's allies did not necessarily have the best interests of Black people in mind. An article in the *New York Times*, entitled 'A Paradise for Negroes', praised Redpath's project for its capacity to remove 'the race element which the North can so well spare'.[33] Thinking of populations as 'race elements', and ones that can be removed, comes dangerously close to a genocidal logic. Black writers were alert to this fact. In 1860, an essay in the *Anglo-African Magazine*, 'What Shall We Do With the White People?' had brilliantly skewered the emigration movement. Written by an anonymous writer, 'Ethiop', the article proposed to think about the real source of America's race problem: white people. 'This is a grave problem,' the writer says, 'and gravely we shall consider it.'[34] From the genocide of Native Americans to the War of Revolution, white people had made a mess of America. 'What then shall we Anglo-Africans do with them?' Ethiop asks. The solution is not emigration for all white people, 'Ethiop' concluded even-handedly. These schemes are 'wrong in conception'. Instead, white people must find a way to live peacefully alongside other races.

In 1862, New York's Black intelligentsia turned against Redpath. Robert Hamilton started to raise funds to revive his magazine. Redpath was bitter about this. Although he had changed the name of the paper to the *Pine & Palm*, to reflect its new concern with the Caribbean, he had bought the rights to the *Anglo-African* name. In a letter to one of his agents, Redpath admitted that he had bought the newspaper for the sole reason of stopping the Black writers of the 'New York clique' from attacking his movement.[35] It had effectively been a hostile takeover. The newspaper, Redpath complained, had been on its 'last legs' before he stepped in and they had gratefully accepted his offer of $1,100. That was more than it was worth, and all he had got for that was the name and subscriber list. But now Hamilton was proposing to start up the *Anglo-African* again, and telling all his subscribers that Redpath's newspaper was untrustworthy. Redpath felt that no one had been a more sincere and energetic friend to Black people: he had even helped to negotiate the diplomatic recognition of Haiti by the US government. He had been imaginative, hoping to start a Haitian cotton industry to compete with the American South. But for the pickle with the *Anglo-African* he had no one to blame but himself.

Redpath had become a little dictator. It was surely he who wrote the 20 April editorial in the *Weekly Anglo-African*, enlisting Milton's poetry for an insurrection against slavery. In his book *The Roving Editor*, Redpath had made a similarly complex allusion, comparing a pro-slavery newspaper editor to Beelzebub.[36] The resemblance between the two allusions means we should probably see Redpath's hand in the editorial, even though it pretends to be written by a Black person. This would make it an instance of what today is called 'blackface'. Redpath's critics in Boston were surely right to say that he was using his Black editor Lawrence as a mere 'figure-head'.

But there may have been more to the editorial than this. In April 1861, the *Chicago Times* reported rumours of an army of free Black people planning to march into the South and incite the slaves to rise up with them:

> a daring scheme is on foot among the free negro population of the Northern States and the Canadas; that, under the direction of such

> turbulent agitators as Redpath, Fred. Douglass, and young John Brown, on whose shoulders has fallen most fully the mantle of his father's bloodthirsty fanaticism, they are proposing to take advantage of the first outbreak of war to consummate a raid upon the South, in which all the horrors contemplated by John Brown, Sr., will find their full realization.[37]

The *Chicago Times* alleged that Redpath and John Brown Jr had at their disposal 'an army of 8,000 Northern negroes, armed, equipped and well drilled . . . ready to march at a moment's warning'.[38] This army could cross the Canadian border in two days, and after that would incite insurrections across the South, marching through Texas, before founding a new home in Central America. The rumour was lurid but it was useful: Frederick Douglass republished it in his newspaper without denying the accusation against him, commenting that anything that scared the slave owners was a good thing. Was this the event that the *Weekly Anglo-African* was advising Black Americans to prepare themselves for? It would explain why the radical Redpath had so quickly converted to the controversial cause of emigration: not to deport Black Americans but to seek support for a more effective insurrection against slavery.

To some Black readers in the uncertain early days of the American Civil War, the *Weekly Anglo-African* editorial must have seemed like the work of a White agent provocateur, recklessly trying to incite an uprising before the right time had truly come. It is often the fate of radicals to come before their time, to be called crazy or irresponsible. The accusation might be true here. Redpath's editorship was seen by members of the Black community as an abuse of open debate, like Beelzebub standing up in Pandaemonium to make Satan's argument. He had dedicated himself to the interests of Black people, but he had become a nuisance – or worse. His adventurism, energy and self-belief had turned him into a dictator in his own sphere. During the war, emigrationism almost became federal policy. Abraham Lincoln started to look into the possibility of colonisation. In August 1862, he invited some leaders of the Black community to the White House and proposed that they start a colony in South America or the

The 'meteor of the war', abolitionist John Brown.
Photograph by Augustus Washington (*c.* 1846–7).

Caribbean. But the Civil War changed things. Ever since the war's beginning, enslaved people on Southern plantations had downed tools and fled to the Northern army, joining in their hundreds of thousands, and leaving the plantations unworked and unprofitable. In the words of the historian W. E. B. Du Bois, this was a 'general strike', and it badly weakened the Southern economy. But the war was not yet won, and Lincoln realised that he needed Black soldiers. In July 1862, Black men were finally permitted to fight for the Union army. Soon, Frederick Douglass was recruiting soldiers, and Robert Hamilton was the first Black journalist to be embedded with Union troops.[39] In January 1863, Lincoln made the Emancipation Proclamation, announcing that the slaves in any state still resisting the Union army were now considered free. This sounded the death knell for the emigration movement. The slave uprising had happened.

★

The main action of *Paradise Lost* – the heroic fighting that is characteristic of many epics – comes at the centre of its twelve-book structure. Raphael's task is a hard one: to tell Adam and Eve of a war between spirits.

One day in Heaven, before the creation of the world, God the Father gathers all the angels. He is sitting on the throne with the Son at his right side. God makes a declaration: On this day, I appoint my Son the sole ruler of the angels. Anyone who disobeys him, disobeys me, and will be cast out of Heaven. The angels are thrilled and spend the rest of the day in celebratory song and dance and feasting. All of them, that is, except one. Evening falls and the angels retire to 'Celestial tabernacles' (V:654) cooled by natural fans. One remains awake. He is an archangel, high up in the angelic hierarchy, and he feels diminished by the Son's promotion. Stewing with envy, he wakes up his subordinate, and tells him they are to leave Heaven's capital with all their troops, pretending that they have been instructed to do so by God. Under the cover of night, they lead a third of the angels, as many as the stars, to the far northern part of the celestial main. On top of a mountain, Satan raises a palace and sets himself up as God's equal. He now asks his followers if they are willing to submit to God's Son:

> Will ye submit your necks, and choose to bend
> The supple knee? (V:787–8)

Not for the last time, Satan sounds like Milton, fulminating against kings. Among the misguided horde is Abdiel, an angel who loves God more than any other. Standing boldly forward, Abdiel replies to Satan. Abdiel says the Son is naturally above the angels, since it was the Son and not God who created the angels.

'Strange point and new!' Satan replies scornfully. 'Who saw/When this creation was?' (V:855–7). He doesn't remember his birth: 'We know no time when we were not as now' (V:859). We shouldn't take any account of our origins on someone else's authority, Satan declares. Abdiel urges the other angels to return to God, and they jeer at him. So he flies away, returning to God's faithful, who welcome him as a hero. Milton no doubt saw himself as an Abdiel figure, urging his own countrymen to reject tyrants as they mocked him.

God now sends his faithful out to meet the rebels, moving as one across the darkened landscape. The two armies, once used to meeting in 'festivals of joy' (VI:94), now encounter each other as enemies. Abdiel steps up to Satan. Reasoning, rather foolishly, that someone who is morally right should also win a physical fight, Abdiel challenges him to individual combat. 'I see that most through sloth had rather *serve*' (VI:166; my italics), Satan says scornfully.

'This is servitude, / To serve the unwise' (VI:178–9), Abdiel responds. Then he swings his sword against Satan's shield, driving him back ten huge paces.

The archangel Michael sounds his trumpet, and the War in Heaven breaks out like an orchestra of cymbals. The battle hangs in the balance, until the archangel Michael spies Satan:

who that day
Prodigious power had shown, and met in arms
No equal (VI:246–8)

Soon, Satan meets Michael. They circle each other like planets. Michael lands a blow on his opponent's right side: 'then Satan first knew pain' (VI:327). Bright liquid oozes from the wound, and he is carried away by his followers, 'Gnashing for anguish and despite and shame / to find himself not matchless' (VI:340–1). He heals quickly: angels don't die except by total annihilation. Night falling, both armies retreat across the wrecked battlefield of Heaven.

In their camp, the rebel angels debate what to do. One argues they should escape: any life would be better than this pain, unless they can invent some new way to win. This is Satan's cue. Under our feet, he says, are 'materials dark and crude' (VI:478). The rebels must dig them up and use them to make war machines. The other rebels are impressed, each one wishing they had thought of this. They set to work and, the next morning, Satan leads his army into the field. Their new weapons are hidden in trenches. Satan turns to his troops and gives a speech full of innuendos, which are a signal for the artillery to start firing. Their missiles hit the faithful angels, knocking them back. Satan starts to mock them, asking why they are dancing so awkwardly.

God now decides to give his angels a special power. They throw down their spears and pull up the hills – dripping rocks, rivers, and trees – to launch at the enemy. This war isn't fair: one of the participants is omnipotent. God now tells his Son to drive the rebels out of Heaven. The Son agrees, then adds that God will eventually relinquish his power:

> thy giving, I assume,
> And gladlier shall resign, when in the end
> Thou shalt be all in all, and I in thee
> For ever, and in me all whom thou lov'st (VI:730–3)

At the end of time, there will be no more hierarchy or authority. Like a dictator, God promises that he will devolve power to everyone – just not yet.

On the third and final day of the war, the Son goes down in the 'chariot of paternal deity' (VI:750). This is a contraption of many wheels, each containing the faces of cherubs, and wings with eyes inside them, and eyes with wheels inside them. As the Son approaches, the whole of Heaven shakes – except, that is, God's throne. (Satan was lying when he said his rebellion had shaken it.) The Son holds 10,000 thunders in one hand. His enemies drop their weapons in terror, and they crunch under his almighty wheels. The Son drives them back, until at last they throw themselves out of Heaven, jumping of their own accord like frightened sheep off a cliff.

The War in Heaven is dynamic, but excessively so, even to the point of becoming cartoonish. This is one reason why the part of the poem most often used by revolutionaries is Satan's glittering speeches. The *Weekly Anglo-African* editorial found an ingenious solution to the problem of identifying one's own cause with Satan. Redpath (if that's who wrote it) took Satan's rhetoric, called it God's, and put it in the mouths of Union cannons. This allowed him to recruit Milton's epic poem for the abolitionist struggle. After the end of the American Civil War, others would do the exact opposite, putting Milton at the disposal of white supremacy.

6. The Mistick Krewe Turns Carnival on Its Head

Ninth Ward, New Orleans, 1857

On the evening of 4 January, six men met in a drugstore on the corner of Jackson Avenue and Prytania Street. At that time, New Orleans was the largest and richest city in the South. It had been part of the United States since 1803, when Napoleon negotiated the Louisiana Purchase with Jefferson, selling territories that he could no longer afford to defend after the loss of Haiti. The 1850s was a boom time and the city was growing fast, with newcomers flooding in from the North. The white population of New Orleans was now divided between the French inhabitants, and the newer, Anglo-Saxon population. In Louisiana, the white French inhabitants were called 'Creoles'. The newcomers were flooding into the Garden District, where the streets were lined with grand new villas belonging to sugar barons and plantation owners, and young businessmen would congregate at the drugstore to smoke cigars and talk business. It had become known as 'The Club'. The drugstore's owner was Dr John H. Pope, a recent transplant from New York. He was a man well acquainted with the classics, and the meeting on 4 January had literary ambitions. That evening, in the back room of the drugstore, he and the five other men decided to found a secret society. They were imitating the Cowbellion de Rakin Society, a carnival society established some years earlier in Mobile, Alabama. Some of the Cowbellions had moved to Louisiana from Mobile. There, they would establish another carnival society, and it would help make New Orleans the hedonistic capital of America.

Known as the Crescent City because it crept around a bend in the Mississippi river, New Orleans was a place of dazzling and disturbing contrasts. After the Louisiana Purchase, Jefferson sent a man to survey it. God 'made this country into Paradise', the surveyor reported, 'but Man has converted it into a *Pandemonium*'.[1] Like Milton's demonic parliament, it was a place of splendour and sin. Cries of Sicilian fruit sellers mingled with the French of the Creole inhabitants, and the Spanish chatter of sailors from Cuba. Visitors found it difficult to believe it was North America. The market was bright with flowers: 'jessamines, modest knots of white roses, glorious orange blossoms, camel[l]ias, red roses, tender pansies, exquisite verbenas, the luscious and perfect virgin's bower, and the magnolia in its season'.[2] Writers became excessive in describing New Orleans. The historian Charles Gayarré called it 'a vile compound of marshes, lagoons, swamps, bayous, fens, bogs, endless prairies, inextricable and gloomy forests, peopled with every monster of the natural and of the mythological world'.[3]

It was a city built on sugar, cotton, and tobacco, all of them produced by slave labour. New Orleans was where bales of cotton from the plantations crossing the Deep South were loaded on to ships bound for the factories of England. It was where slaves were imported, until the trade was outlawed in 1808, and where they were smuggled into America after that. In Congo Square, to the north of the city, enslaved people had congregated to play music, dance, and practise voodoo, rituals that had survived from West African religion – some say it was the birthplace of jazz.[4] The Crescent City had the largest community of free Black people in the South, many of them French speakers, wealthy, and highly refined, educating their children in Paris. It was also a bastion of resistance to change.

New Orleans had a long Mardi Gras tradition. The celebration has its roots in the religious festivals of ancient Greece and Rome, appropriated by the early Christian Church, which turned it into a feast day – 'carnevale', meaning 'farewell to the flesh' – before the forty days of fasting before Easter.[5] But the memory of ancient debauchery survived, and in cities including Paris and Venice, it was an opportunity for masking, dancing, and promiscuity. Carnival mocked power, letting the people be king for a day, reminding the governed of their strength but ultimately restoring the status quo. It was a careful exercise in social control. The first Mardi Gras celebration in Louisiana took place in 1699, on a spot they named Pointe de Mardi

Gras. New Orleans was founded in 1718, on land inhabited by the Chitimacha Tribe and known as Bulbancha, 'place of many tongues'. Within a few decades, it was a French city hosting balls. In 1790, the French Revolution had tried to prohibit carnival, which the revolutionaries saw as an instrument of tyranny.[6] Napoleon, wanting to harness its power, had restored it. After the Louisiana purchase, many Creoles feared that the Americans would ban the festivity, but it had survived. In the winter, steamships brought hedonists all the way from St Louis.

During Mardi Day, people walked the streets masked. Cross-dressing and blackface were common. So was interracial sociability. (It was difficult to segregate a masked ball.) With the balls came drinking, gambling, and prostitution. The celebrations had a violent side: the custom of *entrudo*, where 'rude boys and silly, loose women' threw flour at passers-by.[7] In 1849, they threw quicklime and bricks, knocking one woman unconscious.[8] The *Daily Crescent* called it 'a diabolical abomination'. The city council began to look into it. Some feared that the courtly extravagance of the French carnival had evaporated.[9] This is where Dr Pope and his associates came in. In early February 1856, they met again in the club room above the Old Gem Saloon. This time, they had gathered others. They were mostly merchants, accountants, lawyers, and bankers – men on the make.[10] They elected Charles M. Churchill, the owner of a hardware store, as their president. They rented rooms for their meetings, which were guarded by a sentinel and a password. And Dr Pope came up with a name: the Mistick Krewe of Comus.

Comus is the god of revelry in Greek myth. He is the son of Dionysus, god of wine, and the enchantress Circe. But the use of the word 'krewe' suggests something else is going on – Pope was invoking an early work by John Milton: *A Masque Presented at Ludlow Castle*. A masque is a private drama performed for an aristocratic audience. Milton wrote the masque for the family of the Earl of Bridgewater, and it was performed by them in 1634 to mark his appointment as Lord President of Wales. Milton's masque tells the story of a young woman, called the Lady, who gets lost in a forest, where 'Comus and his crew' encounter her. In Milton's masque, Comus is an evil spirit. He worships Hecate, goddess of enchantment, and his cup transforms the drinker into a beast.

> Come, let us our rites begin,
> 'Tis only day-light that makes sin,
> Which these dun shades will ne'er report.
> Hail goddess of nocturnal sport[11]

Later, Comus tries and fails to seduce the virtuous Lady, who is finally saved by Sabrina, a feminine spirit of chastity. The masque was meant to be a celebration of chastity but – as in *Paradise Lost* – Milton's rich description of temptation overpowers its moral purpose. Because of this, Comus became a byword not only for the triumph of chastity but for the pleasures of temptation.

The Mistick Krewe were using Milton to make carnival Protestant, distinguishing it from the older French customs. Dr Pope suggested they use the old-fashioned spelling 'krewe', emphasising the English origins of the myth.[12] They produced a constitution, which begins:

> Holding it to be a self-evident truth that man at his creation was so constituted that social and intellectual enjoyment should ever be the accompaniment of labor . . .[13]

In this parody of the Declaration of Independence, humour mixes with a serious message. Comus was more about ecstasy than equality. Unlike the other readers we have met in this book, Dr Pope and his associates left no written record of their encounter with Milton. But they put his poetry at the heart of their ritual, which stands as one of the most enduring modern interpretations of *Paradise Lost*. They were turning Milton's authority upside down, using his masque about chastity to celebrate excess, plucking a figure of Cavalier desire from the Puritan poet. Their Milton wasn't a dry theorist but a purveyor of an intoxication that was distinctly English, Protestant, and white. For Milton, the word 'crew' has a derogatory sense: he uses it nine times in *Paradise Lost* and always to describe an evil gathering. The men in New Orleans were dressing themselves in the elite

Anglo-Protestant culture that Milton represented but also specifically identifying themselves with his evil spirits.[14] This decision anticipated the sinister future of their society.

The first parade took place on 24 February 1857. Its theme was 'The Demon Actors of Paradise Lost'. A company of masked men paraded through the city, lit with torches carried by slaves. Satan was borne aloft on a great throne. (They had borrowed floats and costumes from the Cowbellions, who had held a 'Pandemonium' parade a few weeks earlier.) The Mistick Krewe called on the mayor, who was present, to give them a licence to 'raise the supernatural' inside the Gaiety Theater. This being given, they ended their parade at the doors of the theatre.

Inside, the elite of Louisiana waited in their finery, brandishing their invitations. Then the Krewe appeared on stage in new costumes. A reporter for the *Daily Crescent* described it:

> The masks displayed every fantastic idea of the fearful and horrible, their effect being, however, softened down by the richness and beauty of the costumes, and the evident decorum of the devils inside.[15]

On their heads were huge papier-mâché masks, obscuring their identities. The exhilarated reporter continues:

> they were beautiful in their ugliness – charming in their repulsiveness. Such masks were never seen in New Orleans before. There were upwards of a hundred of them, and no two alike, whilst all were grotesque to the last degree.[16]

The Krewe acted out four *tableaux vivants*, each one based on a passage from *Paradise Lost*. They had changed the order of Milton's story: the first *tableau* was Raphael's account of the Creation of the World (in Book VI); the second, the expulsion of Adam and Eve from Eden at the very end (Book XII); the third, the conference between Satan and Beelzebub (Book I); and the fourth, the devils' council at Pandaemonium (Book II). After that, the Krewe members joined the audience in a dance, 'in a manner which showed them to be very gentlemanly and agreeable devils'.[17] As the evening swam, the Krewe melting away at midnight, and the guests dancing on until daybreak,

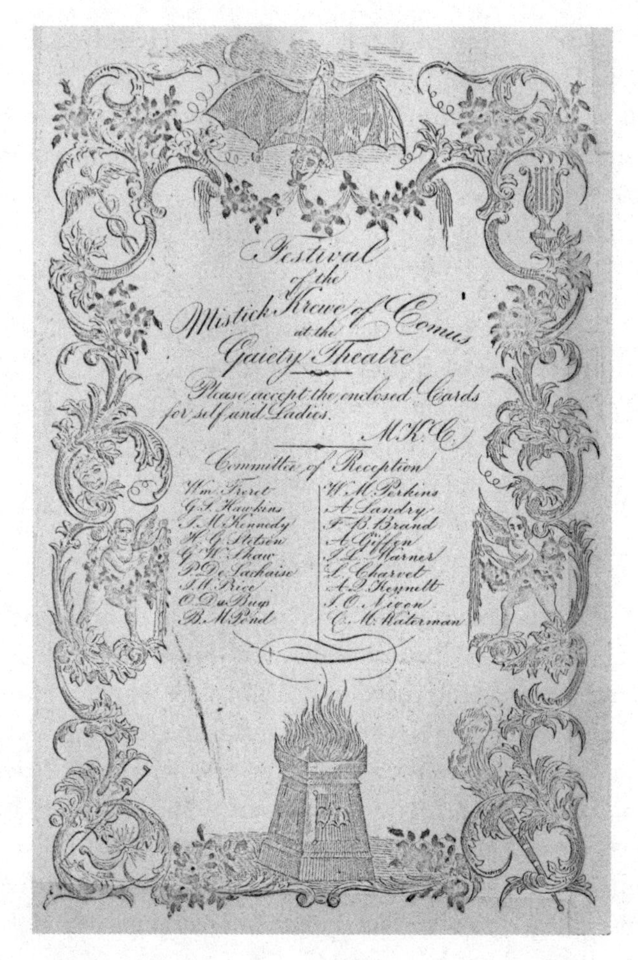

Invitation to the 1857 Mistick Krewe of Comus ball.

did anyone think about what they had seen? Most people on the street, seeing Satan pass by, would not have thought automatically of *Paradise Lost*, but surely some of the guests in the theatre would have known it. Why had the Krewe chosen those particular scenes? To answer this, we must see how Milton recreates the Creation.

After hearing about the War in Heaven, Adam is entranced. Wanting more, he asks Raphael to tell him how the heavens were made. So the angel begins his second story.

After casting a third of the angels down to Hell, God decides to repopulate Heaven. He announces that he is going to create a new world as an incubator for the angels of the future. God's decrees are immediate, so the world is created 'more swift / Than time or motion' (VII:176–7). The Son is the agent of creation. He goes out of the gates of Heaven in his chariot, and rides into the depths of Chaos. There:

> He took the golden compasses, prepared
> In God's eternal store, to circumscribe
> This universe, and all created things:
> One foot he centred, and the other turned
> Round the vast profundity obscure,
> And said, Thus far extend, thus far thy bounds,
> This be thy just circumference, O world (VII:225–31)

The Son draws a circle: inside is the world, and all order, light, and beauty, and outside is Chaos. Creation causes a waste product – 'The black tartareous cold infernal dregs' (VII:238) – which is purged out and down. 'Tartareous' refers to the Latin name for the underworld, Tartarus, and here it means tar-like, sludgy. When the Mistick Krewe performed this as a *tableau vivant*, they were doing so in a city that was racially segregated but also constantly threatening to dissolve. There is no hint that their performance had anything to do with race, at least not explicitly, but the moment comes suspiciously close to an idealised vision of racial segregation.

But if Milton's account of the Creation seemed to contain an aesthetics of segregation, it also contains the opposite. God creates the land, dividing it from the waters. This is all in the Book of Genesis, of course, but Raphael's account is more visceral. The surface of the Earth is covered in a womb of waters, until mountains rear up. At first the land is bare, but soon plants grow through. Life teems. Not the divine act described in other accounts: a sudden fact like a light switched on. Bushes grow frizzy hair and trees unfurl. Up from the depths come 'bended dolphins' (VII:410) and whales that look like moving islands. Everything that can fly now hatches. The lion shakes out his mane. The world is created like the gestation, birth, and growth of an infant. The fact that Creation is a dynamic process helps to explain why Charles Darwin loved *Paradise Lost*. In 1831, he took it on his early voyage to South America aboard HMS *Beagle*, where his observations of nature became the foundation of his theory. He later recalled: 'when I could take only a single volume, I always chose Milton'.[18] In Uruguay, he saw a toad that made him think of Milton's Satan, 'squat at the ear of Eve'.[19] Darwin was a passionate abolitionist, who wanted to prove the shared origin of all human beings. Because of this, his theory was derided by white supremacists, who believed he had 'bestialized the white man'.[20] Likewise, Milton's vision of creation also departs from the absolute opposition of light and dark, and this becomes clearer when the angel describes the finished universe.

After he has heard of Satan's downfall, Adam's head rings like a struck bell. No sooner has he thanked Raphael than he asks another question. It is one that Eve asked him earlier in the poem: Do the stars exist only to light the night on Earth? Do other worlds contain other creatures, who share the universe with us? Seeing Adam's perplexed expression, Eve withdraws to let them talk, and goes to tend her garden. Milton says she prefers to hear what the angel says from her husband, who will mix his lesson with 'conjugal caresses' (VIII:56). In this poem, women may ask fiendish questions but they are only half-interested in the answers.

Raphael tells Adam it's okay to be curious: God has set the universe in front of them like a book to be read. Just because the Earth is only one planet, Adam shouldn't assume that the whole universe *wasn't* invented just for him: 'bright infers not excellence' (VIII:91). The world may not be as it seems. Raphael refuses to satisfy Adam's doubts, instead framing his answer as a series of questions:

> What if the sun
> Be centre to the world, and other stars
> By his attractive virtue and their own
> Incited, dance about him various rounds? (VIII:122–5)

Raphael's speech invites the reader of *Paradise Lost* to confront the greatest scientific problem of Milton's century. In 1514, the Polish astronomer Nicolaus Copernicus had found that his observations of the planets fitted better with a Sun-centred model of the universe than the orthodox Earth-centred one. There was a serious lag between this discovery and its acceptance: after Copernicus's death, his theory was taken up by a handful of other scientists, but it was only after Newton's theory of gravity, published in 1687, that physics supported Copernicus's discovery. Until then, even highly educated people didn't have enough to go on. This is especially true of Adam, who is only one day old. 'Dream not of other worlds' (VIII:175), Raphael tells him. This exchange resembles Galileo's *Dialogue on the Two Chief World Systems*, the book defending the Copernican hypothesis and mocking the older system, and which had been suppressed by the Pope.[21] Raphael advises Adam not to speculate, but reading Milton's epic, it is impossible not to dream of other worlds.

If the Mistick Krewe performed Milton's creation as a story of the world as segregated from the start, it is, in another sense, a vision that resists the very possibility of segregation. Raphael's message is about the dangers of curiosity and taking things by their appearances. The claim 'bright infers not excellence' (VIII:91) recalls a phrase in Milton's *Areopagitica:* 'excrementall whitenesse'.[22] Just because something is white, that doesn't mean it's virtuous. This lesson was missing in New Orleans, where the Mistick Krewe used Milton as a symbol of white culture. After the American Civil War, the gentlemanly devils would turn from whimsical impresarios to fully fledged white supremacists.

In 1858, the Mistick Krewe of Comus marched for the second time. They had spent $10,000 on the first parade, and the second cost twice as much. The Krewe had also doubled in size. They now performed *tableaux roulants*, mobile spectacles on floats. Their parade became the most sensational spectacle in the nation. In 1860, their theme was 'Statues of the Great Men of Our Country' – Columbus followed by the generals and presidents of the United States, their faces whitened with chalk. The politics of carnival became more pronounced as relations soured between the North and South. In 1861, Comus threw a parade in which four Krewe men marched in blackface

The 1867 Mistick Krewe of Comus parade. Engraving based on a contemporary sketch by James E. Taylor.

holding an effigy of Abraham Lincoln.[23] A month later, the Civil War had begun.

There's no doubt which side the Mistick Krewe were on. In February 1862, the Washington Artillery, a Confederate battalion from New Orleans, held a Mardi Gras ball in which fresh-faced young soldiers took the women's part in the waltz.[24] In March, Comus proclaimed: 'War has cast its gloom over our happy homes and care usurped the place where joy is wont to hold its sway. Now, therefore, do I deeply sympathizing with the general anxiety, deem it proper to withhold your Annual Festival.'[25] In April, two members of the Krewe died at the Battle of Shiloh, one of them a Confederate general. That same month, the Union fleet broke through the defences at the mouth of the Mississippi, and sailed up the river towards New Orleans. On 26 April, Marines from USS *Pocahontas* were sent into the city to raise the Union flag above the New Orleans city mint. The same day, a local gambler called William Mumford scaled the flagpole and pulled it down. Later, the rebel was seen disappearing into Dr Pope's pharmacy. This did not stop him from being executed by the leader of the Union army, General Benjamin Butler, several days later. New Orleans was the first Southern city to be occupied by the Northern army and so it was the first one in which the emancipation of slaves took place. In the years to come, it would also lead the counter-revolution.

After the war, during the period of Reconstruction (1865–77), Louisiana, like all formerly Confederate states, was ruled by a governor who represented Lincoln's abolitionist Republican party. Across the South, this led to conflict between Northern occupiers and disenfranchised Southern elites. The general occupying Louisiana warned Lincoln that his reforms would produce a counter-revolution. But the reforms were too important. Reconstruction was a crucial and long-overdue opportunity to fulfil the Declaration of Independence, bringing about equality for all.[26] In April 1865, the Thirteenth Amendment was ratified, making emancipation part of the constitution. This transformed Southern society overnight. Many Southern whites were furious about it, and days after its passing, Lincoln was assassinated. The counter-revolution had begun.

By the end of 1865, Southern states were passing laws to control the recently freed Black population. The new Black Codes were modelled on the old Slave Codes, often merely swapping the word 'slaves' for 'negroes'.[27] They inhibited voting rights, freedom of movement, and attempted to compel Black people to return to work on the plantations, instituting harsh penalties for disobedience. Even within the Thirteenth Amendment a form of slavery had been preserved:

> Neither slavery nor involuntary servitude, *except as a punishment for crime whereof the party shall have been duly convicted*, shall exist within the United States, or any place subject to their jurisdiction [my italics].[28]

Prisons were a way to preserve slave labour. Outside New Orleans, a plantation called Angola, named after the country where many slaves had come from, started using the new system of convict leasing. For some, the new conditions of labour were just as harsh as they had been under slavery. The Senate had also created the Freedmen's Bureau, which looked after the material needs of millions of people, providing food and clothing, founding hospitals, public schools and universities. There was talk of the redistribution of land but it came to nothing. When the former slaves found out they had to leave their homes and carefully tended gardens, freedom took on a colder aspect. According to the historian W. E. B. Du Bois, it broke their faith in politics.

Carnival returned to a society transformed but also substantially the same. The parade of 1866 had as its theme 'The Past, the Present and the Future'.

> The Past was represented by strife, destruction, want, grief and terror; the Present by Washington, surrounded by industry, commerce, science, agriculture, history and art, while peace and plenty attended the Future. Behind these came Comus, attended by his followers in the form of animals.[29]

The torch bearers in the parade were now freedmen, rather than slaves, and the men behind the masks were no longer the city's rulers. Nevertheless, they were still the dominant social class, and carnival was a way to remind the Northern politicians of their enduring power. Their mockery of authority became harsher. The parade was a public-facing performance for all the world to see, but the Mistick Krewe was a private, creaturely thing, laughing at the world behind their masks. In the coming years, carnival alternated with insurrections in the Crescent City.

Tensions between Southern whites, Northern 'carpetbaggers' (people who moved to the South after the war) and 'scalawags' (their Southern allies), soon erupted into violence. In July 1866, a convention met in downtown New Orleans to discuss voting rights for Black men. They were set on by white rioters, many of them former Confederate soldiers. Thirty-four Black men and three white radicals were murdered, and over a hundred injured. When the police arrived, they did nothing. Some even helped the white rioters, and it was only when the Federal Army arrived that peace was restored. The late 1860s also saw the emergence of white supremacist organisations across the South, including the Ku Klux Klan in Tennessee. This development also registered in the parades of the Mistick Krewe. On Mardi Day, 1871, a krewemen dressed as King Arthur rode a horse through the city's streets. The theme of the parade was Edmund Spenser's epic romance *The Faerie Queene*. One contemporary report remarked:

> It was a pity that so few persons had read this exquisite poem of Edmund Spenser, because very few of the lookers-on could fully appreciate the procession, although they all knew it was beautiful.[30]

Spenser's poem, dedicated to Queen Elizabeth I, aimed to instil in its readers the virtues of good leadership; likewise, Comus's enactment of the poem was a barb aimed at the state's governor, a Northerner implementing unpopular Reconstruction policies. The multicultural city's other inhabitants, watching a masked white man riding a white horse, followed by other masked white followers, must have understood its meaning, whether or not they knew who Spenser was.

In the 1870s, other krewes were founded – the Twelfth Knight Revellers, Rex, and Knights of Momus – and the politics of Mardi Gras became unignorable. In 1871, the Twelfth Night Revellers held a parade in which a 'Council of Crows' float mocked the state legislature. In 1872, Rex's parade featured members of the Klan and effigies of President Ulysses Grant and Abraham Lincoln.[31] In 1873, Comus's parade was 'The Missing Links' – a parody of Darwin's theory of evolution, and its scandalous levelling of racial hierarchy. It was a time of mounting tension in the city. The 1873 election for governor was contested between a Democrat candidate, John McEnery, and the Reconstruction candidate, William Kellogg. Both claimed victory and started to make appointments. McEnery raised a militia and appointed as its leader a member of Comus: a handsome, moustachioed cavalry officer called Frederick Nash Ogden. Soon afterwards, Ogden founded the Crescent City White League, an organisation dedicated to restoring Southern leadership of New Orleans. In September 1874, Ogden led 3,000 men – many Krewe members among them – to Jackson Square in downtown New Orleans. They occupied the city hall, statehouse, and arsenal, holding the city for forty-eight hours, and dispersing only when President Grant sent in the Federal Army. After the insurrection – known as the Battle of Liberty Place – not one person was prosecuted.

The following year, carnival wasn't held, but the Mistick Krewe soon returned to their political antics. In 1877, Comus's parade had as its theme 'The Aryan Race', and featured pictures of the progress of the race from ancient Egypt down to 1976, when women would be 'carrying on all the trades and professions now usurped by man, while the men, in hoops and skirts, are nursing the children or attending to household duties'.[32] But that year the parade by a new krewe, the Knights of Momus, managed to be even more controversial. Their parade, 'Hades', included effigies of the abolitionists Frederick Douglass and Wendell Phillips, as well as Charles Darwin. This caused outrage throughout the United States, and brought censure from President Grant. The Krewes had turned carnival on its head: it was not a topsy-turvy spectacle but a top-down one, consolidating white unity. And it succeeded. The presidential election of 1877 was won by Rutherford Hayes, but he lost the popular vote. In order to maintain power, Hayes promised to end Reconstruction. Across the South, the Reconstruction governors were replaced by men more amenable to white elites.

After the end of Reconstruction, the carnival parades were less fraught. Mardi Gras was always meant to be a refuge from politics, and now it became an image of what had existed before the war. In the words of the *Daily Picayune*:

> As dance followed dance, and flirtation succeeded flirtation, the thought occurred to this reporter, if such joy and such happiness can be ours now, what would it have been if Eve had not eaten that abominable apple, and the miscreant tenant, Adam, had not been ejected from his residence in Paradise.[33]

This idyllic vision was no less political. After the end of Reconstruction, the Mistick Krewe helped to produce the myth of the Lost Cause of the Confederacy, a society that had passed away because of its genteel ways and not its addiction to the compulsory labour of others. In 1884, Comus's ball was attended by the daughters of four Confederate generals: Jefferson Davis, D. H. Hill, Robert E. Lee, and Stonewall Jackson. Comus led Lee's daughter in the dance. In 1892, Davis's daughter was chosen as Comus's carnival queen. This was the confirmation of something many had been waiting for, and the *Picayune* reported that it was 'the happy signal for thousands of war veterans to sound off their famous rebel yell after 27 years of unreconstructed silence'.[34] Mardi Gras offered a vision of the unreconstructed South. This was a fantasy, as the founders of Comus had been newcomers to the South, but it was a powerfully political one.

The Mistick Krewe was the beginning of New Orleans's Mardi Gras as it is known today. Once the tensions of Reconstruction had dissipated, it was free to become a more artistic version of itself, thrilling the streets with the finest Parisian costumes and splendidly horrific floats. In 1897, Nereus Krewe set loose on to the streets a one-hundred-foot Kraken. In the final decades of the century, in the Black neighbourhoods of the city, men started to parade the streets in six-foot-tall costumes of feather and beadwork. Known as the Mardi Gras Indians, they combined West African and indigenous American masquerading traditions, a practice autonomous from the white carnival. The official Mardi Gras stopped when the US joined the First World War, and when the soldiers returned, individual neighbourhoods started to fund their own trucks. In 1916, Zulu became the first African American krewe to parade. The Mistick Krewe continued to parade until 1991, when a city council ordinance required them not to discriminate on the basis of gender or race, and they withdrew from public parades like the evil spirits at the end of Milton's masque. By then, they had Protestantised carnival, and helped to Creolise Anglo-Saxon culture. Some say it was the origin of modern America.

When Dr Pope and his associates reinvented carnival, they had effectively segregated it, distinguishing their white parade from the rest of the multicultural city. This was surely the meaning of the first *tableau vivant*, when they enacted Milton's creation of the world, separating light and order from darkness and chaos: that the coming of the Anglo-Protestant elite into New Orleans was the beginning of order and civilisation. But if racial segregation was the intended message, carnival continued to be a teeming, populist event, which could never be contained.

7. Virginia Woolf Is Denied Access

The day casting longer shadows, Adam tries to delay his guest by offering to talk of his birth, as Eve has already done. Raphael, who didn't witness the creation of the humans, readily agrees.

One day, Adam says, he had woken up on a flowery bed, springing to life and testing out his new limbs like a happy Frankenstein. A divine shape appeared and spoke to him. This was God, and he told Adam that Paradise was his to rule over. With one rule: not to eat the fruit.

Adam then began to name the creatures, and in naming them, to know them. Noticing they came in pairs, he asked his Creator: How can I enjoy this alone?

God replied: Do the creatures not keep you company?

This didn't make sense. Adam asked: 'Among unequals what society / Can sort, what harmony or true delight?' (VIII:383–4). Societies are made between equals, and only creatures of equal reason can enjoy conversation.

God responded: Do you think I am unhappy, since I am alone?

You are infinite, and perfect, Adam answered. You don't need company. I can't be happy on my own.

Then God admitted that he was testing Adam. He would make him a companion. God put Adam to sleep, giving him an 'internal sight' (VIII:461) so that he could watch one of his ribs being removed and then be used to form another body. This was Eve.

But then Adam mentions to Raphael an awkward fact: when he looks at Eve, he experiences a 'Commotion strange' (VIII:531).

> when I approach
> Her loveliness, so absolute she seems
> And in herself complete, so well to know
> Her own, that what she wills to do or say,
> Seems wisest, virtuousest, discreetest, best (VIII:546–50)

Eve's beauty makes Adam's superior knowledge seem foolish. His praise collapses into a complaint: she doesn't need him the way he needs her. It is a common complaint in Renaissance love poetry that the beloved is *too* perfect. Since God is the only being who doesn't need anyone, the indifferent beloved seems godlike. He's lost in her beauty.

Raphael is unimpressed. He tells Adam not to blame Eve for his loss of judgement. Don't let sexual passion rule you, Raphael says. This is the law of patriarchy in Milton's poem: man must wield his natural authority over woman.

Finally, Adam asks Raphael how angels procreate and Raphael smiles blushingly. But his description of angel sex has no shame in it. No puritan in this respect, Milton insists that bodily pleasure can be sacred. The same is true for angels. Angel sex is an infinitely flexible form of total union:

> Easier than air with air, if spirits embrace,
> Total they mix, union of pure with pure
> Desiring; nor restrained conveyance need
> As flesh to mix with flesh, or soul with soul (VIII:626–9)

But humans can only imagine this: we have more complicated desires and must manage them. The afternoon departing, it's time for Raphael to leave, telling Adam one final time to obey God. Neither knows how brief a time this will last.

By the start of the twentieth century, *Paradise Lost* was 'something everybody wants to have read and nobody wants to read'.[1] With the birth of cinema, there were other things to do than read Milton and melt into tears like William and Dorothy Wordsworth. Critics worried that true readers were a dying breed.[2] Milton wasn't read by one in a hundred people.[3] His epic started to seem more and more outdated: the Copernican revolution, the physics on which it was based, was superseded by Einstein's theory of relativity, and new technologies made its descriptions of war seem quaint. Yet even if it was old-fashioned, many readers still cherished Milton's epic. '*Paradise Lost* is not the less an eternal monument,' wrote one critic, 'because it is a monument to dead ideas.'[4] The twentieth century wouldn't treat

Paradise Lost with the reverence of the eighteenth century or the disturbed fascination of the nineteenth, but it survived, even in the writings of those who sought to render it obsolete.

Modernism was an aesthetic revolution with no single origin. It happened in French painting in the mid-nineteenth century when the impressionists broke from the reigning academic style to paint from their own subjective viewpoints, and then the symbolists, Fauvists, and Cubists proclaimed their successive rejections of their predecessors. In 1908, Arnold Schoenberg announced a new atonal music, and in 1913, the primitive rhythms of Stravinsky's ballet *The Rite of Spring* caused an uproar in Paris. The French poets Stéphane Mallarmé and Guillaume Apollinaire exploded poetic metre, anarchically scattering words across the page. In each medium, forms were found to express the disruptions of modern life. By 1929, a modernist journal could announce: 'The revolution in the English Language is an accomplished fact.'[5] But this revolution was one that involved a preoccupation with the past, and with Milton. The most acute dissection of Milton's haunting of modernism is by Virginia Woolf. With two American migrants, Ezra Pound and T. S. Eliot, she swept away Victorian literature like a pair of moth-eaten curtains. *Paradise Lost* had been so much imitated that it, too, had to go. But in their efforts to overthrow him, the modernists gave Milton new life.

An energetic twenty-nine-year-old Pennsylvanian with a pointed beard and the wardrobe of a circus magician, Ezra Pound arrived in London in 1914 looking for 'giants & dragons'.[6] What he found was a decadent culture dominated by dull poetry. The most 'modern' poets appeared in the *Georgian Anthology* (1913), named after King George V. The Georgian poets were obsessed with their own experience, the passing of time, and the fleeting present.

> Deep meadows yet, for to forget
> The lies, and truths, and pain? . . . oh! yet
> Stands the Church clock at ten to three?
> And is there honey still for tea?[7]

Ezra Pound began a one-man crusade to disturb their quiet. He declared that 'no one cares to hear, in strained iambics, that he feels sprightly in spring, is uncomfortable when his sexual desires are ungratified'.[8] Pound used shards of older literature to disrupt Georgian platitudes. His poetic time machine flew past Milton back to the troubadours of mediaeval France, poet-singers who Pound believed were the origins of modern poetry. He wrote under personas, including the troubadour Peire Vidal, who went mad for love. He used a mixture of archaic words and slang to make jarring, extravagant pronouncements.[9] A critic from the *Evening Standard* newspaper called his 1909 collection *Personae* 'A queer little book which will irritate many readers.'[10] His publisher included the quote in his next book. But soon Pound realised that archaic spellings were an unhelpful eccentricity. In 1911, he began championing a new approach to poetry: imagism. The imagist poem was compact and economical, a collection of 'luminous details'.[11] This, Pound believed, would prove more enduring than sentimental Georgian verse. It would also be a profoundly un-Miltonic poetry.

'Milton is the worst sort of poison,' Pound said.[12] He referred to the 'sin or error of Milton', as if Milton himself were the snake in the garden of English poetry.[13] Pound wasn't even talking about Milton's ideas: 'I am leaving apart all my disgust with what he has to say, his asinine bigotry, his beastly hebraism, the coarseness of his mentality, I am dealing with a technical matter.'[14] The phrase 'beastly hebraism' refers to Milton's imitation of the inspired poetry of the Hebrew Old Testament, which was grounded in his Puritan religion.[15] (There is also the undeniable hint of anti-Semitism, something emerging elsewhere in Pound's writing at this time.) Pound's main objection was that Milton had tried to turn English into Latin, changing native sentence structure, and importing loan words like the awkward coinage 'irriguous' (meaning irrigated).[16] By 1915, Pound's preferences were notorious:

> I am known to hold theories which some people think new, and which several people know to be hostile to much that hitherto has been accepted as 'classic' in English poetry . . . for Milton and Victorianism and for the softness of the 'nineties I have different degrees of antipathy or even contempt.[17]

Pound had raised the question of how English poetry could become truly modern, but his own poetry did not provide the most convincing answer.

Thomas Stearns Eliot was born to an elite family in St Louis, Missouri. A sensitive and precocious child, he read Milton's poetic drama *Samson Agonistes* at the age of twelve.[18] He attended an elite school in Massachusetts, Milton Academy (no relation to the poet), and then Harvard, where he studied ancient and modern languages. In 1914, he moved to Oxford to begin a PhD in philosophy, but Pound managed to lure him to London. There, the two men launched what Eliot later called a 'revolution in poetry'.[19] Where Coleridge and Wordsworth had launched their own poetic revolution in the 1790s by disavowing Milton's bad imitators and proposing to return to his true spirit, the modernists wanted to depose Milton altogether. Eliot dismissed Milton's Heaven and Hell as 'large but insufficiently furnished apartments filled by heavy conversation'.[20] Like the Great Wall of China, *Paradise Lost* was long, old, and no longer useful.[21] Worst of all, Milton had helped to create a 'dissociation of sensibility': a division of thinking and feeling that had never been mended – a kind of fall in English literature and society more generally for which Milton was partly responsible.[22] Rejecting their admired predecessor also cleared the way for the modernists' own epics.

The young Eliot believed that *Paradise Lost* was hopelessly cut off from modern life, which was precisely what animated his modernist verse. Eliot's first published poem as an adult, 'The Love Song of J. Alfred Prufrock' (1915), is a vision of alienated life in a nameless industrial city.[23] Eliot's cautious, ageing Prufrock – wondering if he dares to eat a peach – sounds like a cartoonish parody of the banal poets of the *Georgian Anthology*, a boring modern Adam, worrying about his waistline. The poem moves dizzyingly between neurotic monologue and sing-song couplets. But the figure of Prufrock still gives it some psychological coherence – the revolution was not yet complete. In June 1921, Eliot complained that 'the twentieth century is still the nineteenth'.[24] Soon, that was no longer true: in February 1922, James Joyce's *Ulysses* was published. Eliot and Pound were among its earliest readers, and they realised that it heralded a new era. Eliot said: 'I wish, for my own sake, that I had not read it.'[25]

Ulysses tracks a single day in the life of several Dubliners, using Homer's epic *The Odyssey* as its structure, and including pastiches of writers like Milton. This is not a sign of reverence. The Irish novelist complained: 'I cannot express myself in English without enclosing myself in a tradition.'[26] In *Ulysses,* the young schoolteacher Stephen Dedalus fantasises about rewriting *Paradise Lost* as a novel, *The Sorrows of Satan* – it is a hackneyed idea, in thrall to a deadening tradition. Years earlier, Joyce said: 'Epic savagery is rendered impossible by vigilant policing.'[27] But by 1922, he completed his modern epic. Poetry had not yet followed in his footsteps but, the following year, it would do just that. T. S. Eliot's next poem was written after a nervous breakdown and a spell in a Swiss sanatorium, and described a world dissolved into fragments. Pound slashed it into shape, removing the last vestiges of the nineteenth century, and reducing its lines to shards of modern music.

The Waste Land is a contradiction: literature is thrown into the vortex of modern life. The reader is disoriented by multiple personas, unattributed speech, and fragments of ancient and modern languages. Apocalyptic visions are superimposed on everyday images. London becomes Hell, where the poet hears the voices of the dead. Surprisingly, given Eliot's aversion, Milton is one of them. There are echoes of Milton's 'Lycidas' and *Comus*, and of four passages from *Paradise Lost*.[28] This isn't fanciful thinking: Eliot admits it. His American publisher needed to fill space to make a book out of his slender epic, so Eliot added some endnotes.[29] More intriguing than helpful, they link Milton with a passage describing an ornate interior decorated with a mosaic of Philomel, the woman who in Greek myth was raped by her sister's husband:

> Huge sea-wood fed with copper
> Burned green and orange, framed by the coloured stone,
> In which sad light a carvèd dolphin swam.
> Above the antique mantel was displayed
> As though a window gave upon the sylvan scene
> The change of Philomel[30]

The poem is itself a mosaic, and in one of the endnotes, Eliot confesses that the phrase 'sylvan scene' comes from *Paradise Lost*, in which it describes the wooded Eden where Eve is violated by Satan. But poetic influence isn't always a matter of acknowledgement or open allusion. It happens more often in the repetition of musical phrases, slightly changed: in this same passage, the phrase 'carvèd dolphin' echoes the 'bendèd dolphins' in *Paradise Lost* (VII:410). *The Waste Land* seemed so modern that its early readers failed to recognise its echoes of Milton. Milton's epic survived in the work of the modernists, precisely where it had been superseded. For a time, this contradictory fact lay dormant.[31]

The Waste Land was published as a book in New York in 1922, and then the following year in the UK by the Hogarth Press, which was run by Virginia Woolf and her husband Leonard. They were part of the bohemian Bloomsbury group rather than the more male-dominated circle that gathered around Pound. Woolf met Eliot for the first time in 1916. Initially, they were mutually distrustful acquaintances; later, intimate friends. Woolf was trying to move away from her pre-war style and find one more attuned to the disorientation of modern life. She was also writing criticism, which was less bombastic than Pound's and Eliot's but no less acute. Of the three, she was the most generous to Milton – perhaps because she was not a poet.

Born in 1882, Virginia Stephen grew up in the upper-middle-class idyll of Hyde Park Corner, London. Her father, Leslie Stephen, was an eminent Victorian man of letters. He wrote a life of Milton for the *Dictionary of National Biography*, the monumental series that he presided over as general editor, and a patronising biography of George Eliot. He knew much poetry by heart, and recited Milton to his children.[32] The boys were sent to Eton, where they learnt Greek and Latin, while the girls were taught at home, but Virginia worked to keep up with her brothers in ancient and modern languages. Her father fell apart after the death of her mother, Julia, in 1895, and this cast a long shadow over his family. On Christmas Day 1903, Leslie tried to read Milton's 'Ode on the Morning of Christ's Nativity' to his family – an annual tradition – but he was too weak to finish it.

After his death two months later, Virginia and her sister, Vanessa, moved across the city to Bloomsbury. There they formed the nucleus of a bohemian set of writers and artists, and her independent thinking about literature flourished.

From her father, Virginia Woolf inherited a set of Milton's prose. Instead of reading it, she gave it a new binding, and turned more often to Milton's poetry.[33] In 1906, she read his poetry to her brother Thoby, as he died from typhoid aged only twenty-six. In 1907, the siblings formed a play-reading society with their friends: the unmarried Virginia played the part of the temptress Dalila in Milton's late poetic drama *Samson Agonistes*, and Sabrina, the spirit of chastity, in *Comus*.[34] Allusions to Milton appear in Woolf's first two novels, *The Voyage Out* (1915) and *Night and Day* (1919), but it's in her diary, a place to think expansively, that she thinks most seriously about him. (Years later, she encouraged the novelist Elizabeth Bowen to keep a diary: 'I mean not tea parties but Milton and so on.'[35]) In these private pages, she could express thoughts without fear of censure, and rehearse her own critical revolution.

During the First World War, Virginia and Leonard rented a house in rural Sussex. In 1918, she read *Paradise Lost*, and it penetrated her thoughts. One day, watching a friend talk to a German prisoner of war, she thought to herself that 'the existence of life in another human being' is as difficult to understand as a book like *Paradise Lost* when it is shut.[36] A month later, Woolf felt put out by hearing that her friend Janet Case had been reading Milton too: 'My intellectual snobbishness was chastened this morning by hearing from Janet that she reads Don Quixote & Paradise Lost, & her sister Lucretius in the evenings.'[37] This clearly inspired a competitive urge, and Woolf writes: 'Though I am not the only person in Sussex who reads Milton, I mean to write down my impressions of *Paradise Lost* while I am about it.'[38] Then she did so. The novelist Geoff Dyer says that Woolf's diary entry is 'one of the best things ever written about Milton'.[39] He's not wrong.

The entry documents Woolf's awe. She knows she hasn't fully grasped *Paradise Lost*, writing: 'I have left many riddles unread. I have

Virginia Woolf and her father Leslie Stephen in 1902.

slipped on too easily to taste the full flavour.'[40] But who has fully grasped *Paradise Lost*? To her credit, she stays with her impressions rather than worrying about it. 'I am struck by the extreme difference between this poem & any other,' she writes. 'It lies, I think, in the sublime aloofness & impersonality of the emotions.'[41] Milton's 'aloofness' is something she both admires and feels disturbed by:

> He deals in horror & immensity & squalor & sublimity, but never in the passions of the human heart. Has any great poem ever let in so little light upon ones own joys & sorrows? I get no help in judging life; I scarcely feel that Milton lived or knew men & women . . . He was the first of the masculinists; but his disparagement rises from his own ill luck, & seems even a spiteful last word in his domestic quarrels.[42]

Milton was the '*first* of the masculinists' – meaning that his epic was influential among later, muscular English poets. Was Woolf, perhaps, also thinking of her male contemporaries, Pound and Eliot, with their hard, impersonal poetry? Then, as if prevailing over the negative thought, Woolf interjects:

> But how smooth, strong & elaborate it all is! What poetry! I can conceive that even Shakespeare after this would seem a little troubled, personal, hot & imperfect. I can conceive that this is the essence, of which all other poetry is the dilution.[43]

Her judgement is finely balanced: an attempt to grasp the best and worst of *Paradise Lost*. Her final thought is that it is all grandeur and masculinity: 'the figures are majestic, in them is summed up much of what men thought of our place in the universe, of our duty to God, our religion'.[44] Milton's masculinity, she hints, limited his work.

Some years later, Woolf turned Milton into a monster. This happened in 1928, when she was invited to give lectures at Newnham and Girton, the two women's colleges at Cambridge. By that time, she had written her masterpiece *To the Lighthouse* (1927) and *Orlando: A Biography* (1928), a novel about an aristocratic young man in the seventeenth century who wakes up one day having turned into a woman. Orlando befriends the male poets of the seventeenth century, but they think little of her. She outlives them all, surviving for centuries in a happy, if unpoetical, existence. When she visited Cambridge to lecture, Woolf spoke of relationships between women and the cult of poetry. She had just returned from France with her lover Vita Sackville-West. *Orlando* was breaking new sales records. Woolf was becoming famous. But the lectures were an awkward affair. At Newnham, she was late, and brought her husband unannounced, prompting last-minute seating changes. At Girton, the room was dark and she read almost inaudibly. At the dinner, she made awkward conversation with the students. After returning to London, she wrote:

> Thank God, my long toil at the women's lecture is this moment ended. I am back from speaking at Girton, in floods of rain. Starved but valiant young women – that's my impression. Intelligent, eager, poor; & destined to become schoolmistresses in shoals. I blandly told them to drink wine & have a room of their own.[45]

The following year, this bland advice became a book-length essay and, in time, one of her most famous works. *A Room of One's Own* (1929) is a fictionalised account of the lecture: invited to lecture on the subject 'Women and Fiction', Woolf imagines the fate of Shakespeare's sister if she had been a gifted writer. But Milton looms no less large in it.

At the beginning of *A Room of One's Own*, an unnamed woman novelist sits by a river, contemplating the university on the far bank. She thinks about how women had been denied access to education, how they had been shut in the home and prevented from developing their powers in so many ways. Even after they had been permitted to attend this hallowed university, they had been cloistered in colleges at its outskirts. On a whim, she decides to visit a library in one of the nearby colleges, where one of Milton's manuscripts was kept. She wants to witness the accident of genius: to see which words the young poet had crossed out as he tried to finish his poem 'Lycidas'. She walks with purpose towards the library, crossing a lawn. Suddenly a man appears, telling her that walking on the grass is a privilege reserved for fellows of the college. She returns to the gravel path and finally arrives at the door of the library:

> I must have opened it, for instantly there issued, like a guardian angel barring the way with a flutter of black gown instead of white wings, a deprecating, silvery, kindly gentleman, who regretted in a low voice as he waved me back that ladies are only admitted to the library if accompanied by a Fellow of the College or furnished with a letter of introduction.[46]

This is communicated in the dull tones of the establishment. A passer-by might not notice it: the woman quietly turned away. It is as if Milton himself had risen from the dead to prevent her.

Woolf's being denied access confirms Milton's repressive figure. Milton, and the culture of classical learning that he represents, has become a problem. Like George Eliot, Woolf described him morph from an 'affable archangel', someone willing to educate women, to a joyless tyrant. When she mentions him again, on the final page of *A Room of One's Own*, he is a terror. If women have 'five hundred pounds a year to live and rooms of our own', she says, in a hundred years, they might achieve something great:

> if we look past Milton's bogey, for no human being should shut out the view; if we face the fact, for it is a fact, that there is no arm to cling to, but that we go alone and that our relation is to the world of reality and not only to the world of men and women, then the opportunity will come and the dead poet who was Shakespeare's sister will put on the body which she has so often laid down.[47]

Milton had become a 'bogey' – meaning a devil or goblin. In saying this, Woolf was militating against the Victorian culture of poetry, in which gazing at nature had become a mere opportunity to quote the poets. Someone would look at a mountain, mention a phrase from Milton or Wordsworth, and in doing so substitute for nature itself the name of a man. Her father had this habit.[48] Even the modernists, Pound and Eliot, with their learned fragments, were guilty of the same substitution. When a woman writer looked at the sky, her own thoughts would be crowded out by her predecessors, who were largely men. But with money in her pocket and a room with a lock on the door, she could become free to see the sky for herself and write about it. Only writing would banish 'Milton's bogey'.

This didn't mean not reading him. Woolf's exorcism was successful: having developed her own modernist art, she could consume the past without herself being consumed by it. The essays collected in *The Common Reader* (1925 and 1932) range across the centuries, covering both male and female writers, major and minor, as if trying to gather them all. She wrote about Mary Wollstonecraft ('we hear her voice and trace her influence even now among the living'), Dorothy Wordsworth ('her powers of observation became in time so expert and so acute'), and the minor eighteenth-century writer George Crabbe ('his father, a short powerful man, who used sometimes to read poetry – Milton or Young – to his children but was fondest of mathematics, became, owing to the death of his only daughter, violent sometimes').[49] Milton is again associated with overpowering fathers. But Woolf was unintimidated and this is reflected in her increasingly ambitious plans. In

1941, as German planes flew over Sussex on their way to London, she wrote to a friend:

> Did I tell you I'm reading the whole of English literature through? By the time I've reached Shakespeare the bombs will be falling. So I've arranged a very nice last scene: reading Shakespeare, having forgotten my gas mask, I shall fade far away, and quite forget . . . Thank God, as you would say, one's fathers left one a taste for reading![50]

Woolf wanted to write a complete history of English literature but feared that she would be killed before she had read 'Ben Jonson, Milton, Donne and all the rest!'[51] It is extraordinary that she believed this was possible, let alone wanted to do it. But she didn't get a chance to finish the task, dying in 1941 – not by a German bomb but by her own hand. She lived the truth of her earlier statement about *Paradise Lost* – that it was 'the essence, of which almost all other poetry was the dilution' – she wasn't a poet and didn't have to labour in Milton's shadow.

Woolf's modernism was less bombastic than that of Pound and Eliot. She didn't disavow Milton, but found a way to incorporate his voice in it. Her stream-of-consciousness novel *Mrs Dalloway* (1925) follows Clarissa Dalloway, a society hostess, as she travels through London, preparing for a party that evening. Later, at the party, she observes her guests. A Milton expert talks to a 'very bad' young poet, and 'even at this distance they were quarrelling, she could see. For Professor Brierley was a very queer fish'.[52] As she approaches the unfortunate pair, the hostess observes the Milton expert as a naturalist catalogues a rare species:

> his prodigious learning and timidity; his wintry charm without cordiality; his innocence blent with snobbery; he quivered if made conscious, by a lady's unkempt hair, a youth's boots, of an underworld, very creditable doubtless, of rebels, of ardent young people; of would-be geniuses[53]

Mrs Dalloway may be frivolous, someone who can't understand the pleasures of great poetry, but in this we can hear some of Woolf's indignation about male-dominated universities and her suspicion of

Virginia Woolf in 1924. Photograph by her friend Ottoline Morrell.

anyone who would devote their lives to Milton's sublime aloofness. Mrs Dalloway's assessment of the professor, horrified by women, rebels, young people, and geniuses, is devastating. She interrupts the two, gaily telling the young poet: 'He knows everything in the whole world about Milton!'[54] Then she glides on.

Clarissa Dalloway doesn't read Milton. When she was young, she read the poetry of Shelley, at a time when she almost confessed her love for her friend Sally, and daydreamt about a more bohemian life. She had listened to her lover Peter, who she believed would become a writer, talk about Wagner, Pope, and Addison. But then she had married the dull, safe Mr Dalloway, who believes that no decent man should read Shakespeare's queer sonnets. Mrs Dalloway is not the adventurous, ambitious Woolf, who not only read *Paradise Lost* but prided herself on being the only person in Sussex reading it in 1918, and when she found out she wasn't, wrote two pages in her diary that brilliantly capture Milton's divided legacy.

For a long time, it seemed as if the modernists had toppled Milton.[55] In 1936, T. S. Eliot gave a lecture in New York in which he stood over his predecessor in judgement: 'by the ordinary standards of likeableness in human beings, Milton is unsatisfactory'.[56] This seems rich coming from a man who worked in a bank and (according to Queen Elizabeth II, after she met him) dressed like it; who embraced the worst part of English culture – snobbery – and sullied his undeniably great poetry with anti-Semitism. In 1928, Eliot became a naturalised citizen of the UK, and soon after that called his views 'classicist in literature, anglo-catholic in religion, and royalist in politics'.[57] Conservativism was Eliot's solution to the dissolution of self that his poetry described, and it helps to explain his rejection of Milton. In the lecture, Eliot declared that 'the Civil War of the seventeenth century, in which Milton is a symbolic figure, has never been concluded'.[58] Someone who called themself a 'royalist' could never love Milton.

After the Second World War, however, Eliot softened. He gave another lecture on Milton in 1946. This time, he compared Milton to Joyce, who had published his own epic retelling of the Fall of Adam and Eve, *Finnegans Wake* (1939), part of it dictated to his long-suffering daughter. Then Eliot declared that 'poets are sufficiently liberated from Milton's reputation, to approach the study of his work without danger'.[59] The revolution was complete. Milton was safe to read! The young American modernist William Carlos Williams attacked Eliot for this betrayal:

> That Mr T. S. Eliot is an idiot I see no reason to insist. No one who has wheedled himself into the good graces of the Church of England, in fact the British Empire, Harvard University (an honorary LLD) and the Nobel Prize Committee can be considered that.[60]

Williams believed that Eliot had softened his view on Milton as he sought to ingratiate himself with the English establishment. The modernist writer Wyndham Lewis agreed: 'I think that our old friend

T.S.E.'s business about Milton was merely a feature in his long build-up of self.' But it seems just as likely that Eliot the royalist simply had been unable to prevail over Eliot the poet, who had for a long time been secreting Milton's gem-like phrases into his own poems.[61]

Only Ezra Pound never recanted. He had moved to Italy in 1924 and spent the next two decades working on his fragmentary epic, the *Cantos*. When the war broke out, Pound gave a series of anti-Semitic radio addresses in support of Mussolini's government. Pound's eccentric but deeply held fascism infected the *Cantos*, in which he argued that America needed a dynamic leadership, not the more democratic republic desired by Milton. For this, Pound called Milton a 'dithering idiot'.[62] In 1945, Pound was captured by the Italian resistance and turned over to the US army. They put him in a cage in a military detention centre in Pisa, where he prowled around like an animal, and wrote some of his best poetry, the 'Pisan Cantos', on toilet paper. Pound was transported back to America to stand trial for treason, but eventually they declared him insane. He was put in a mental institution in Washington DC, where he was free to receive visiting poets and members of the American far Right.[63] By then, the modernist project was no longer new. After the Second World War, their criticism seemed politically suspect, even as their poetry was canonised. A new age of political revolutions took place in the 1940s and '50s, as England lost its colonies, and they required new ways of reading and writing. The modernists had disrupted poetic form in a way that was powerfully expressive of the modern world. At the same time, what made their poetry appear great was its continuity with the past. Even as they had dismissed *Paradise Lost*, their own writing made Milton's poem look like an immense accumulation of luminous fragments.

8. Hannah Arendt Begins Again

Our story turns away from bliss. 'I now must change / Those notes to tragic', Milton says (IX:5–6). Satan having fled from Eden now returns. He circles Earth for seven nights, and on the eighth finds his way in, via a fountain near the Tree of Life, shooting up into the garden like a child on a water slide. Once there, he gives another soliloquy. Revenge is his addiction: a moment on the lips, an eternal life in Hell. But still he thinks it's worth it. He creeps around Eden. Finally, he finds his vessel, the serpent, and 'In at his mouth / The devil entered' (IX:187–8). He is ready.

In the Garden, the humans are at work pruning the greenery, when Eve poses a seemingly innocent question. Do we always need to work together? Would it not be more effective for us to work apart? He can guide honeysuckle around the elm, while she tends to a bush of roses a little way off. Concerned, Adam responds:

> The wife, where danger or dishonour lurks,
> Safest and seemliest by her husband stays (IX:267–8)

No one wants to be called 'The wife', but Eve responds with 'sweet austere composure' (IX:272). She knows about Satan, having overheard Raphael telling Adam about him. Do you really think so little of me? she asks. After all, 'what is faith, love, virtue unassayed' (IX:335)? That is, how can virtue survive without being tested? In *Areopagitica*, Milton writes: 'I cannot praise a . . . cloistered virtue.'[1] Virtue requires a struggle, and Eve echoes this argument. Eden is not Eden, she says, if we are not free. Eventually, Adam concedes. If he forced her to stay, she would be absent in spirit. You could accuse him of being melodramatic, but the fate of humanity resides in her heels. Once she goes, Milton laments, never again will she find true rest.

In the twentieth century, some readers saw *Paradise Lost* as a fable about capitalism. Gender is the 'natural' reason that Adam and Eve divide their labours: he receiving the angel, and carrying out rational conversation, and she preparing the food. But when Eve proposes to work separately from him, this mirrors a division of labour that was taking place in modern Europe, one divided between specialised workers in a factory. This transition brought workers from the countryside to the city, the emergence of global trade on a new level, and a rift between humanity and nature. In Germany, a kind of political philosophy arose to describe it. *Sozialphilosophie* is a catch-all term for a philosophy describing modern society, and it includes the work of the most influential thinkers of the nineteenth and twentieth centuries: Karl Marx, Friedrich Nietzsche, Max Weber, and Hannah Arendt. Coming in the wake of the high-flown idealist philosophy which reigned in Germany until the 1840s, these thinkers attempted to describe politics in more realistic terms. They came up with ambitious theories about the transformations that made the world modern. To describe it, they turned to Milton's epic.

German was the first language into which *Paradise Lost* was translated. Theodore Haak, an experimental scientist and friend of Milton, started his translation in the years after the poem's publication.[2] Haak's loyalty is reflected in his attempt to keep to the exact numbers of lines in the original, but he didn't get beyond Book IV. A prose translation by Johann Bodmer followed in 1732 – one that authorities in Prussia and Switzerland tried to suppress. Even in the absence of a good translation, German readers still saw Milton as the great English poet. The religious poet Friedrich Klopstock wrote an epic poem, *Messias* (1748–73), that was so obviously written under Milton's influence that he became known as 'the German Milton'. Milton was the classic example of poetry's difference from painting, of artistic inspiration, of the sublime.[3] 'A poet must be able to substitute shadow for things, since he can create shadow,' Kant said, a skill epitomised by *Paradise Lost*.[4] But Milton's star fell in the 1800s, when Schelling's revered translations of Shakespeare began to appear. *Paradise Lost* couldn't stand up to the introspective *Hamlet*. In 1799, Goethe says of Milton's epic: 'The subject is detestable; externally not without a certain imposing grandeur, but internally worm-eaten and hollow.'[5]

Goethe was horrified at Milton's biblical subject, which was far too familiar to be interesting in 1799, but he still judged *Paradise Lost* to be 'majestic'.

Milton was more appealing to thinkers concerned with politics. G. W. F. Hegel argued that epic was impossible in the modern world, as the nation state made heroic action outmoded. Accordingly, Hegel judged *Paradise Lost* more a drama than an epic, a genre that had fallen off since Dante.[6] The young Karl Marx agreed that epic poetry 'can no longer be written in our day', contrasting Homer's *Iliad* with the forgettable epics of the eighteenth century.[7] Marx littered his brilliantly satirical anti-capitalist writings with literary quotations, including *Paradise Lost*.[8] In 1871, writing about the short-lived Paris Commune, Marx compared the communards, who had filled the government posts without expectation of financial reward, to Milton, who sold 'his *Paradise Lost*, for a few pounds'.[9] This is true: in 1667, Milton received £5 from the publisher Samuel Simmons as an advance: he would receive £5 more if the first edition sold out, then the same amount again if the second and third editions sold out. For Marx, this humble sum was a sign of capitalism's priorities.[10] Later, in a manuscript of his own epic work *Das Kapital,* he wrote:

> Milton, who wrote *Paradise Lost* for five pounds, was an *unproductive labourer*. On the other hand, the writer who turns out stuff for his publisher in factory style, is a *productive labourer*. Milton produced *Paradise Lost* for the same reason that a silk worm produces silk. It was an activity of *his* nature.[11]

Marx is speaking from the dollar-eyed perspective of capital, from which only those forms of labour that gain capital are considered 'productive'. When Milton wrote *Paradise Lost*, therefore, he was doing something 'unproductive'. Only when he sold the poem did he become productive. Marx's point is satirical: only the most perverse system would consider Milton to be unproductive. Marx used Milton's poem for a comedy about the impossibility of unalienated labour in a world obsessed with profit. In 1875, Marx's wife, Jenny, joked that Englishmen were better acquainted with pork pies than *Paradise Lost*.[12]

A few years later, a philosopher suspicious of revolution turned Milton into a symbol of contamination. Nietzsche saw art as the highest form of individual freedom, not to be mixed with politics, and he didn't approve of Milton. In *Human, All Too Human* (1878), Nietzsche writes:

> When an artist wants to be more than an artist, for example the moral awakener of his nation, the retribution is that he ends up enamoured of a moral monster – and the muse laughs at him: for this goddess, otherwise so good-hearted, can grow malicious out of jealousy. Consider Milton.[13]

Nietzsche did not believe an artist could pursue poetry and politics at the same time. He saw Milton as a cautionary tale, turning his poetic muse into a monster. But if Nietzsche saw Milton as a backward puritan, another important political philosopher would place Milton at the very beginning of the modern age.

Born in Prussia in 1864, Max Weber was beaten as a child by a female servant, and this event informed a lifelong fascination with the relationship between sex and morality.[14] As a promising young economist, he was sent to East Germany to undertake a study of agriculture, and he claimed that the peasants had sex 'before the eyes of onlooking travellers without the slightest feeling of shame'.[15] In 1893, having become a professor of economics, Weber married his cousin Marianne. Soon it became apparent that he was incapable of making love to her, and he made up for this by drinking competitively with his students and exercising vigorously.[16] In 1897, he bought a series of provocative etchings by the symbolist artist Max Klinger as a gift for his wife.[17] One of the etchings shows a tough-looking Adam with Eve flung over his shoulder: a vision of the German 'he-man' Weber was trying to be. But, in 1898, he had a nervous breakdown. This forced Weber to give up his professorship and stop lecturing. In this state of involuntary leisure, he wrote an immensely influential study of modern work.

Weber wanted to understand the transition from an agrarian society, where peasants work the land for a feudal lord or for their own profit, to a modern capitalist one, where work is exchanged primarily for

Max Klinger, *Eve from the Future* (1898). One of a series of provocative etchings given by Max Weber to his wife, Marianne.

money. *The Protestant Ethic and the Spirit of Capitalism* (1904–5) draws on Weber's studies of peasants in eastern Germany. He offers the following fable. Once upon a time, peasants produced linen in their villages. They grew and harvested the flax, leaving it to soak in pools of water, and then separated the fibres and processed them. After spinning the linen, they took it to town, to a person called the 'putter-out', who would inspect its quality and give the peasant an established sum of money. This system was called 'putting-out', because the work was outsourced to peasants, to be done in their homes.[18] In those days, Weber says, they didn't have to work too hard – five or six hours a day at most. They spent long hours in the local tavern. Life was good. Then one day, an enterprising young man from a 'putting out' family went into the countryside. He decided to turn the linen producers into his employees. He would supervise them, making sure they were disciplined, helping them to produce more. He improved the marketing of his products, making his profits grow. In the beginning, only a small sum had been invested, but the effects were enormous. People started to abandon the village, leaving behind a common relation to the land and to each other. They flocked to the cities, where they lived a more regimented and alienated existence. It was a modern Fall.

Weber didn't believe that capitalism had arisen from moral causes like greed. It surely would have happened earlier if that were the case. Distinguishing himself from Marx, Weber offered an account of the origins of capitalism based not on economic relations but a change in the *spirit* of society. In the mediaeval period, Christian society deemed profit-making a sin. What changed? Weber noticed that Protestants were more likely than Catholics to be leaders of industry, owners of large companies, and skilled workers.[19] This was true not only in Germany but everywhere transformed by capitalism. Weber wondered what it was in the values of Protestantism that had enabled this devotion to capital. He turned to the writings of the Protestant Reformation, where he found a 'Protestant ethic' emerging in the course of the sixteenth century. Unlike the mediaeval Catholic theologians, who saw the contemplative life of monks as the highest form of living, Protestants emphasised the worldly, active life. For them, a merchant was potentially no less virtuous than a monk. They could devote themselves to money-making so long as they did not spend it on frivolous things. It became acceptable to accumulate wealth, which is why the Protestant Dutch Republic and England became centres of finance. Making money was not only acceptable, it became a vocation. This 'Protestant ethic' emerged long before weavers were brought to the city and capitalism properly took hold. On this insight, Weber built a theory of the modern world that has proven as influential as it has been controversial.[20]

The Protestant ethic is exactly what Weber saw in *Paradise Lost*. At the conclusion of Part I, Weber offers as a culminating proof of his thesis a comparison between Dante's mediaeval epic and Milton's modern poem:

> Take for instance the end of the *Divine Comedy*, where the poet in Paradise stands speechless in his passive contemplation of the secrets of God, and compare it with the poem which has come to be called the *Divine Comedy of Puritanism*.[21]

The 'Divine Comedy of Puritanism' is none other than *Paradise Lost*, for Weber sees expressed in Milton's Eden the ethic that paved the way for modern capitalism:

> One feels at once that this powerful expression of the Puritan's serious attention to this world, his acceptance of his life in the world as a task, could not possibly have come from the pen of a medieval writer.[22]

Milton, the son of a middle-class urban moneylender, framed his poem with the values of early modern bourgeois society. Weber's analysis might lead us to notice that the division of labour in Eden also anticipates another important aspect of capitalist society. Eve's proposal to Adam that they work separately anticipates the story Weber tells about linen-making, and the emergence of a modern society, where everyone works in their own cubicle, their minds blinkered by increasingly specialised knowledge.

Twenty years later, Weber returned to lecturing at Munich University's Große Aula, a grand lecture hall. The walls were white with gold ornaments like a wedding cake; behind the stage was a golden mosaic of a god riding a chariot drawn by four horses. It had been built before the war, in a moment of high imperial ambition. But Germany's fortunes had changed. In 1918, a general strike had forced the Kaiser to end the First World War and abdicate his throne. A socialist revolution had then taken place in Bavaria. It was a productive time for Weber: he had emerged from premature retirement to be the voice of realism. The new socialist president, Kurt Eisner, had accepted Germany's responsibility for the war, and Weber publicly decried this as a shameful act. He had his own answers to his nation's burning questions. His friends lobbied for him to be offered a position in government. But he was not universally popular. Radicals protested at his speeches, throwing chairs at him. Weber was undeterred, thrilled with his new platform. In Munich, some in the Große Aula that day noticed that he had grown his beard long, like an Old Testament prophet. He was here to speak not only to the students but to his nation, to light the path ahead.

Weber's lecture 'Politics as a Vocation' described two approaches to politics, one of which would save Germany, the other condemn it. The first is an 'ethics of conviction', in which a politician draws their authority from God or some idea of Utopia. This was also true, Weber believed, of the new socialist republic in Bavaria. He contrasted this approach with an 'ethic of responsibility', in which politicians did not rely on super-human authority – whether God, Utopia, or Marxist logic – but assumed responsibility for their own decisions, appealed to widely held social values, and drew their authority from the people. Like Nietzsche's comment about Milton's confusing of the muses of poetry and politics, Weber believed that charisma alone should not be the basis of political authority. 'Politics', he said, 'means a slow, powerful drilling through hard boards.'[23] This grim realism had its own charisma. Weber's favourite catchphrase was: '*Lasciate ogni speranza.*' Abandon all hope – the inscription on Dante's Gates of Hell. Weber invented a resolute but grimly realistic mood that he believed was what Germany needed. It is a mood conjured up by Max Klinger's provocative etching on the wall of Weber's house, in which a macho Adam carries Eve heroically out of Eden.

In May 1919, Weber accompanied the German delegation to Paris where they were negotiating the peace terms. He came to see the Treaty of Versailles as a calamity. He believed his nation was being castrated, and feared it would lead to a backlash. In particular, he was concerned that the delegation had so many Jewish members, who would be blamed for the treaty's harsh effects. These warnings were not heeded. The following year, Weber died in the Spanish Flu epidemic. The harsh terms of the Treaty of Versailles impoverished Germany, then a global financial crisis created rampant inflation, causing the Weimar Republic to fail. With the rise of Hitler, Weber's warning against the 'ethics of conviction' proved to be prophetic, and some wondered what would have been different if the gloomy sociologist had been in charge. Where Weber had seen *Paradise Lost* as the beginning of an irredeemable fall into the modern world, another social thinker, writing after the rise and fall of Nazism, would see Milton's poem as a work with which to remake the world.

Morningside Heights, Upper Manhattan, 1950s

In the early 1950s, the philosopher Hannah Arendt started writing the book that would become the most enduring expression of her thought: *The Human Condition*. She and her husband, Heinrich Blücher, were living in Upper Manhattan, in an apartment that looked out over Morningside Park towards the Hudson river. They had fled Nazi Germany, arriving in New York in 1941. Ten years later, they finally became naturalised citizens. It was a time of rising prosperity for post-war America and a new life for them. Beginning again is also the subject of *The Human Condition*, but writing it took Arendt back to her student days in Germany, before the war, and to the man who was her teacher.

In 1924, the eighteen-year-old Arendt had arrived at Marburg University, where she was to study philosophy.[24] There, she came under the influence of 'the little magician of Messkirch'. Known by the provincial town where he was born, Martin Heidegger was a stocky man who wore quasi-military collared shirts. In the 1920s, he launched an assault on Western philosophy, proposing to recover something that had been eclipsed by the modern age and its furious technological progress: the ancient concept of 'Being'. Later in life, Arendt described his reputation among the students of Marburg:

> Thinking has come to life again; the cultural treasures of the past, believed to be dead, are being made to speak, in the course of which it turns out that they propose things altogether different from the familiar, worn-out trivialities they had been presumed to say. There exists a teacher; one can perhaps learn to think.[25]

Heidegger, a 'hidden king in the realm of thinking', would teach the students about this apparently mysterious concept: 'Being'. In his philosophical masterpiece, *Being and Time* (1927), Heidegger described

Hannah Arendt as a young woman, *c.* 1930.

how we are 'thrown' into the world and must work out how to live authentically in relation to Being. A non-moralised fall into existence, his philosophy would later inspire the French existentialists to develop their philosophy, in which the fact of existence precedes any attempt to make sense of its essential meaning. The students in Marburg encountered it first, and Arendt came to have a close connection to it.

In her first term, Arendt went to meet her professor in his office. The thirty-five-year-old Heidegger was married, but this did not prevent him from pursuing a romance with his student. It lasted until Arendt graduated, when she finally called it off. She moved to another university and started to develop her own philosophy. She married, and Heidegger took a new mistress – who was, like Arendt, Jewish. Soon after that, Germany became possessed by fascism. It was only in 1933, when news of Heidegger's anti-Semitic activities reached

Arendt, that she broke off all contact with him. That April, he had been elected Rector of Freiburg University, and the following month, he joined the Nazi Party. Soon afterwards, Arendt fled Germany. She went first to Paris, where she got divorced and met her second husband. Then, after a period in a French internment camp, they escaped to Spain and from there to New York. The day after disembarking, Arendt wrote in a telegram to her ex-husband: 'We're Saved'.[26]

In America, Arendt learnt English by working as a maid before establishing herself in New York as a writer, thinker, and teacher. In 1950, she returned to Europe for the first time as part of a mission to recover Jewish property looted under the Nazis. While she was there, her former teacher and friend Karl Jaspers showed her the evidence of Heidegger's Nazism, which Weber's widow Marianne had helped to circulate. Heidegger had been far more complicit with Nazism than he let on.[27] Arendt told Jaspers that Heidegger's 'mendacity' was an established fact.[28] But when she returned to Germany, for the first time, she wrote to Heidegger. She was in Freiburg to give a lecture and he came to her hotel. She later wrote: 'it was as though time had stopped'.[29] She was happily married and he was still married to Elfride, who Arendt said 'is ready to drown any Jew in sight'.[30] But he was the thinker whose path she had followed, and she was the most important of his former students. The bond endured.

What did it feel like to go, as a Jewish person, into the Bavarian countryside less than five years after Hitler's downfall? The area was still populated by many of the people who had supported the Nazis, including Heidegger. The Jewish poet Paul Celan wrote a poem about visiting the philosopher in the *Hütte*, a rural cabin in the Black Forest that Heidegger used as a retreat. When he signed the visitors book, Celan wondered whose names had been written in there before his.[31] Heidegger never confronted his complicity with Nazism and Arendt may not have known the extent of it. She believed he hadn't read *Mein Kampf* until the late 1930s, by which time he had grown disillusioned with Nazism. In fact, he read it in 1931, urged to do so by his wife. Arendt didn't know that Heidegger had been quietly covering up evidence of his earlier fervour in the new editions of his writings. An acquaintance compared him to a fox who sweeps away his own tracks with his tail.[32] But he was still her teacher, they still had a deep love for each other, and she learnt to accept his error. That year she started making notes about forgiveness and reconciliation that would be the culmination of her next book.[33]

The Human Condition was published in 1958, by which time post-war prosperity had soured into Cold War paranoia. Arendt no longer wrote in her mother tongue, preferring the language of her new home. Her philosophy also started to reflect the hawkish liberalism of Cold War America.[34] Her first work in English was *The Origins of Totalitarianism* (1951), which analysed the similarities between fascism and communism, contrasting them with a democracy that guaranteed freedom of thought and association. Likewise, *The Human Condition* takes on another enemy of capitalist America: Karl Marx. Arendt argues that Marx's philosophy failed to distinguish between 'labour' and 'work'. She points out that many modern languages possess two different words for work and labour. Labour, she says, is the activity with which we reproduce our basic existence: 'Whatever labor produces is meant to be fed into the human life process almost immediately.'[35] Work, on the other hand, results in things that have a greater permanence – poetry, laws, buildings, games etc. Work is what allows us to be objective, creating things that are distinct from us. 'The world . . . consists not of things that are consumed but of things that are used.'[36] Arendt believed that the modern world – both in capitalist and communist countries – had privileged consumption, forgetting the importance of work. She believed that only works, which are used but not consumed, could create the shared world necessary for a functioning democracy. This is why she wrote about *Paradise Lost*.

Arendt believed that Marx's comparison of Milton to a silkworm was a classic example of his failure to distinguish between work and labour.[37] *Paradise Lost*, she maintained, is a work. This disagreement captures the curious hybridity of Milton's poem. Milton claimed that it was 'unpremeditated' (IX:24), delivered at night. As noted earlier, he called the process of dictation being 'milked', which does resemble Marx's image of the poet as a silkworm producing silk: more labour than work, according to Arendt's distinction. The poem's music would delight the ears of its readers in a way that wasn't entirely conscious. However, it was also clearly the result of a great deal of conscious activity: Milton was not only being milked but producing something deliberate. *Paradise Lost* was a composition aimed at educated readers, who Milton hoped would be inspired to found new republics. It did become a semi-precious commodity when Milton sold it, but it also became a work in Arendt's sense: something that enables us to begin again to make the world.

One of the activities fundamental to beginning again, Arendt writes in *The Human Condition*, is forgiveness. Forgiveness is necessary in an unpredictable world where we bind ourselves to others through promises. When we fail to act as we have promised, the options are punishment or forgiveness. Arendt writes:

> The discoverer of the role of forgiveness in the realm of human affairs was Jesus of Nazareth. The fact that he made this discovery in a religious context and articulated it in religious language is no reason to take it any less seriously in a strictly secular sense.[38]

Only forgiveness, she says, allows us to 'begin something new'.[39] It is the opposite of vengeance, which binds us to the past. There are some crimes, to be sure, which do not merit forgiveness: 'men are unable to forgive what they cannot punish and . . . unable to punish what has turned out to be unforgivable'.[40] Arendt would later confront an unforgivable crime in *Eichmann in Jerusalem: A Report on the Banality of Evil* (1963), her book about the trial in Jerusalem of Adolf Eichmann, a Nazi who had escaped to Argentina and then been hunted down by the Israeli secret services. There, she argues that the Holocaust had been carried out by dull bureaucrats like Eichmann, who exhibit the 'banality of evil'. She concludes that Eichmann deserved the death penalty, since no one could be expected to want to share a world with him. But what evil did she ascribe to the philosopher-magician who was her lover?

Arendt saw Heidegger's mistake as one that could be forgiven. In the decades to come, she championed his work and even befriended his wife. They remained in touch, on and off, for the rest of their lives.

Hers was an extraordinary act of forgiveness. But there was another aspect to her beginning again. She thought about dedicating *The Human Condition* to Heidegger, telling him that the book 'came directly out of the first Freiburg days and hence owes practically everything to you in every respect'.[41] It was their reconciliation at Freiburg in 1950 that led to this major new work. But Arendt realised that she couldn't dedicate the book to Heidegger. Among her unpublished papers, there is a poetic piece of reasoning that explains why:

> The dedication of this book is omitted.
> How could I dedicate it to you,
> trusted one,
> whom I was faithful
> and not faithful to,
> And both with love.[42]

This paradoxical relationship to the past – at once a bond to it and a freedom from it – characterises forgiveness. To forgive someone is not to be beholden to them. *The Human Condition* departs from Heidegger's thought, returning to it in order to go beyond it. Whereas Heidegger insisted that death is the defining event of human existence, Arendt privileged the concept of natality. In order to exist and have Being, Arendt argues, we have to begin. Beginning is not only a kind of labour performed by mothers and midwives; it is also a kind of work, something that lawmakers and writers are responsible for. She returned to Heidegger and overcame his influence in the very same work. *The Human Condition* is full of references to the defining works of the modern world – including *Paradise Lost* and Weber's *Protestant Ethic* – but Heidegger is not named once. She had truly begun again.

When Satan encounters Eve, she is 'Veiled in a cloud of fragrance' (IX:425), tying the drooping heads of roses to stems. It is both erotic and innocent. Satan is so captivated that he becomes for a moment 'Stupidly good' (IX:465). For Milton, to perceive beauty is to become good, however briefly. Then, remembering himself, Satan returns to the task at hand.

The serpent approaches Eve and speaks to her. Don't be surprised to see a creature capable of language, he says, surprisingly. Dumbfounded, Eve asks him how he's not mute like other animals. He tells her it is the fruit of a certain tree and then he leads her to it. When she sees which tree it is, Eve tells him that he might have spared her the trouble. She can't eat its fruit. The serpent now rises up and asks the tree: Why can't your fruit be eaten by these humans? Why shouldn't they eat it? Could God be *envious* of their freedom?

Eve is affected by this. She starts musing to herself, nervous to transgress, longing to find out the truth, and already partly convinced. Why should I fear knowledge? she wonders, giving in to it.

> So saying, her rash hand in evil hour
> Forth reaching to the fruit, she plucked, she ate:
> Earth felt the wound, and nature from her seat
> Sighing through all her works gave signs of woe,
> That all was lost (IX:780–4)

Notice the harshness of these lines, especially the spondee (two stressed syllables in a row): 'her **rash hand**'. This is the first catastrophe. The serpent slinks away as Eve gorges herself on the fruit, drunk with new knowledge. She wonders if she should hide her new power from her husband, using it to make herself superior: 'for inferior who is free?' (IX: 825). But she doesn't want to die without Adam, leaving him to replace her with 'another Eve' (IX: 828). She decides to tell him, and make him fall with her.

In her absence, Adam has crafted a flower garland like those worn by harvest queens in English villages. But he's anxious. Eve returns and tells him she has eaten the fruit.

> horror chill
> Ran through his veins, and all his joints relaxed;
> From his slack hand the garland wreathed for Eve
> Down dropped, and all the faded roses shed (IX:890–3)

There's something tragically cartoonish about the roses wilting before they hit the ground. Notice the harshness of this second spondee: 'his **slack hand**'. Adam is slack where he should be firm. He asks himself:

> How can I live without thee, how forgo
> Thy sweet converse and love so dearly joined
> To live again in these wild woods forlorn? (IX:908–10)

Even if God were to make a 'second Eve', Adam wouldn't want her. He's in love. He decides to eat the apple out of love. In the ruthless language of today's misogynists, Adam is a *cuck*. For himself, Milton may have felt he made the same mistake with his first wife, and his poem now seems like a cautionary tale against excessive love. He eats the fruit and once again, the whole of creation responds:

> Earth trembled from her entrails, as again
> In pangs, and nature gave a second groan,
> Sky loured, and muttering thunder, some sad drops
> Wept at completing of the mortal sin
> Original (IX:1000–5)

It's difficult to say when the Fall actually happened. Was it when Adam ate the apple, or when Eve did? Was it when Eve began to believe Satan, or when he visited her in her dream? Or even earlier, when God lifted Satan out of his chains, or in Heaven, when Satan raised the first rebellion? We could keep following the chain of events back until the blame rests with the Creator, or we could conclude that this is a story in which there is not one Fall but many. In this way, Milton departs from a theological narrative of history, with its absolute beginnings, and instead approaches something more like a political account of causality. Just as there is no absolute beginning in this story, so there is no immediate end. Like Arendt, emerging from the shadow of Heidegger to insist on the importance of beginning again, Milton doesn't end his epic with the Fall. It stays with Adam and Eve as they work out how to live after they have made their catastrophic error.

9. Malcolm X Startles His Visitor

If you've ever made a serious mistake, you'll know what it feels like to wake up the next day. The dawning memory of what happened, the sadness that comes hand in hand with shame, the nostalgia for what things were like before.

After eating the fruit, Adam and Eve become drunk on their new power. Adam seizes Eve by the hand, leading her to a sofa of flowers, and they have sex for the second time. This time it is profane. After sleeping restlessly, they wake and realise that everything has changed. Their minds are now 'darkened' by sin (IX:1054). A 'newcomer' is there with them: it is 'shame' (IX:1097). They decide to clothe themselves with fig leaves.

Adam now tries to blame Eve, saying that she shouldn't have left his side.

She asks whether she was to stay by his side all the time, a 'lifeless rib' (IX:1154). If he is meant to be in charge, 'the head' (IX:1155), why didn't he command her to stay?

He says he didn't want to force her. They find themselves at an unhappy impasse, neither of them willing to concede.

God comes down to the garden and the humans hide. He asks them what has happened and they tell him, everyone trying to blame someone else.

Adam blames Eve: 'She gave me of the Tree, and I did eat' (X:143).

The Son asks: 'Was she thy God?' (X:145). She was made to be his companion.

Eve also tries to shift the blame: 'The serpent me beguiled and I did eat' (X:162).

The Son now pronounces a curse on the guilty parties: the serpent will crawl on his belly, and be crushed by the heel of humankind; women will suffer pain in childbirth and submit to their husbands' rule; men will have to work for their daily bread; they will all die.

The Son then clothes them tenderly and disappears up to Heaven. Milton is staying close to the Book of Genesis. This is why Thomas Jefferson accused him of 'servile plagiarisms'. Milton likely just accepted it as truth.

Meanwhile, Sin and Death are sitting in Hell, and they feel new strength rising in them. They follow Satan up to the world, like vultures to a battlefield. As they do so, Death creates a bridge between Hell and the world, which will lead their human prey back down. God decides that he can't allow Sin and Death to feast on his perfect creation. So he says to his Son that they must spoil the world. Once Sin and Death are finally defeated, they can make it pure again. He sends the angels down to the world to tip the Earth off its axis. It's now no longer always spring in Eden. The angels instruct the moon to exercise her toxic astrological influences. And violence breaks out among the creatures. Adam watches his perfect world turn to horror. He complains:

> Did I request thee, Maker, from my clay
> To mould me man, did I solicit thee
> From darkness to promote me . . .? (X:743–5)

Who hasn't hurled this bitter accusation at their parents? *I didn't ask to be born*. It's an adolescent thought but also a reasonable one. Mary Shelley put these lines on the title page of *Frankenstein*. If we are not made to be happy, why are we here? It's a painful, profound question. Adam and Eve will find an answer together.

It's now cold in Eden, and Adam lies foetal on the ground. He cries out: 'why do I overlive?' (X:773). Eve tries to talk to him, and he curses her: 'Out of my sight, thou serpent' (X:867). He says she is crooked like a rib. He wishes God could have allowed men to reproduce without women.

Eve falls on her knees, asking his forgiveness. Even if they are alive only one more hour, she says, they should make peace. She wants to take responsibility for the Fall. Adam is moved by her humility and his anger relents.

Eve then suggests that they should not have sex so their children won't have to experience death. If abstaining proves too difficult, they can just kill themselves: 'Destruction with destruction to destroy' (X:1006). With this, Milton has done what he first thought he would do in 1640: turned the Book of Genesis into a tragedy. These star-crossed lovers are ready to kill themselves for love, the ultimate sacrifice. But the story doesn't end here.

We can't kill ourselves, Adam says, in case it's the wrong way to receive our punishment. Maybe God will be merciful. If I have to earn my bread, what's so bad about that? Fire will protect them from the cold. They don't need a satanic Prometheus to bring fire to them; God lets them discover it. Now they must both do for God what Eve has already done for Adam, and throw themselves at his mercy. They kneel on the ground in prayer. Forgiveness allows them to begin again, to repair their relationship with God and with each other. Beginning again was exactly what Malcolm X had just done when he read *Paradise Lost*. But unlike Hannah Arendt, his interpretation of Milton's epic turned it against liberal America.

Norfolk Prison Colony, Massachusetts, September 1949

The twenty-four-year-old Malcolm Little looked out of his window. In the yard, there were men, taking their recreation, talking in little groups. There was thunder in the sky but the men kept on talking, no one taking much notice of the weather. The thunder grew nearer and louder, and still they didn't move. Suddenly the heavens opened, and the men now began to run for cover. Before they could find shelter, they were all drenched. In a letter to his brother, Malcolm turns this into a parable.[1] Since his conversion, he had come to see everything as events in a great drama of good and evil, black and white, salvation and damnation. A great change was going to come, and he wondered how many would be prepared for it.

Malcolm Little was born in Omaha, Nebraska, in 1925. His parents were members of Marcus Garvey's pioneering Pan-Africanist organisation, the Universal Negro Improvement Association (UNIA), which promoted Black pride, economic self-sufficiency, and unity between Africa, Black America, and the Caribbean. Malcolm's father, Earl Little, was a Baptist lay preacher and local leader in Garvey's movement, and his mother, Louise, wrote for the UNIA's newspapers about Black pride and self-elevation. From the beginning, Malcolm's life was shaped by racial violence. When his mother was pregnant with him, a group of Ku Klux Klan on horseback came to their home to intimidate them. The family moved to Lansing, Michigan, where their political activities continued to attract attention. When Malcolm was six, Earl Little was found dead on the streetcar tracks, and his family believed he had been murdered. Louise raised her eight children alone, but eventually her mental health deteriorated, and she was institutionalised in 1939. Malcolm had been a promising student, hoping to become a lawyer. But he was discouraged by white teachers, dropped out of high school and drifted into a life of crime. In 1946, he was arrested for selling stolen goods and given an eight-to-ten-year prison sentence.

Soon after entering Charlestown, the crowded state penitentiary in Boston, Malcolm was given the nickname 'Satan' because of his unrepentant attitude, propensity to curse, and refusal to work. Then something prompted him to change. An older man known as Bimbi made an impression: 'we would sit around, perhaps fifteen of us, and listen to Bimbi. Normally, white prisoners wouldn't think of listening to Negro prisoners' opinions on anything, but guards, even, would wander over close to hear Bimbi on any subject.'[2] Bimbi, who has been identified as John E. Bembry, had gained his learning in the prison library.[3] His influence brought Malcolm back into the world.[4] He took a correspondence course to improve his reading and writing skills, then started learning Latin. In March 1948, thanks to lobbying efforts by his relatives, he was moved to Norfolk Prison Colony. An experimental 'community prison', there were no bars on the windows, and when his brother Reginald came to visit, they didn't have to talk through wire mesh or reinforced glass.[5] There were opportunities for education and a debating club that competed against teams from the Ivy League (and often won). And there was an extensive library. In 1947, Malcolm's older brother Wilfred had joined the Nation of Islam. He started to convert his family members, and together they lobbied Malcolm to join 'the natural religion of the black man'.[6] By the end of 1948, they had succeeded.

Administration building, Norfolk Prison Colony, *c.* 1934.

The Nation of Islam was established in 1930. The nationality, background, and fate of its founder, Wallace Fard Muhammad, remain unknown. After the Wall Street Crash of 1929, he was selling products door-to-door to the poor Black community of Detroit.[7] He soon noticed that his customers had a different need, as one of them later recalled:

> He told us that the silks he carried were the same kind that our people used in their home country and that he had come from there. So we all asked him to tell us about our own country.[8]

Fard had travelled over the world, and he told his customers about Africa and the Middle East. He knew what their diet should be, and told them how to cure their everyday aches and pains. Soon, he was giving them a whole new account of their origins: telling them that Black people were the original people. He said that Islam and not Christianity was their true religion. He made a stirring critique of white America, calling white people 'devils', and claiming that Christianity had taught Black people to love their oppressors. Soon, Fard's sermons were attracting crowds.

The Nation of Islam followed some of the tenets of orthodox Islam. Its members weren't meant to drink, smoke, eat pork, or engage in extramarital sex. There were strict dress codes for women. Gay men were not admitted. But they didn't fast on Ramadan, and the pilgrimage to Mecca was not yet part of their faith. It was a liberation theology: 85 per cent of Black people were 'dead' and had to be resurrected. Islam was a vehicle for Black freedom and separation from a society of white devils. Some took this literally. In 1932, a follower called Robert Harris killed his room-mate and called it a ritual sacrifice. This led the *Detroit Times* to call them a 'voodoo cult'.[9] After that, the police told Fard to leave Detroit. He disappeared in 1934, never to be seen again. The new leader was Elijah Muhammad, and he said Fard was God, and he, Elijah Muhammad, was his prophet. For a while, the Nation of Islam remained small. When America entered the Second World War, Muhammad was arrested for refusing the draft and when he was released, in 1946, the Nation had only 400 members. But soon after that, Muhammad gained his most effective – and most troublesome – follower.

Malcolm X described conversion as rising from the dead.[10] It gave his life direction, channelled his energy, and increased his appetite for knowledge. Elijah Muhammad taught him that history had been 'whitened', and Black people had been left out. Malcolm now read as widely as possible about colonialism, slavery, and race. He didn't want to be taught by the volunteer instructors, who came from Harvard and Boston Universities. He began to teach himself. 'No university', he later declared, 'would ask any student to devour literature as I did when this new world opened to me.'[11] Poetry offered him a special kind of illumination. 'I've become a real bug for poetry', he wrote to his brother Philbert. 'When you think back over all of our past lives, only poetry could best fit into the vast emptiness created by man.'[12] Malcolm littered his letters with quotations from the mystical Islamic poetry of Hafez and Rumi, in turgid nineteenth-century translations.[13] *Paradise Lost* may have been a Christian poem, but it offered a more intense experience, giving colour to the world he had discovered through the Nation of Islam.

Malcolm read Milton's epic in the *Harvard Classics*, a fifty-volume, cloth-bound series known as the 'Five Foot Shelf', which offered an education to readers not fortunate enough to go to college. Its editor presents Milton as a proto-American writer: an early champion of the freedoms later enshrined in the Declaration of Independence. Malcolm came to a radically different conclusion, and he told Reginald about it in the visitors' room:

> The devil, kicked out of Paradise, was trying to regain possession. He was using the forces of Europe, personified by the Popes, Charlemagne, Richard the Lionhearted, and other knights. I interpreted this to show that the Europeans were motivated and led by the devil, or the personification of the devil. So Milton and Mr Elijah Muhammad were actually saying the same thing.[14]

Many radical readers had seen themselves in Milton's Satan, but not Malcolm. Having embraced a new religion, and cast off the name 'Satan', he could not do that. Instead, like Vastey, Malcolm saw Satan as a symbol of his white enemies: the kings and popes of Europe and also the white-supremacist USA. This encounter has often been mentioned by modern scholars of Milton, hoping to make *Paradise Lost* seem relevant, but they have rarely, if ever, explored what it was in the poem that resonated with the young militant.[15]

Malcolm's interpretation rests on the Nation of Islam's origin myth. This exists in multiple versions, and Muhammad's followers understood it in ways not accessible to the uninitiated, but the basic story is well known. The original people were Black, created 76 trillion years ago. They lived in Mecca, and all was well, but a third of them were often discontented. One of the discontented was a Black scientist called Yakub, who even as a child had promised that he would one day wipe out Black people. Yakub was so clever that he had a large head, or two brains. He did create a new people – the white race – and designed them so that they would take over the world and dominate the Black race. Eventually they did take over the world, subjugating all races. Black people were the lost Tribe of Shabazz, the original people, and they would be oppressed by Yakub's ugly creatures for another 6,000 years until one great man arrived to rule them for a millennium of peace. At first glance, this seems alien to the Christian origin myth. However, some versions do bear similarities to the Old Testament's brief account of Lucifer's expulsion from Heaven. For example, when Elijah Muhammad writes: 'Yakub rebelled against Allah and the righteous people and was cast out of the homes of the righteous into the worst part of our planet.'[16] This is strikingly close to the plot of *Paradise Lost*: Mecca is like Heaven and Yakub and his white creations are like the fallen angels. This is surely why, to the young Malcolm, Milton's poem did sound a lot like Elijah Muhammad.

This connection is also a sign of Malcolm's ingenuity as a reader. In a letter to his brother Philbert, he recognised that his conclusions were 'violently contrary' to the usual interpretations.[17] He often read the Western tradition in an oppositional way: Socrates got his wisdom from ancient Egypt. King James I was the real author of Shakespeare's works, and he had also 'fixed' the Bible, in the King James translation of 1611, which had 'enslaved the world'. Spinoza's philosophy impressed him briefly, while he believed Spinoza – a Dutch Sephardic Jew – was Black. He read Kant, Schopenhauer, and Nietzsche, and believed they were the foundations of Nazism. He called Western philosophy a 'cul-de-sac'.[18] Malcolm's rejection of Western civilisation was an epic act. Just as Milton, when he describes how the fallen angels were later worshipped as gods in pagan societies, folded the entire history of ancient civilisation into the backstory of his Christian epic, Malcolm had consumed works representing the whole of Western culture; now he was declaring it dead, and proposing the new nation that would supersede it.

But Milton represents an exception. Malcolm's interpretation of

Paradise Lost was certainly 'contrary to popular belief', but it also grasped something true about Milton's poem. Malcolm wasn't the first Black radical to interpret *Paradise Lost*: as we've already seen, Equiano quoted it in his 1789 slave narrative, Vastey referenced it in Haiti in 1816, Frederick Douglass used Milton as a cardinal example of the 'self-made man', and more recently, Anna Cooper had quoted Milton in her 1892 call for Black women's education, *A Voice From the South*.[19] Malcolm was right to say that *Paradise Lost* asserts a link between Satan and Christian rulers. Milton compares Satan's army of fallen angels to crusading armies (I:582–7); he twice compares Satan to European merchant ships travelling to Africa and Asia in search of precious commodities (II:636–40; IV:159–65); Death wears a 'kingly crown' (II:673) and builds a bridge that is 'pontifical', a pun on the Latin name of the pope, *pontifex* (X:313). To appreciate this, Malcolm seems to have understood Milton's Latin wordplay – a true feat of reading. He had read, understood, and recruited Milton's epic.

He read Milton at the time when he was becoming Malcolm X. Reading was fundamental to that transformation. In the Nation of Islam, X was a sign of a follower's unknown original name, and it was usually later replaced by an Islamic name. A month later, he signed a letter 'Malcolm X'. But he gave the custom his own original meaning, connecting it symbolically to Christ, and the x in algebra. By January 1949, Malcolm Little was no more and a new man had been born. Malcolm's ability to interpret was the foundation of his political activism. In 1950 there was a typhoid epidemic: Malcolm refused a vaccine, so he was transferred back to Charlestown State Prison, where literature was in limited supply. He wrote to the prison commissioner to complain about his lack of access to reading materials. At that time, prisoners were considered 'slaves of the state', and did not enjoy the rights guaranteed in the constitution.[20] Malcolm asked:

> Can the 'laws of this state' deprive one from one's God-given *Rights*? Can it deprive one from the Right to exercise in one's Speech, Thought, and Practise, one's conscientious views concerning one's

> people, one's God, and one's conception of what constitutes 'a devil,' simply because one is an inmate in a penal institution, and because one's skin is Black? . . . Is there a monopoly on Truth?[21]

This final question was the basis of Malcolm's critique of white America, which he took from Elijah Muhammad and ran with. He was overturning a view in white America that Black power was a demonic threat to social order. One translation of the Qur'an appeared to support this: 'the Day when the Trumpet shall be sounded and We shall muster the sinners, their eyes turned blue with terror' (20:102). White people were the real devils.

Malcolm's education at Norfolk Prison Colony would prove crucial to his rise within the Nation of Islam. Malcolm X left prison in 1952 and became minister of Harlem's Temple No. 7 two years later. He travelled regularly as Muhammad's representative, opening temples in Boston, Philadelphia, Harlem, and Atlanta. In 1956, he appeared on the front cover of *Muhammad Speaks* next to his leader. The number of young members increased tenfold during this time, and they were a key demographic for him. In 1958, two NYPD officers invaded Malcolm X's home without a warrant, and arrested his pregnant wife, Betty. At her trial, Malcolm stood on the courthouse steps and told his followers: 'Any policeman who abuses you belongs in the cemetery.'[22] (In this, he was like Milton, declaring that any king could justly be killed if he became a tyrant.) Statements like these made him famous and vulnerable.

In 1959, the FBI launched a media campaign to smear the Nation of Islam. This was part of the Counter Intelligence Program (COINTELPRO), which aimed to discredit many different radical groups. Soon the campaign began to take effect: cracks emerged in the relationship between Muhammad and Malcolm, and within the Nation more generally. Some of the younger members were frustrated with the lack of direct political action: the Nation criticised other Black civil rights leaders as 'Uncle Toms' but they were not doing enough to fight real inequality. By 1963, Malcolm was talking more about social problems and less about Islam. When JFK was assassinated, the young minister commented that 'the chickens are coming home to roost'.[23] The violence of white America against Black people had come back to haunt them. Muhammad, who was trying to make the Nation of Islam both more orthodox and more mainstream, silenced Malcolm for ninety days. Their relationship deteriorated further and, the following year, the disciple left the movement.

After leaving the Nation of Islam in March 1964, Malcolm was free to think for himself. A Sudanese student called Ahmed Osman told Malcolm he had misread the Qur'an verse about blue-eyed devils: instead, it meant that the wicked would *turn* blue out of fear, not that the wicked were all naturally blue-eyed.[24] Malcolm started to be more orthodox in his religion and to reconsider his politics. Having bitterly criticised civil rights leaders, he became more conciliatory. When he met Martin Luther King, Malcolm said: 'I'm throwing myself into the heart of the civil rights struggle.'[25] That same year, he went to Mecca to perform the Hajj, and he said that the experience of worshipping alongside white Muslims had shown him that American whiteness was a state of mind. He still thought Black political groups should exclude white people, but he now spoke of them as hypocrites rather than devils. He no longer believed that Elijah Muhammad was Allah's prophet, and he didn't want to be a leader like him. Instead, he wanted to be like the celebrity evangelist Billy Graham, a minister without a church.[26] Muhammad was suspicious of African liberation but Malcolm increasingly saw his politics as international.[27] After meeting the ambassador of Algeria, he realised that the struggle extended beyond Black people. Mao's support for the African American struggle, and the Cuban revolution, expanded his understanding even further. He wanted to take a case against America to the UN Court of Human Rights, and tried to persuade African leaders to support it.

Malcolm was now able to speak freely, and it was during this time that his speeches developed their own distinctive poetics. He had a talent for creating simple, memorable images. In 'Message to the Grassroots' (1963), he asked: 'when you've got some coffee that's too black, which means it's too strong, what do you do? You integrate it with cream, you make it weak.'[28] His speeches didn't only communicate his message of Black power, they embodied it. He

Malcolm X speaks at a rally in Harlem, 1963.

established himself as an alternative to Martin Luther King by rejecting non-violence, which he associated with the Christian doctrine of turning the other cheek and forgiving one's enemies. Instead, he promoted self-defence by any means necessary. In 'The Ballot or the Bullet' (1964), he said: 'A ballot is like a bullet. You don't throw your ballots until you see a target, and if that target is not within your reach, keep your ballot in your pocket.'[29] Whether through politics or violence, power should be used. He used his knowledge of history to demonstrate that his revolution was faithful to the spirit of the American Revolution. In 'The Black Revolution' (1964), he declared: 'George Washington didn't get independence for this country nonviolently.'[30] It was at this time of heroic self-reinvention that he returned to *Paradise Lost*.

In 1963, Malcolm started to write his autobiography with Alex Haley. Haley was a Black journalist, who had written articles that demonised the Nation of Islam during the FBI's media campaign against it, but he was perceived to be one of the more fair-minded mainstream journalists. Malcolm told Haley that he only trusted him '25 per cent'.[31] The autobiography tells the story of Malcolm's conversion: his dark night of the soul in Charlestown State Prison followed by the daylight of conversion, then, later, his disillusionment with Elijah Muhammad and departure from the movement. Because of this, there may be an irony in recalling his former zeal as a new convert, reading *Paradise Lost* and seeing, even in the heart of Western culture, the evidence of his new religion. But there's more to it than that. When Malcolm told his brother Reginald about *Paradise Lost*, it was a demonstration of his ability to make his own poetry to fill the emptiness of the world, rather than relying on the teachings of Elijah Muhammad. His encounter with *Paradise Lost* contains seeds of that future discord in the very beginning.

On 21 February 1965, Malcolm X was assassinated. He was giving a speech in Harlem's Audubon Ballroom, when two men stood up and started firing. One of the men was apprehended, and later confessed, but the other escaped into a police car, and was never identified. Two other men were framed for the murder and given long sentences. It is alleged that Muhammad's loyalists in Newark's Mosque No. 25 plotted it, after Elijah Muhammad made insinuations about Malcolm getting what he deserved. But the state is widely believed to have had a hand in it. The government's war on Black political groups was discovered in 1971, when anti-war activists invaded an FBI office in Pennsylvania and exposed the existence of COINTELPRO.[32] The programme was stopped – at least officially – but by then damage had been done. Black radicals had always maintained that the white media was to be treated with suspicion. These revelations validated the Nation of Islam's long-standing belief that America was run by devils.

In death, Malcolm's influence only grew. His *Autobiography* soon became a bestseller, and has remained so, an enduring story of self-education and mental emancipation. His speeches were printed on vinyl records – *Malcolm X Speaking* and *Message to the Grassroots* – preserving their distinctive poetry. In the 1980s, amid the War on Drugs and rising rates of incarceration, his speeches were sampled on rap tracks. 'Bring the Noise', on Public Enemy's incendiary record *It Takes a Nation of Millions to Hold Us Back* (1987), opens with his words: 'Too black . . . too strong . . . Too black . . . too strong'. Malcolm's epic rhetoric, first developed during his early years in prison, had become the voice of a collective rage.

10. C. L. R. James Is Deported

After tempting Eve, Satan slinks off into a bush. He watches the Son of God come down to the Garden and he flees. On his way down to Hell, Satan meets Sin and Death coming the other way. He tells them to continue up to Earth, where they will be able to feast on freshly mortal humans. Satan finds the Gates of Hell open. Inside, the place is strangely empty.

The devils are all in Pandaemonium, waiting to greet their triumphant returning leader – just as the English greeted King Charles II when he restored the monarchy in England. Satan steals among them disguised as an ordinary foot soldier. He slips into the great hall and ascends his throne. Then his head suddenly appears, his lustre tarnished but still glittery, like an entertainer on his final cruise. The crowds rush forward, adoring. He silences them.

We now are the 'lords' of 'a spacious world' (X:467), Satan says, a world hardly less perfect than Heaven. He won't tell them how much he had to suffer to get there: it would take too long. He went to Paradise and seduced the humans, and God cursed the serpent, instead of him! Well, he concedes, maybe he did get cursed too. God said that Satan will bruise man's heel when man bruises Satan's head. But isn't a world worth a bruise? He concludes with the triumphant command: 'up and enter now into full bliss' (X:503). He expects rapturous applause, but none comes; instead, there is a 'dismal universal hiss' (X:504–8). At first, Satan doesn't understand. Then, he feels his face become sharp, his arms stick to his sides, and his legs wrap around each other. He falls to the ground. He has become a snake. The same fate has befallen the other devils. Pandaemonium swarms with tangled serpents. They are drawn by some invisible force to a grove where there is a tree not unlike the one in Eden. The snakes fall on its fruit, greedily, but it turns to dust in their mouths. Milton says that each year they are destined to repeat this 'annual humbling' (X:576).

This is the last we see of the character who at first seemed to be the poem's heroic protagonist, now its villain. If Satan was a revolutionary, he has been brought low. It's necessary to reconcile the claims of Satan in the early books with this conclusion. If we were supposed to sympathise with Satan, the revolutionary, what are we to make of his humbling? Is this a sign that all revolutions must fail? A few years after Malcolm X, another incarcerated radical turned to Milton, and came up with an ingenious reading of *Paradise Lost*, which cast light on his own situation.

Cyril Lionel Robert James was born in Trinidad in 1901. The son of a schoolmaster, he mastered Greek and Latin at a young age. From his mother, he inherited a love of reading and started to devour English literature in his early teens. Raised with puritan, middle-class strictness, James was taught to see Trinidad's native calypso music as 'the road to hell'.[1] He was sent to a school where the English principal instilled respect for imperial culture: 'How not to look up to the England of Shakespeare and Milton, of Thackeray and Dickens, of Hobbes and Rhodes, in the daily presence of such an Englishman?'[2] Education was the key to social mobility in colonial Trinidad, and a literary sensibility was a sign of belonging to an elite.[3] But for James it was more than opportunism: he was a passionate reader and an aspiring writer. He became a schoolteacher, wrote a novel, and set up a magazine called the *Beacon* to promote Trinidadian literature to a mostly indifferent anglophone world.

Like many young writers in England's colonies, James felt that his destiny was to leave Trinidad. In 1932, he emigrated to Britain, hoping to pursue his ambitions as a writer, leaving his wife, Juanita, behind. He moved to Bloomsbury, and one evening went to a lecture by Virginia Woolf's friend Edith Sitwell, an eccentric and grand literary critic. From his account of the meeting, James was eager to impress with his knowledge of art, literature, and music. He succeeded, and soon they were duelling over the merits of English poets. James proclaimed: 'Keats' poetry is very beautiful but it is not strong as the work of Shakespeare or Milton is strong.'[4] Hostile to modernism, James maintained that a great poet would still write in regular metre.

If he had gone to London to become an English man of letters, it was there that his ambitions changed. He fell in with other men who had sought education in England and found their vocation in revolutionary politics: Trinidadian communist George Padmore, Barbadian trade unionist Chris Braithwaite, Guyanese activist T. Ras Makonnen, African American actor Paul Robeson, and the future President of Kenya, Jomo Kenyatta. They gathered at the International Afro Restaurant on New Oxford Street, run by the Pan-Africanist Amy Ashwood Garvey, to talk politics and seek refuge from 'inedible' English food.[5]

Back in Trinidad, a movement for self-government was under way, and James was following it closely. In 1933, Leonard and Virginia Woolf's Hogarth Press published his pamphlet *The Case for West Indian Self-Government*, which describes the mediocrity of the colonial administration. Quoting Shakespeare, James says that the colonial administrators are enhanced by 'all the large effects / That troop with majesty'.[6] Even when the Englishmen sent to Trinidad are mediocre, their office makes them seem majestic. The well-chosen quotation serves a second purpose, implicitly demonstrating by his impeccable education the capacity for self-government in the West Indies. Having been exposed to the world, in London, he soon decided to put his literary skills to the service of post-colonial revolution. Everything changed when he read Trotsky's *History of the Russian Revolution* (1932). 'At the end of reading the book, Spring 1934, I became a Trotskyist – in my mind, and later joined. It was clear in my mind that I was not going to be a Stalinist.'[7] By that time, Trotsky was in exile, having been outmanoeuvred by Stalin, but he still had many supporters outside Russia. James began to write a history of the Haitian Revolution – an event that, astonishingly, had been left out of the histories of the age of revolutions. When it had not been ignored by white historians, the Haitian Revolution was diminished as a provincial imitation of the French Revolution or an outbreak of barbarism. He also wrote a play called *Toussaint Louverture*, with Paul Robeson playing the main role. But his history was to become the more famous work. By this point, his literary success was less important than revolutionary struggle.

C. L. R. James speaks on behalf of the International African Friends of Abyssinia at a rally in Trafalgar Square, 1935.

James believed that a great revolutionary had to be a great artist. A cadre of revolutionaries had to help the masses to realise victory over capitalism: not by leading them, as Lenin had argued, but by inventing a language for them to grasp their revolutionary situation. This was a kind of literary work. It involved thinking, writing and public speaking, and James excelled in all three. In 1938, he was invited to lecture in America by the Socialist Workers Party (SWP), a new Trotskyist party. He stayed in Harlem, the cultural centre of Black America, but soon after arriving, he informed a writer friend: 'I'm afraid my interests now are almost entirely political.'[8] In 1937, the SWP sent him to visit Trotsky in Mexico, at the house of artists Frida Kahlo and Diego Rivera. James was not a natural follower: he disagreed with Trotsky's analysis of Stalinism, but he came away charmed by the diminutive Russian revolutionary, who three years later would be killed by a Stalinist's ice axe to the head. By then, the imperial powers were gearing up for war. James believed the British Empire would not survive another world war, and it was with the goal of accelerating its collapse that his next book was written.

In lean, dynamic, and ironic prose, *The Black Jacobins: Toussaint Louverture and the San Domingo Rebellion* describes the slave uprising of the 1790s, Louverture's betrayal and death, and the completion of the revolution by Dessalines. James writes:

> The revolt is the only successful slave revolt in history, and the odds it had to overcome is evidence of the magnitude of the interests that were involved. The transformation of slaves, trembling in hundreds before a single white man, into a people able to organise themselves and defeat the most powerful European nations of their day, is one of the great epics of revolutionary struggle and achievement.[9]

The Black Jacobins belongs to the Haitian tradition of epic histories going back to Vastey. For this reason, perhaps, Milton was on his mind: James describes how a European visitor would often be 'enchanted at his first glimpse of this paradise'.[10] This is a subtle allusion to Satan's view of Eden in Book IV of *Paradise Lost*, which is confirmed when, shortly afterwards, James says that the visitor's excitement morphs into a 'longing for the season returning with the year'.[11] This is an echo of Milton's lament about his blindness:

> Thus with the year
> Seasons return, but not to me returns
> Day (III:40–2)

James was making fun of the French colonists, thinking themselves as unfortunate as the blind Milton as they suffered Haiti's monotonous climate. *The Black Jacobins* doesn't make the story of Toussaint Louverture a tragedy, as he had done on the London stage.[12] Instead, Toussaint's death is followed by the continuation of the struggle by Dessalines and Christophe, who triumph over Napoleon against all odds. The real tragedy, James says, occurred when the massacres started under Dessalines: 'It was not policy but revenge, and revenge has no place in politics.'[13] This was a tragedy for Haiti, trapping it in a cycle of violence. However, James ends on a note of optimism: if the slaves of Haiti were at the vanguard of history, Africa in the 1930s is far more advanced, despite what its colonisers say about it being 'backward'. Africa was primed for post-colonial revolution.

Charismatic, handsome, and eloquent, James soon became a prominent Trotskyist at a time when they were bitterly divided. One of the causes of this was the pact of non-aggression that Stalin signed in 1939 with Nazi Germany. Eventually, the SWP split over this issue. James believed Russia was now 'state capitalism' and he left the SWP. Several years later, he formed a reading group with a Chinese American philosopher Grace Lee, and Raya Dunayevskaya, who had been Trotsky's personal secretary. In the late 1940s, this group became its own 'tendency': a party that wasn't a party, with James a leader who wasn't a leader. The 'Johnson–Forest Tendency' – named after James's and Dunayevskaya's party aliases – was born from the experience of poring over Hegel's *Logic*, the philosophy that provided the underpinnings of Marx's analysis of capitalism. In doing so, they were imitating Lenin, who had turned to Hegel's philosophy of logic in the years leading up to the Russian Revolution. James believed that this was the key to understanding revolution. At one point in his notes, Lenin writes:

LEAP
LEAP
LEAP
LEAP[14]

This became a catchphrase for James. It was what he and his comrades wanted to do: leap in their thinking past the ossified forms of thinking of the past and discover the language to describe a new revolutionary situation. James now believed that revolutionaries should abolish all parties and convince the working classes to organise themselves.

As the Johnson–Forest Tendency gained followers, they also attracted suspicion. Some believed that James had created a 'cult'.[15] James's charisma extended to a disconcerting ability to command love and acts of service from his younger followers. One day, his girlfriend was disconcerted to see a male member of the tendency scrubbing the leader's back as he took a bath.[16] At this contradictory moment, as a charismatic leader of a movement that opposed charismatic leaders, James returned to *Paradise Lost*.

The year 1949 was the 300th anniversary of the culmination of the English Civil War, and James turned his attention to it. Like Trotsky, James saw the English Civil War as the beginning of the modern revolutionary tradition, and it was the starting point of his analysis.[17] He focused on the Putney Debates of 1647, when the radical elements in Parliament's army – known as the Levellers – discussed reform with the leaders of the army, including Cromwell. James lists their most radical ideas:

> All power comes from the public.
> The foundation of government is the free choice of parliamentary representatives.
> The House of Commons must be supreme.
> Parliaments must be biennial.
> They are to be elected by manhood suffrage.[18]

Cromwell and the other army leaders quickly moved to crush the Levellers' power base, in their place instituting a 'bourgeois revolution', winning political rights only for property-holding men. James saw Cromwell as a Stalin-like figure, who had suppressed the radical revolution and replaced it with a bourgeois one. And he believed Milton was complicit. Having worshipped English poetry, James now saw Milton in purely political terms. 'Milton was an intellectual aristocrat,' James says. In saying this, he was attacking Stalinist critics, who made an 'idol' of the revolutionary poet.[19] Trotsky said that the 'nightingale of poetry . . . is heard only after the sun sets', meaning that poets are never ahead of their time.[20] They only ever seem to be ahead when the rest of society is so far behind the time. Likewise, James consigns Milton to the past: 'Today it is quite clear that the Milton of *Paradise Lost* and *Samson Agonistes* represented the *end* of an age.'[21] Milton wasn't ahead of his time; he belonged to the Elizabethan period, which ended before he was born. But if the times required James to see Milton as obsolete, he would nonetheless speak of him repeatedly in the years to come.

★

In 1952, James gave a series of lectures at Columbia University in New York. The subject was 'The Human Personality in Great Tragedy', and one lecture was devoted to Milton.[22] The lectures don't survive, but in his other writings from that time, James was looking at literature to understand the problem of personality in politics – most obviously embodied in the cult of personality that had developed around Stalin. We don't know exactly what James said about Milton, but some fragments of his thinking are preserved in his next book. By the time he wrote that, his life had been turned upside down.

In the early 1950s, James had been in America for more than a decade without a visa. His second wife was a young model and actress called Constance Webb, and she had given birth to a son, Nobbie. Their marriage drew attention to the fact that James had overstayed his visa, and in 1952 he was arrested. He applied for citizenship, but the FBI informed the immigration authorities of his political activities, and his application was refused. In 1952, they sent him to Ellis Island. The symbolic gateway to America, it was also the point of departure for those denied entry: the sick, superfluous, and un-American. During the Second World War, it became a detention centre for enemy aliens – condemned as 'a concentration camp' by the *New York Times*.[23] Those detained on Ellis Island could look across at the lights of Lower Manhattan, as they sat in the shadows of the American dream.

In 1950, Senator Joseph McCarthy whipped up an anti-communist panic in the US Congress. That year, the McCarran Act was passed, requiring subversives to be deported, including anyone who had ever been affiliated with an organisation advocating 'totalitarian dictatorship', whether fascist or communist. Ellis Island began to fill with undesirables, most of them Europeans whose lives had led them, by necessity or choice, to associate with fascism or communism. President Truman opposed the legislation and tried to veto it.[24] When it became law, he ordered that it be enforced as strictly as possible – hoping it would become so controversial that it would quickly fail. This meant that people were sent to Ellis Island whose association with totalitarianism was accidental, glancing, or entirely misunderstood. As the President intended, newspapers soon featured stories of

New York Bay, with Ellis Island and the Statue of Liberty in the foreground and Lower Manhattan in the background (*c.* 1934).

people unjustly detained. When James arrived, there were only thirty detainees on Ellis Island. He was put in a cell for political prisoners, along with five communists. As a Trotskyist, he was their enemy. They watched each other in mutual suspicion. James feared making a complaint in case they found out. But they proved excellent comrades to him. The de facto leader of the communists was a Christ-like figure, who looked out for the injustices of the detention centre, defending the detained from unjust punishments, protesting for the right to exercise in the open air, bathing a disabled detainee, and coming to the aid of his cellmate. James suffered from a chronic stomach ulcer, made worse by the food in the detention centre. This landed him in the hospital wing, and his communist cellmates went on hunger strike to force the authorities to give him appropriate food.

James protested that it was a mistake to deport him, and he had lawyers appeal the decision. He claimed to believe in the democracy and egalitarianism promised in the Declaration of Independence. He loved Hollywood, hamburgers, and romance novels.[25] He was at work on a monumental study called *American Civilization*. But as a Marxist, he saw America as the most advanced form of capitalism and therefore believed it was a society that held the secrets to overthrowing capitalism. What was the truth? Had James come to destroy the American dream or fulfil it? Was he committed to continuing the revolution or had he found something else? He desperately wanted not to be deported back to Britain, and even less to Trinidad, where he would be far from the action. He wrote to the British Prime Minister, Anthony Eden, to complain. Eden responded that life in Britain wasn't to be considered a punishment.[26]

After being released on bail, in 1953, he turned to literary criticism to protest his treatment. *Mariners, Renegades, and Castaways* is ostensibly about the great American novelist Herman Melville, but it's really about the threat that McCarthyism poses to American democracy. James used Melville's fiction, especially *Moby-Dick*, to identify a character in American politics: a 'totalitarian type'.[27] In the 1950s, totalitarianism had become a fashionable term for liberals wanting to critique Nazism and Stalinism in the same breath: Hannah Arendt did so in her book *The Origins of Totalitarianism* (1951). James used the term in a characteristically ingenious way. In *Moby-Dick*, he says, the totalitarian type is represented by Captain Ahab, who leads his crew on a suicidal mission to hunt a whale that tore off his leg in a previous encounter. Melville had recognised something: a special way in which America could become a totalitarian state. The rise of a personality who, in championing American values, would lead America astray. The final chapter gives an account of his detention. The spirit of immigration law is 'the extermination of the alien as a malignant pest'.[28] While not as bad as the gulags or the concentration camps, this represents a form of totalitarianism latent in America.

James was using literature to shame the US government. 'Aeschylus, Shakespeare, Milton – I felt them real and living,' he wrote.[29] Literature was an act of speculative thinking, perceiving a totalitarian future in the paranoid present, and this is close to what James believed his own task as a revolutionary to be. Rather than seeing Melville's characters as timeless symbols of essential human evil, they were a comment on the historical movement of American society towards totalitarianism. After James left America, the Johnson–Forest Tendency had *Mariners, Renegades, and Castaways* privately printed and sent to every member of the US Senate. The book is divided against itself: both an epic 'fuck you' to the USA and a plea to be let back in. James attacks US policy but he also excoriates his former comrades of the Left. He describes how the communists on Ellis Island were more humane than the government officials, but he also argues that they are a danger to the USA. He even includes his former comrades the Trotskyites in his warning. Sounding repentant for his radical past, James says he now understands the values of liberalism and the freedom of speech that it champions.[30] In this, he was a victim of anti-communist paranoia turned state's witness. He left the United States voluntarily in 1953. This meant he was absent for the era of the civil rights struggle, where his political analysis of Black struggle was borne out by events.

Further south in the Atlantic, another revolutionary thinker was returning to Milton at this same moment. In 1954, Fidel Castro was in a prison on the Isle of Pines, off the coast of Cuba. The previous year, he and 130 followers had made an assault on the Moncada garrison, hoping to overthrow General Batista, the unelected President of Cuba. The coup had failed, and half of Castro's followers had been killed. Thanks to his family connections, instead of being executed, Castro was sentenced to fifteen years and was granted a relatively comfortable situation in the prison, permitted to send and receive letters. There, he returned to the speech he had given at his trial. Castro had summoned the long history of rebellions against unjust authority, including the English Civil War, as precedents for his own rebellion. 'The right of insurrection', Castro claims, 'became a fundamental tenet of political liberty.' The execution of the English King was the beginning of something, Castro argued: 'As far back as 1649, John Milton wrote that political power lies with the people, who can enthrone and dethrone kings and have the duty of overthrowing tyrants.'[31] He concluded with the declaration: 'History will absolve me.' This became the title of a pamphlet secretly published in Havana, containing the speech, which would prepare the way for the Cuban Revolution in 1960. Milton had appeared in the Cuban courtroom in his capacity as a political thinker, but his fame as a poet made the claim resonate.

In 1958, James returned to his native Trinidad for the first time in twenty-six years. He was soon at the heart of things. His former student Eric Williams was the Prime Minister of the island, which was gradually gaining its independence from Britain. Williams often sought James's advice, and James used his influence to promote an idea close to his heart: a West Indian federation uniting the Caribbean islands, giving them a power apart from the European colonial powers and the United States. This was established in early 1958, and James worked to forge stronger bonds between the islands' leaders. His influence waned as the federation encountered difficulties. This led him back to his books. In 1962, he revised *The Black Jacobins*, arguing that the Cuban Revolution was heir to that of Haiti, the beginning of a new age of West Indian independence, and maintaining, even in the final year of the West Indian federation, that the masses could be convinced to rise up.

In 1966, James travelled to Montreal at the invitation of some Caribbean militants – Robert Hill from Jamaica, Alfie Roberts from St Vincent, Anne Cools of Barbados, and Tim Hector from Antigua. They had organised a lecture tour for him. The purpose was political, but as ever with James, literature came hand in hand with politics. During a lecture on Lenin and trade unions, he suddenly started talking about the English Civil War. He recommends that his listeners study the life of Cromwell: 'It's worthwhile if you are interested in personality.' Tim Hector asks him about Milton, and James responds:

> I believe that Milton, in *Paradise Lost*, was saying, 'Look here boys. This man of great power and authority, Cromwell, upsets the regime.' He had been with Cromwell all the time but in the end he was doubtful.[32]

James's thinking was always making leaps, and his interpretation of *Paradise Lost* had turned inside out:

> I believe that Satan in *Paradise Lost* was developed from his knowledge of Cromwell and the rest. That is what I think. I cannot prove that. I will have to spend ten years on it. I cannot do that. But somewhere I am going to write that down so that it will be left for somebody to take up.[33]

James now saw *Paradise Lost* as a criticism of the dictatorial Cromwell in the person of Satan. In this ingenious argument, James turned Milton into an anti-Stalinist.

Between 1970 and 2000, a great change occurred in the afterlife of *Paradise Lost*. Milton's fame had tracked the rise of revolutionary hopes in the West and now it fell with them. His work's charge was increasingly preserved as a memory of revolution rather than a present reality.[34] It featured in the degradation of the radical hopes of the 1960s, when the counterculture turned to drugs and cynicism. Frank Reynolds, a leading member of the San Francisco chapter of the Hells Angels, was writing his memoir with the poet Michael McClure, who had given the biker a copy of Milton's epic. Reynolds read it as he descended into LSD-induced hallucination. He came to believe he was Satan:

> I'm dipping into the middle of John Milton's loss of Paradise, and I've got into about six pages of it that are giving me the rundown on what would not be allowed to be said in the manner of students. Wowow-owowow! Dig, this book gave me such a rhythm of words of *my* inborn instincts which gives me the flourish of mind of being reborn. The old one-armed butcher up above curses this book as he smells the bloody burning offerings of his ignorant what he calls sacred *lambs*. Meaning the majority, the Lame.[35]

Like William Blake, Reynolds sympathises with Satan against God, 'the old one-armed butcher'. *Paradise Lost*, for the Hells Angel, is a resolutely Satanic book, guiding him to his destiny:

> A few pages from John Milton's Paradise Lost have put me exactly on the positive track that I am following. I am a child of his. I am a Hell's Angel. Along with all the brothers in the Hell's Angels I no longer

> have to stammer and stutter: I will be able to lay down the trips of the righteousness of Lucifer.[36]

When Reynolds comes to speak of his motorbike, he does so in Milton's words: 'I like to think of my motorcycle as Milton's reflected vision of a *sturdy chariot led by fiery steeds.*' Milton's poem feeds the biker's commitment to the negation of all deemed good by a conservative Christian society. Hunter S. Thompson quotes Milton in his book *Hell's Angels*, a work of reportage about the bikers' notorious gatherings, where rape, theft, and murder took place: 'Better to reign in Hell than serve in Heaven'. Milton's immortal line became a catchphrase for a counterculture that was pure demonic contrarianism.

In another drug-addled part of California, *Paradise Lost* influenced one of the most influential dystopias in modern literature. In November 1971, someone broke into the house of science-fiction writer Philip K. Dick in Marin County. They removed the locks from the doors, took his gun and stereo. They destroyed a filing cabinet using plastic explosives, or so he claimed. At that time, Dick was addicted to amphetamines, and his house had become a meeting point for hippies, junkies, and dropouts. The paranoid writer feared investigation by the FBI, CIA, and IRS, as well as reprisals from communists, religious fanatics, Black militants, drug dealers and vengeful former housemates. He paid local muscle to give him security. He expected the police to raid, but he had called them so many times that they gave him a wide berth. The police, like some of his friends, thought Dick had staged the break-in himself. Several months earlier, he had entrusted some valuable manuscripts to his lawyer that might otherwise have been destroyed in the explosion. Whatever the truth, after the break-in he spiralled further. Then, in February 1974, a dark-haired young woman visited his house to deliver prescription painkillers. Dick, who had a penchant for dark-haired young women, saw her as a divine revelation.

The encounter precipitated a series of visions. Dick referred to them as '2-3-74' since they occurred in February and March 1974. Dick had been experiencing paranoid fantasies of a hostile universe,

God's Son drives Satan and the other rebel angels out of Heaven.
Painting by William Blake 1807–8.

and the new visions were, he said, the inversion of paranoia. He turned to God and sought to reconcile himself with the state, sending a confession of his trespasses to the FBI. He believed he was possessed by the spirit of an early Christian believer named Thomas. He baptised his young son Christopher with hot chocolate. He was guided by a pink light. He received messages in his dreams. One prophecy was that his son had a birth defect that urgently needed to be operated on, and this turned out to be true. Some of his friends wondered if Dick was making the whole thing up. His visions are curiously similar to Milton's visitations by his divine, feminine muse. Dick said the visions happened around the 'vernal equinox', which was the yearly terminus for Milton's poetic composition. Did Dick take his dubious account of these visitations from Milton?

Dick's interest in Milton at that time is undeniable. In his manuscripts from that period, 8,000 pages of speculations on the meaning of his visions which were posthumously published as *The Exegesis*, Dick discusses Milton. He wants to turn Milton's myth of the Fall upside down: 'Man, to be saved, must commit an act of disobedience to this system of things to restore his pristine state now lost.'[37] At that time, Dick was working on a novel, *Through a Scanner Darkly*, and he refers to it as 'my true Paradise Lost'.[38] His grandiosity expressed itself in comparison to Milton. Dick's final vision came in early 1975, described in a letter to his mother: 'Somehow goodness has arrived . . . As Milton wrote, "Out of evil comes good."'[39] But his most Miltonic work from the period is his novel *Do Androids Dream of Electric Sheep?* (1968), a futuristic adaptation of *Frankenstein*. Dick's novel, which was made into the film *Blade Runner*, preserves some of what Shelley took from Milton. For this reason, *Blade Runner* is the most influential cinematic version of *Paradise Lost*.

In a dystopian future America, humans have created a class of humanoid clones, called 'replicants', to work for them. The protagonist must track down a replicant called Roy, who has gone rogue and is trying to kill his creator. As he dies, the replicant delivers a speech that demonstrates his disarmingly human sensibility. Like Mary Shelley, from whose monster Philip K. Dick adapted this speech, *Blade Runner* gives the villain a tragic ending, something Milton denies to Satan.[40] Instead, in *Paradise Lost*, Satan degrades to the point where his angelic nature is no more. His ending can't be tragic, and win the reader's sympathy: it has to be comic. Milton expects us to enjoy the humbling of Satan, just as seventeenth-century crowds flocked to watch the execution of criminals. The modern age abolished the culture of public punishments, and this has influenced narrative expectations. Satan's humbling by an all-powerful God is less likely to produce the satisfaction it might have done for a seventeenth-century reader.

In modern liberal democracies, criminal punishment is most often justified on the basis of rehabilitation, deterrence, and incapacitation. Retribution appears increasingly old-fashioned. But what C. L. R. James noticed in the detention centre was that, while the degradation of life was inconsistent with the values of liberal democratic society, it had remained fundamental to it. Prisoners and illegal migrants were still humiliated, but this happened behind walls and barbed-wire fences. Citizens might know that this was happening, but they didn't have to watch it. What is most uncomfortable about Milton's treatment of Satan is that we are expected to enjoy it.

Satan became corny around 1980, when the commodification of the counterculture led to a commercial satanism espoused by rock bands like Kiss and AC/DC. By then, you'd more likely see Satan's words on the bumper sticker of a family car than on a biker jacket. Going through security on his way into a football stadium, Michael Foot, the leader of the British Labour Party in the 1970s, declared that he had a copy of Milton on him. The joke is that Milton is an instrument of unrest, but the marginalisation of revolutionary politics in the West meant that Milton was less a powerful totem than a toy mascot. The canon of English literature was losing its purchase on the imagination. C. L. R. James noticed this.

In 1982, James appeared on a TV programme called *Arena*. Then in his early eighties, James was filmed in bed in his Brixton apartment, with a shock of white hair and a thick red turtleneck. Two younger poets, Linton Kwesi Johnson and Michael Smith, are visiting him. They write in Jamaican patois rather than James's received English. James tells them about his love for English poetry as a boy in Trinidad.

'They were the finest poems in the world,' he says. 'But when I came here, and got interested in politics, and began to talk to English men who were not as committed to the English system as I was in literary matters, I began to lose my sense of what Wordsworth meant. Wordsworth declined in my opinion.'

Johnson then asks Michael Smith if he is interested in the same literature. 'Never have any influence on me, Linton,' Smith replies.

'Didn't have any impact. As a matter of fact I detested . . . a lot of . . . what is it CLR? Words . . . wort?'

'Wordsworth. That's no pronunciation. That's his name!'

'That's his name? Well I hope I get the pronunciation of his name correct. And Shakka-speare. Or Shakespeare.'

'Nobody in the Caribbean have I heard say Shakka-speare,' James says in a dignified way, as the two young men collapse in laughter.

Unruffled, he continues: 'For you, poetry was part of the awakening of the Caribbean people. And that's what you are all making a contribution to. It was not so for me. And you are all turned to the native speech. And it is a rejection of the English domination. Not so much the speech as such you rejected, if I may say so, but the Rastafari people said: we are dominated by the English King, the English Queen, the English language, the English religion, every God damn thing is English!'

Michael Smith replies: 'Words . . . *wroth* . . . Keats . . . Shelley. We have to write something that is identified with our own.'

'You tackled the most fundamental part of the business. You tackled the language! And created the dialect that is part of the language. But your own use of it. Which I think is splendid!'[41]

In a good-humoured way, James was observing the passing of his own generation, where literature was a means of self-advancement in a colonial society, and a way to communicate revolutionary ideas. To the younger men, Wordsworth, Keats, Shelley – and surely Milton too – were no longer relevant. James has become old, and the young men laugh at him without malice. Smith leans towards him on the bed, affectionate, even as they are talking about something that made the old man's literary tastes obsolete.[42] As a revolutionary who had spent his life conceptualising the leap from one period to another, James thought this was 'splendid'.

James's commitment to the literature of the past was also a knowledge of the future. In a lecture about how he came to write *The Black Jacobins*, James thought of Milton. 'Milton has a great phrase,' he said. 'A good book is the precious life-blood of a master's spirit.'[43] Never content to simply idolise the past, James modifies Milton's argument: 'But it is more than that. It is the result of the circumstances of the age playing upon a mentality and the circumstances of people who are central to it.' Great men and women don't make history alone, they make it with the collectives that are central to their age, whether it is the working classes, the enslaved, or post-colonial nations. But if they do that, like James and Milton, individual writers can take part in the changing of their times.

11. Jordan Peterson Gets Lost

If in England, Milton's revolutionary legacy had begun to seem outdated, this wasn't the case everywhere. A Catalan translation was published in Barcelona in 1953, under a dictatorship that suppressed the region's language.[1] In 1963, imprisoned Yugoslav politician Milovan Djilas translated Milton's epic into Serbo-Croatian, writing it on toilet paper.[2] Translations multiplied, often inspired by movements for national self-determination and liberal reform. In 2011, an Arabic translation of *Paradise Lost* was published, with a picture of Suzanne Mubarak, the wife of the Egyptian dictator Hosni Mubarak, on its back cover.[3] The translation was to be published as part of a literature festival that she had founded.[4] However, the festival was cancelled when Arab Spring protests led to the toppling of Mubarak's regime. That same year, in Syria, a translation by Hanna Aboud was published by the Syrian General Organization of Books. No doubt thinking of the protests against Syria's dictator Bashar al-Assad, which would soon develop into an open uprising, the Ministry of Culture cautioned that readers should be careful in the connections they draw between *Paradise Lost* and Milton's politics. An editorial in the Assadist newspaper *Al-Thawra* (*Revolution*) insisted that Milton's epic showed the defeat of Satan's rebellion by God, the absolute ruler of Heaven, to be inevitable.[5] If the regime wanted to show that *Paradise Lost* had become a fable for the failure of revolutions, it's surely because they recognised it also had the capacity to say the opposite.

While the Arab Spring was the resurgence of revolutionary possibility, the fallout of those protests was no certain proof of the effectiveness of regime change. In Egypt, the revolution was replaced by a military leadership. In Syria, Assad remained the absolute ruler of most of the country. A bookshop in Kuwait was shut down in 2013 by the Ministry of Information for selling a copy of *Paradise Lost* – on the state's list of prohibited books.[6] Meanwhile, in the West, the

Occupy Wall Street protests of 2011 called attention to increasing economic inequality and political stagnation. Marginalised after the downfall of the USSR in 1989, the Western Left had become plausible for a new generation. At the same time, there was the rise of a new progressive politics of identity, promoting protections for sex and gender identity and new sensitivities towards everyday racism and misogyny. At its most radical, this new politics of identity proposed to rethink Western history, and because of this, it was vigorously opposed by conservative elements. University campuses became a crucible for this new 'culture war'. For these reasons, in those years, Milton became attractive to a new generation of conservative revolutionaries.

Edmonton Institution, Alberta, Canada, 1990s

A young psychologist was visiting a colleague in prison when he lost his way. He found himself in the prison gym, his colleague nowhere to be seen. The visitor, who was wearing a woollen cape and a pair of tall leather boots, suddenly found himself surrounded. Men crowded around him, curious about his eccentric costume. Suddenly, one man pushed through the crowd and led him back to safety. Later, the psychologist was shocked to hear that his rescuer had once murdered two policemen. How could that ordinary-looking man have been capable of such extreme violence? He began to think deeply about evil and to meditate on his own capacity for evil. As he did so, he changed.

Jordan Peterson was born in 1962 in Alberta, Canada. In his teens, he volunteered for Canada's left-wing New Democratic Party, but became disillusioned. Writers like Ayn Rand convinced him that left-wing politics were based not on sympathy for the poor but resentment of the rich. He became obsessed with the totalitarian regimes of the twentieth century, the Cold War, and the possibility of nuclear apocalypse. While undertaking a PhD in psychology, he read the Swiss psychoanalyst Carl Jung's writings on mythology. Later, he gained a reputation as a popular if eccentric teacher of psychology at Harvard.[7] He lined the walls of his home with Soviet propaganda to remind himself of the danger of totalitarian ideologies. He moved back to Canada to teach at the University of Toronto, and it was here that he started publishing his thoughts to a mass audience. In the process, he became the most famous living interpreter of *Paradise Lost*.

In 1999, Peterson published his first book. *Maps of Meaning* is an eclectic mix of clinical psychology, myth-analysis, and autobiography. In the preface, entitled 'Descensus ad inferos' (Descent into Hell), Peterson describes getting lost in the Edmonton prison as a mythic voyage into the underworld: a beginning of his investigation of evil. The phrase '*descensus ad inferos*' comes from Christian theology: Jesus going down to Hell to redeem the virtuous souls of those born before him. It is also a task carried out by the heroes of ancient epic: in the *Odyssey*, Odysseus travels to the underworld; in the *Aeneid*, Aeneas goes down to Hades to visit his father; in *The Divine Comedy*, Virgil guides Dante through Hell; and, of course, Milton does the same. Peterson was following a more recent precedent. Carl Jung's *Red Book* (1913–30) describes his exploration of the forgotten, repressed, buried parts of himself as a descent into Hell. Inspired by Jung, the American mythologist Joseph Campbell claimed that all human myths could be reduced to one story: the hero's journey. Campbell's theory became a popular self-help guide, *The Hero with a Thousand Faces* (1949), advising people to think of their own lives as a hero's journey. Following Jung and Campbell, Peterson frames his own life as an epic journey. He went down to Hell, confronted the nature of evil, and emerged as the adversary of liberal society.

Maps of Meaning is as ambitious as it is eccentric. Its subject is the 'architecture of belief', an attempt to explain all religions, myths, and political identities. To do so, Peterson uses Jung's theory of archetypes: symbols that occur in myths, dreams, and writings across all cultures in the world. Peterson relies on two archetypes: the Adversary and the Hero. The Adversary is a son of God who becomes alienated from his father, dominated by envy and resentment. Satan is the most famous example of this archetype. Noting that Satan is only hinted at in the Old and New Testaments, Peterson says: 'All I knew was the outline of the story codified by Milton: Satan, the highest angel in God's heavenly hierarchy, desired to become like the Most High, and fostered a rebellion in heaven.'[8] The psychology of the Adversary is the cause of fascism, Stalinism, and other political evils. Then there is the Hero, who is upright, responsible, and in pursuit of the good. The difference between these two archetypes is the foundation of Peterson's ethics: we must strive to be like the Hero rather than the Adversary. Since myths are inherited, and not invented, we must abide by their truths rather than try to change them. Peterson's eccentric method is the basis of his conservative belief in traditional values. Later this catapulted him to global fame.

Peterson's moment came in 2016. It was election season in the US, and Donald Trump's candidacy led to the emergence of the 'alt-right' in mainstream American politics, an online reaction to the progressive politics of identity. Where many other right-wing thinkers presented themselves as hard-headed rationalists, champions of Enlightenment philosophy, Peterson cast quite a different figure. He believed in Freud's theory of the unconscious, had an interest in myth and literature, and often wept openly in his public talks.

In May 2016, the Canadian government proposed Bill C-16, an amendment to the Canadian Human Rights Act that added gender expression and gender identity to a list of grounds for discrimination. The law proposed to consider hate speech against trans people as similar to racist speech acts. For Jordan Peterson, this was a step too far. He posted a video, 'Professor Against Political Correctness', announcing that he would not submit to the new law. C-16 was designed to address extreme cases of abuse, but Peterson claimed his freedom of speech had been attacked. Even more importantly, he said, those people who demanded that others use their chosen pronouns were part of a new totalitarianism:

> I think they're connected to an underground apparatus of radical left political motivations. I think uttering those words makes me a tool of those motivations. And I'm going to try and be a tool of my own motivations as clearly as I can articulate them and not the mouthpiece of some murderous ideology.[9]

Progressive identity politics, Peterson said, were a danger to liberal society comparable to the totalitarian regimes of the twentieth century. In doing so, he was taking a stand, emulating the solitary heroes of the liberal tradition, including Milton. Peterson now referred to himself as a 'classical liberal'. At a hearing in the Canadian Parliament, the grey-haired professor defended his position in a high-pitched, tenacious voice that would be heard around the world.[10]

Peterson quickly became one of the most divisive public thinkers in North America, viewed by some as a guru, and others as a preacher of hatred. His lectures were increasingly disrupted by protesters. He spoke out about the 'illiberalism' of liberal college campuses. Amid his growing notoriety, in 2018, a second book appeared. Far more accessible than his first, *12 Rules for Life* is self-help literature. Its rules are counterintuitive formulations of simple, powerful truths: 'Treat yourself like someone you are responsible for helping.' This is an old piece of advice, going back to Socrates, who would tell young men intending to go into politics: first you must learn to take care of yourself. Each rule is illustrated by a wide-ranging meditation on biology, clinical psychology, political commentary, and myth. Once again, Peterson is preoccupied by Hell.

> Perhaps, if we lived properly, we wouldn't have to turn to totalitarian certainty to shield ourselves from the knowledge of our own insufficiency and ignorance. Perhaps we could come to avoid those pathways to Hell – and we have seen in the terrible twentieth century just how real Hell can be.[11]

Living responsibly, Peterson says, is the way to avoid ending up producing political Hells. Adopting the envious psychology of the Adversary leads not only to personal unhappiness but also to the totalitarian politics of Hitler and Stalin. To understand Hell, Peterson uses literature: 'I read and perhaps understood much of Milton's *Paradise Lost*, Goethe's *Faust* and Dante's *Inferno*.'[12] In an age where knowledge of classics cannot be taken for granted, even among college students, this list is part of his authority. In one YouTube video, he calls Milton's poem 'one of the prime literary masterpieces of the last five hundred years'.[13] But if Peterson gives off an air of authority, his interpretation of *Paradise Lost* is highly eccentric.

Peterson refers to 'the arrogance and certainty that the English poet John Milton's genius identified with Satan, God's highest angel

White supremacists march through the University of Virginia the night before the Unite the Right rally, Charlottesville, VA, on 11 August 2017.

gone most spectacularly wrong'.[14] This isn't necessarily true. In *Paradise Lost*, Satan is not the highest angel. In Heaven, before his fall, Satan is an archangel, like Michael, Gabriel, Raphael, and Uriel: 'of the first / If not the first archangel, great in power' (V:659–60). This is ambiguous: 'if not' could mean Satan *was* the highest or wasn't. Peterson decides that it means 'the first' (or 'first equal'), because this fits into his two principal archetypes: the Adversary and the Hero. To illustrate this, Peterson quotes a passage about Satan from Book I: 'He trusted to have equall'd the most High' (I:40). The word 'trusted' suggests that Satan was on a par with the most High: not only the other angels but God himself. However, this line is not trustworthy. Satan *assumed* he was the most high, but that doesn't mean he really was. Milton is giving us an insight into Satan's pride: he believes himself to be the equal of God's Son, but he isn't. *Paradise Lost* shows us that Satan isn't equal to the Son, or even, ultimately, to the other archangels. Peterson attacks the idea that 'all interpretations are valid'.[15] He identifies it with 'postmodern philosophy', which is responsible for the crisis of modern life. Interpretations have consequences, Peterson says: 'Some hurt – yourself and others.'[16] This is true, and Peterson's interpretation of *Paradise Lost* mirrors the side of his work that could be construed as harmful.

Within its first year, *12 Rules for Life* sold 3 million copies around the world, and gained Peterson many followers. Many of them are young men, compelled by his powerful way of stating the obvious, and his eclectic thinking. Many see Peterson as a Christlike figure, and credit him as a transformative effect on their lives. There is also something else going on. In *12 Rules for Life* Peterson says: 'I've always thought that if people really noticed what I was teaching there would be Hell to pay. You can decide for yourself what truth there might be in that concern after reading this book. :)'[17] What does this smile allude to? If there is a radical content hidden in Peterson's writing, it is a scepticism about contemporary political struggles, including those against transphobia, misogyny, racism, and climate change. It emphasises the importance of ethics and psychology at the expense of politics. 'Maybe the environment problem is spiritual', he muses.[18] Likewise, he interprets *Paradise Lost* as a caution against politics: 'Milton's great poem was a prophecy. As rationality rose ascendant from the ashes of Christianity, the great threat of total systems accompanied it.'[19] In this interpretation of Milton, which Jung himself had proposed fifty years before, Satan is a symbol of arrogant Western rationality.[20] Peterson argues that this culminated in totalitarian communist regimes in the USSR, China, and Cambodia. As someone whose house is decorated with totalitarian propaganda, it's perhaps not surprising that Peterson sees Canadian legal reforms and student radicals as signs of the most extreme totalitarian ideologies. This leads him to a contradiction: even as he appears to coach his readers not to stew in resentment – to be like the Hero rather than the Adversary – Peterson's own political opinions endorse resentment towards liberal society.

Peterson returned to Hell in his third book, *Beyond Order* (2021). There, he describes his addiction to anxiety medication as his wife Tammy battled cancer. He had been sent to a clinic where he was given strong doses of the tranquilliser ketamine: 'two ninety-minute trips to hell' – presumably a version of what partygoers call a 'k-hole'. For most of the book, however, Peterson is not an inhabitant of Hell but a witness to it in others. He describes a childhood friend, 'Chris', whose battle with drug addiction led him to criticise the world for his own mistakes. In the end, Chris dies, a blunt fable for Peterson's argument that left-wing views are nothing but resentment. The advice, as before, is to take responsibility for yourself – and it is valuable advice. But lately Peterson himself has struggled to embody the Hero rather than the Adversary. Under the glare of global attention, he has become more extreme. It's no longer entirely clear if he is trying to save young men from extremist politics or becoming a demagogue himself.[21] In 2019, he had a meeting with the autocratic leader of Hungary, Viktor Orbán, and he continues to associate with far-right thinkers. Opposition to the liberal establishment has caused him to embrace a variety of bizarre causes, including an all-meat diet and attacking seemingly innocuous targets including transgender celebrities, plus-sized models, and diversity in AI image generation. He has even taken to signing his social media posts 'Satan'.[22]

If *Paradise Lost* is a mountain, it is one whose slopes are scattered with bodies. In Books XI and XII, when the archangel Michael comes down to teach Adam, Milton guides the patient reader to his most important political arguments. Many don't make it that far. Readers like Peterson, who accept Satan's representations of himself, don't appear to have understood Book XII. Milton expected this: he hoped that his poem would 'fit audience find, though few' (VII:31). Few people would finish the poem, and even fewer would do so without going astray. There's nothing wrong with misreading – it can be creative, freeing, generating new ideas and new books. But interpretations, as Jordan Peterson points out, have consequences. Over the centuries, *Paradise Lost* has often resurfaced in moments of political polarisation, and here, it joined a re-energised Right.

Adam and Eve's prayers reach Heaven, and the Son brings them to the Father like a plate of delicacies. God agrees to be merciful but says he has to cast the humans out of Paradise. He sends the archangel Michael down to the garden to prepare them. Eve withdraws as Adam goes out to meet the angel. He is there to give Adam an education, which doesn't make for the most dramatic part of the plot. But this isn't entertainment: Milton wants to teach the reader how to live. Michael tells Adam that God has heard their prayers: he has postponed their death, but they must leave Paradise. Eve cries out from her hiding place: she will have to leave her garden, the flowers she has named, nursed, and now will never see again.

Michael tells her: think of the world, too, as 'thy native soil' (XI:292). God has given them possession of the whole world. If they hadn't fallen, their children would have spread out into it in due time. The difference between Eden and the world is not absolute. God is everywhere. Michael now leads Adam up the highest hill in Eden and puts three magic drops in his eyes, giving him a special inner sight.

Adam's first vision is of a newly harvested field and some pens of sheep and goats, and an altar. From the field, a 'sweaty reaper' brings to the altar a sacrifice from the harvest (XI:434–5), and a shepherd brings 'the firstlings of his flock' (XI:437). The second sacrifice is accepted but the first is rejected. Angry, the reaper fells the shepherd with a stone.

Is this death? Adam asks Michael, horrified. Is this what he too will have to suffer?

Next Michael shows him a leper-house, where people are suffering all kinds of diseases.

Why is life given to us if we have to suffer this? Adam asks, weeping.

Michael then tells him the best way to live: 'The rule of not too much' (XI:531). This means moderation. 'So mayst thou live, till like ripe fruit thou drop / Into thy mother's lap' (XI:535–6). Most people don't get to die like a patriarch, and not for a lack of temperance: in our world, death is not fairly distributed. But Michael isn't wrong to propose moderation as a way to navigate the world's temptations.

Lastly, Adam has a vision of a land where everything has turned to pleasure: feasting, drinking, and dancing. Among them comes 'a reverend sire' (XI:719). He tries to preach to them, but no one listens. He withdraws to a mountain, where he builds a great ship. Rains start, and the waters rise, destroying everything:

> sea covered sea,
> Sea without shore; and in their palaces
> Where luxury late reigned, sea-monsters whelped
> And stabled (XI:749–52)

Milton was surely imagining the English King's palace flooded and filled with mating whales. It is a vision of providential revenge. But Adam doesn't enjoy it. These are his children.

Why would God destroy those peaceful people? Adam asks.

Those people gained their peace by means of war, Michael tells him. They lived violently. It's for this that they deserved God's judgement. Noah, the 'one just man alive' (XI:818), has survived by an act of special grace. His ship has lodged on a mountain. He sends out a dove and it returns with an olive leaf. The appearance of a rainbow tells him that God will never destroy the world again. At this, Adam rejoices. It's enough that one man has survived, even though the rest have perished.

You now have seen one world end and another begin, Michael tells him. The human race is born again from Noah, and for a while they live in peace. This is a period of 'paternal rule' (XII:24), a government austere and righteous. But then, Michael says:

> one shall rise
> Of proud ambitious heart, who not content
> With fair equality, fraternal state,
> Will arrogate dominion undeserved
> Over his brethren (XI:24–8)

This man who claims power over his fellow men is Nimrod. Setting himself up as a king, Nimrod dresses in God's authority. He orders his followers to build a great tower, drawing ore from the mouth of Hell. Nimrod claims a divine right to rule: 'from heaven claiming second sovereignty' (XII:35). This idea casts light on the great mystery of *Paradise Lost*: why Satan at first seems so much like a revolutionary.

As the reader moves through the poem, Satan has morphed from hero into villain. Now we get the explanation why God isn't a tyrant, as Satan claimed in Book I. Milton believes that all power comes from God, the one true sovereign power, and all worldly kings are claiming a 'second sovereignty' from him. This is what he had argued as a political theorist, and now his epic poem finally corroborates it. Adam is outraged by Nimrod's actions, and cries out:

> Oh execrable son so to aspire
> Above his brethren, to himself assuming
> Authority usurped, from God not given:
> He gave us only over beast, fish, fowl
> Dominion absolute; that right we hold
> By his donation; but *man over men*
> *He made not lord*; such title to himself
> Reserving, human left from human free (XII:64–71; my italics)

Countless abolitionists used this passage, claiming that it proved Milton was against slavery. But slavery is only the most extreme instance of this usurpation of natural rights: it could also apply to aristocrats, capitalists, party bureaucrats, and other elites. This is the most radical passage in *Paradise Lost*, a resounding defence of freedom and equality as the fundamental human condition. But Adam has got it wrong.

After the Fall, Michael says, true freedom is lost. When humans allow their reason to be dominated by their passion, 'God in judgement just / Subjects him from without to violent lords' (XII:92–3). Humans are enslaved by their passions, and not only individuals but whole nations. When Adam said that hierarchy was against God's will, he didn't realise that hierarchy was a result of weaknesses that are, indirectly, the will of God. Michael offers an example, and it's an example so disturbing that many readers have completely ignored it.

> witness the irreverent son
> Of him who built the ark, who for the shame
> Done to his father, heard this heavy curse,
> *Servant of servants*, on his vicious race (XII:101–4; my italics)

Michael is talking about Noah's son, Ham, who is said to have seen his father naked and mocked him (Genesis 9:20–7). For this, Ham and his descendants were cursed. In the seventeenth century, some people used this story to justify the African slave trade, calling Africans 'sons of Ham'. Michael's words leave some room for interpretation, and Milton might be justifying the African slave trade or he might be saying something more general: that anyone who mocks their own father (or God the Father) will themselves be brought low.[23] While believing that all men are born free, Milton did seem to believe that pagan peoples deserved slavery, and he confined his politics to defending the freedom of Protestants. Immediately after its exultant celebration of freedom as a natural right, *Paradise Lost* gives us a defence of slavery.

This troubling aspect of the poem has also had a legacy in the modern world. One of Milton's most famous readers, Thomas Jefferson, was partly responsible for the preservation of slavery in America, since the Thirteenth Amendment was modelled on laws that he drafted in the years after independence, in which penal slavery was an exception to emancipation. Jefferson believed it was permissible for the guilty to be used as slaves – something for which he would have found support in *Paradise Lost* – and this view had a considerable influence on America. After the Civil War, the Thirteenth Amendment allowed Southern states to incarcerate free African American people: their labour could still be exploited without recompense. Then, in the late twentieth century, this led to one of the largest systems of unfree labour in the modern world.[24] Today, in federal prisons, all able-bodied adults are compelled to work. Most receive wages, but often as little as sixteen cents per hour. As C. L. R. James recognised, it is a form of totalitarianism native to liberal democracies to treat migrants as 'pests'. And prisoners are often treated no better – this is justified by a notion of citizenship welded on to a Christian notion of innocence. It was only in 1983, after a long campaign by incarcerated members of the Nation of Islam, that prisoners were no longer treated as 'slaves of the state' but, instead, as citizens who have constitutional rights.[25] *Paradise Lost* might not have directly influenced the Thirteenth Amendment, but it helped to fabricate a society in which the guilty deserved no rights. Poetry complements the law, in Jefferson's words, by offering a vision of 'the light side of humanity'.[26] But it also, and this is especially true of *Paradise Lost*, gives us a vision of the dark side: of temptation, weakness, and the cruelty that often lurks within the will to punish. For this reason, Milton has been the unacknowledged legislator not only of modern freedom but also of mass incarceration.

What is true in America has also been true in other liberal democracies. That certain groups – including women, indigenous people, migrants, and prisoners – have often been a silent exception to the famous statement that 'all men are born equal'. To hark back to the origins of the liberal tradition today is to celebrate a politics founded on equality but also marked by those exclusions. This is why the 'classical liberal' politics, revolutionary in the age of Milton and Jefferson, became reactionary.

12. My Students Teach Me About Disobedience

The youth correctional facility lies in the green outskirts of a town on the Delaware river, where the state line between Pennsylvania and New Jersey reaches its westernmost extent. To get there, you drive up a tree-lined avenue with fields on both sides. In winter, the slanted sun makes the frost glow and sometimes a pheasant runs beside the car. Underneath the trees' dark canopy, a building appears ahead. An arrangement of curving planes and dark glass windows, it looks like a regional bank headquarters, neither welcoming nor forbidding. The prison opened in the late 1960s, when President Lyndon B. Johnson reformed America's prison system and expanded it, laying the foundations of mass incarceration.

I was there as a PhD student teaching in a prison education programme run out of Princeton University and part of a state-wide scheme. Our students were working towards an associate's degree, which was accredited by a local community college, and some of them went on to get a BA. The programme's existence raised difficult questions about education and inequality. To teach at the Ivy League school and the prison at the same time was to receive a unique view of two extremes of American society: one group lavished with attention, praise, and opportunities, the other harassed, humiliated, and punished. But there were similarities as well as differences: the conversations we had with our students in prison were no less vital and stimulating than those at the university. Often more so.

Prisons are often intensely literary environments. In an age of technological distraction, they are places where reading is still a form of entertainment. More importantly, the life situations of incarcerated people often inspire them to read ambitiously. A student in the programme once told me he would see other incarcerated men walking around with copies of Jean-Paul Sartre's *Being and Nothingness*. Some of our students were self-identifying scholars, poets, and writers of short stories. But others didn't care about literature. Often it was the only course they were able to take: another handful of credits on the long road to their degree. Not being able to assume their interest, we, as teachers, had to try to make what we taught valuable to them. How could literature speak to their lives and ambitions, without being patronising or depressing? How could it represent the world as it is, with all its suffering and violence, while showing it to be a place in which we should want to live? I came to see *Paradise Lost* as a powerful answer to these questions.

The facility was a thirty-minute drive from the Princeton campus, and every week the PhD students teaching there scrabbled to find someone with a driving licence and a car they could borrow, so it was always a relief to sink into the drive along the grey highways of the Garden State. The facility is for young men. If they turn thirty inside, they are shipped out to a men's prison. To enter the prison, the visitor gives up their ID and receives a name tag in return. I was so nervous the first time I arrived that I shook the hand of the officer when he reached out to take my ID. When all the teachers have arrived, you go through a double gate. The outside gate closes and the inside one opens. An officer arrives to escort you down the curved corridors, which make it impossible to see all the way to the end. We would pass slop buckets containing the remains of dinner: a smell provoking a deep and unforgettable disgust. Then we would wait outside the classroom block, while the officer unlocked the gate.

Inside the classroom block, the corridor was lined with pictures of US presidents and civil rights leaders, and a poster made of neon card that said:

KEEP ALL NEGATIVE
THOUGHTS TO-
SELF

The classes took place in the early evening, when others were exercising in the yard. There were long waiting lists for classes, so our students had to have special determination or luck to be there. They seemed to pride themselves on being different. But still they complained about humiliating strip-searches and arbitrary invasions of their cells. The classroom felt like a refuge from that. There was generally a calm, friendly atmosphere. Lining up in the corridor before class, they would chat with friends from other cell blocks. After the first few weeks, I felt relaxed too.

The students were bored of *Hamlet* by the third week of studying it. They understood the plot and they didn't want to talk about it any more. As an undergraduate in the UK, I had studied the canon of English literature: Chaucer, Shakespeare, Spenser, Milton, Wordsworth, Woolf, and so on. I had learnt what these texts said about the fundamental experiences of life, about love and loss, often before I had had those experiences myself. By my early twenties, pretty much all I knew how to do was to read English literature and write about it. But teaching in prison, I couldn't take its value for granted.

One afternoon, when they were meant to be planning their final papers, one student was distracted. The student – whom I will call Omar – was normally one of the sharpest in the class. But that day he was talking to his neighbours, who weren't listening to him. I sat at the desk next to him. He said he wanted to become a 'sovereign citizen'. He explained what this was: the idea that you could become a citizen of your own nation.

I was sceptical about the practicality of achieving legal separation from other people: 'Isn't it only when your actions harm someone else that you break the law?'

'I'm sick of this place,' he said simply.

'Think about Prince Hamlet,' I said, remembering my purpose. 'He lives under a government that is cruel, arbitrary, that he hasn't chosen, in a country where he is denied the rights he was born to. Hamlet develops a language to describe this condition, a way of speaking that the agents of the state will not understand. It's insane or sounds like it is, but it infects his listeners with doubt. Maybe you could write your paper about this.'

He was quiet for a moment. Then he said: 'Why weren't we talking about this all along?'

*

Slipping along the highway on our drive back from the facility, I would feel exhaustion mixed with relief. There was a natural camaraderie among the instructors: we would chat about what had happened in class, things our students had said, any exercises that had worked especially well. It was worlds apart from the unhappy competitiveness of the university.

After the first semester, I signed up to teach again. I taught a class almost every semester for five years. I don't say this to boast. The role of education programmes in America's prison system is complicated, to say the least. In their teaching evaluation, one student wrote: 'Orlando teaches us to speak right, not to speak street.' I was horrified: their degree required them to write in formal English, but I certainly didn't see it as the correct way of speaking. I sometimes felt that my students would have been better served by a teacher who shared their experiences. There were times of frustration and despair – with the system and occasionally with the students. But it was also an experience that permitted moments of real intellectual intimacy. I can't say what the students got from my classes, but I have often thought about what I learnt from them.

I continued teaching in prison as I lost my way. Crises are common among PhD students: the work is solitary, difficult, and seemingly endless. Those who struggle to find their place often retreat into themselves, growing their hair and beards long, losing the ability to present their thoughts coherently, stuttering and blanching while talking, failing to write or producing knotty, ill-tempered, unreadable tracts, becoming fearful of others and unable to take in new knowledge. The malcontents of graduate school are proud, envious, impotent, and bitter. I had it worse than most. I developed a kind of reader's block, picking up too many books and finishing none. I lost confidence in my work. Teaching in prison seemed like the only thing worth doing. Sometimes, while waiting for the students to arrive in class, I looked out of the narrow windows across the grass, to the basketball court where men in their beige khaki exercised in the dying golden light, and I thought that this unhappy period of my life would eventually end. My students were one thing that made me feel sad at that thought.

The morning after the 2016 election, there was a light but persistent rain. I went to the Princeton campus, where everyone seemed to be in shock. That evening, our escort was unusually cheerful, whistling as he walked us to the classroom block. It was a reminder of the political divide between the liberal America associated with the university campus and the America of the prison. The prison officers' union had been the first to come out in support of Trump. In class, the students were subdued. They seemed to know what the election results meant for them. The funding for their education would be taken away. Sentencing would get tougher. The invisible punishments they faced on being released would multiply.

In the years after that, the classroom felt more political, and our discussions would sometimes zero in on difficult aspects of our students' realities. This wasn't my doing: the students were themselves often thinking about white supremacy and racism. I didn't discourage it. At the same time, it taught me to appreciate literature that created a space to draw connections. A freedom to make meaning for yourself.

After four years at the youth correctional facility, I was assigned a class at a state prison. This was my first time teaching at an adult facility. Some of the students would be inside for life. It was also the first class I ever got to design and teach on my own. I called it 'World Poetry': I wanted to think about poetry in the context of the whole of human history, to take the students from the early writing systems of Mesopotamia all the way to the present. We would discuss Egyptian tomb inscriptions, the Hebrew Bible, Renaissance poetry, and blues music. It was overambitious, but I wanted to put into practice what I had learnt at the youth correctional facility. To use literature to make sense of our world.

To get to the prison, I took the train to Newark, where, from the faded glamour of the station waiting hall, I ordered a taxi to take me out of the city centre – not far from the mosque where Malcolm X's murder is said to have been planned – and on to the highway roaring past the airport. Finally, we would arrive at a security checkpoint. Sometimes the driver didn't want to go through the gates, and I walked the final half-mile along the grassy verge to the visitors' entrance. Inside, I put my phone in a locker, went through airport-style security, and waited for an officer to escort me through the concrete precincts. By then, the yard was empty, but if it was a fine evening, outside the kitchen a few men would be leaning against the wall, relishing the dusk. As we entered the education block, a square of officers waited to frisk the students on their way to class. I greeted the officer on the gate, and he pointed me towards a classroom.

On the day of my first class, I was late. I called ahead to tell the prison, so they wouldn't send the students away. When I finally got to the classroom, twenty unfamiliar students were waiting. I unpacked my materials in a rush, and when a voice offered to help, I hastily refused. As I introduced myself, another asked how long I had been teaching for. I said four years, not unconfident of my experience. I was twenty-nine, and no longer felt young, but I was conscious that some of them were older than my parents. I handed out copies of one of Shakespeare's sonnets. When we were discussing the poem, I mentioned its metre. Several students asked follow-up questions about this unfamiliar system of rhythm, and I agreed to talk more about it in the next class. That's why I decided to bring in the opening of *Paradise Lost*, which Mark noticed could be read disobediently.

After Mark made that comment, the other students kept returning to it. They wanted to learn more about metre, but they didn't want to accept it. In one class, we were talking about another line of verse and I was trying to show them where the stresses went, and one student suggested that I was trying to teach them to speak like me. I was taken aback by this. I racked my brain to find a way to show them that metre wasn't a matter of personal opinion or accent. Finally, I found my example. The next class, I gave them the lyrics to 'Amazing Grace'. We all know how Aretha Franklin sings it, I said, but unless we know that the lyrics follow a particular metre, we can't understand how this song was written.

Am-**az**-ing **grace** how **sweet** the **sound**
That **saved** a **wretch** like **me**
I **once** was **lost**, but **now** am **found**
Was **blind**, but **now** I **see**

However you sing it, each verse has lines of iambic metre, alternating between unstressed and stressed syllables, in lines that alternate between four and three stresses. This is called ballad stanza, and it's the basic structure of the verse. I think this helped to convince the students that metre was not subjective, but they continued to think about it in relation to freedom and oppression.[1]

As the semester went on, I poured more and more time into the class, hoping to arrive at some new understanding by the end. When that came, I was exhausted and uncertain what conclusion we had reached. But the students had taught me to see something that I only realised in retrospect. As we looked at the literature of the past, they were respectful but not reverential. They weren't reading in an abstract, academic way, they were reading in the context of their whole lives, as something that might help to explain why we had ended up where we were, and this was why they couldn't relinquish the idea that poetry had something to do with the inequalities of the modern world. To see that is to want to read disobediently.

Reading disobediently might, paradoxically, be the best way to honour Milton's work. After all, he disobeyed the words of Jesus which forbade divorce when he wrote his pamphlets on marriage reform. When he did so, the young Milton was obeying a higher principle: the principle of charity, or love for others, which requires that we allow them to be free to choose and also to correct their mistakes. This was no pacifist principle: it would later cause him to advocate for the abolition of unjust institutions – state religion, censorship, monarchy – by force if necessary. But Milton's ideas about freedom are not timeless. For him, freedom was above all a question about whether to obey or disobey a Christian God. There is another version of freedom, which people have claimed for themselves in moments of radical self-determination: the capacity to define the meaning of freedom for oneself. This is one meaning of the poetic darkness of *Paradise Lost*.

Milton's poem plunges us into an uncertain world. We meet a kaleidoscopic, seductive Satan, and then a wooden, authoritarian God, and have to weigh their respective arguments for ourselves. In doing so, *Paradise Lost* extends a peculiar kind of freedom to its readers, to make our own choices and our own mistakes. This is a virtual experience of political self-determination and an education. But the lessons we take from it may not be the ones Milton intended. Over the past three and a half centuries, readers have honoured this poetic darkness and radicalised it, reading it on their own terms. As with Virginia Woolf's devouring of the canon, Hannah Arendt's unfaithful fidelity, and Malcolm X's late political transformations, reading disobediently is a way of relating to the past, not as a burden but as a new beginning.

In the final part of Book XII, Michael tells Adam the rest of world history, from Moses to Christ. Then the story speeds up, folding in it all of history up to the Protestant Reformation and Milton's present, then the future dissolution of the world, the defeat of the antichrist by the Messiah, new Heaven and new Earth, endless bliss, and that's it. Adam tells Michael he has learnt that 'to obey is best' (XII:561). This is a disarmingly humble lesson to receive at the end of such a complicated poem. But obedience is a process, and Michael tells Adam that it will lead to knowledge, faith, virtue, patience, temperance, and love. Together, these possessions will be 'A paradise within thee, happier far' (XII:587). Adam is now equipped with the tools to make his way in the world. It is time to go.

The angel tells him to wake Eve. Adam goes to the bower, where he finds her already awake. God has appeared to her in a dream, so she already knows what Adam knows. Eve has the final spoken words in the poem:

> In me is no delay; with thee to go,
> Is to stay here; without thee here to stay,
> Is to go hence unwilling (XII:615–17)

These lines, beautifully balanced, display a happy equanimity. Since Adam's company is a kind of Paradise, Eve is happy to go into the fallen world with him; to stay in Paradise without him would be to lose it. These lines express a more general thought – that free, loving relationships are the best of what we have in this world. The fact that marriage in *Middlemarch* is not an ending but a beginning is the reason

Virginia Woolf said it was one of the few English books for grown-ups. Something similar is true of *Paradise Lost*: to read it all the way to the end is to grow up.

Angels have come down to escort them out of Paradise. Milton compares them to the mist that 'gathers ground fast at the labourer's heel / Homeward returning' (XII:631–2). Adam and Eve are returning home too. The angel catches man and woman by the hand and leads them down to the plain that lies beneath the garden.

> They looking back, all the eastern side beheld
> Of Paradise, so late their happy seat (XII:641–2)

Behind them, the gate of Paradise has closed and God is beginning to turn its green into desert. The final lines are perfectly balanced, and dignified, with their own quiet momentum:

> Some natural tears they dropped, but wiped them soon;
> The world was all before them, where to choose
> Their place of rest, and providence their guide:
> They hand in hand with wandering steps and slow,
> Through Eden took their solitary way (XI:645–9)

This beautiful passage comes as a reward for the substantial work of reading *Paradise Lost*. It draws together images that have occurred throughout the poem – Eve dropping a tear after her dream of Satan, Adam seizing her by the hand, their separation and reconciliation – gathering them all into an image of union. They are alone but together, leaving Paradise but still in Eden, sad but resolute. Epic poems often conclude with homecomings, and this is a strange one, since Adam and Eve have never been in the fallen world before. For the reader, too, it is a homecoming. We are leaving Milton's Eden and returning to our own world. If the poem has done its work, it should look different.

Beginning in Hell but ending in the world, *Paradise Lost* guides us from despair and resentment, through the fantasy of boundless pleasure, into an encounter with the real world. In doing so, it reminds us that it is only in the world and not in any fantasy that we can be happy. Since the world is shared, and people are different, it follows that democracy is the best system of government, because the

Adam and Eve enter the world. Digital image by Alan Best, 2024.

decisions are made through the deliberation of different views rather than the tyranny of a single decision-maker. This is the political argument buried in the end of Milton's epic, one that readers for centuries saw and made sense of in their own ungovernable ways. It should be clear by now that the afterlife of *Paradise Lost* was exactly what Milton hoped for and, at the same time, something he never could have imagined.

★

When spring came, I took my class outside, and we discussed *Paradise Lost* in the shade of a tree. Then I got on a train to Newark to teach in the jaundiced light of the prison classroom. It wasn't until the final week of the semester that I realised why *Paradise Lost* had taken hold of me. As I had been travelling between the university and the prison, I had been travelling between an American version of Eden and an American Hell.

The town of Princeton was founded in 1683, less than ten years after the publication of the final version of *Paradise Lost*. The university was founded sixty years later by men who had likely read Milton's epic and shared many of his religious beliefs.[2] In the seventeenth and early eighteenth centuries, Puritans built America's universities on the model of Eden: green cloisters protecting the innocent beings inside from the world outside. It was common for speakers at graduation events, as they looked out at the happy students ready to enter the world, to quote the end of *Paradise Lost*.[3] During that period, men from the same Protestant ruling class laid the foundations of America's prison system, as an expression of their ideas about Hell, where the guilty could be used as slaves.[4] But if the modern world is still haunted by this cruel will to punish, the best part of Milton's legacy is the belief that unjust institutions should be abolished.

One of the students – I will call him Roger – was a tall, bald man with thick glasses, probably around seventy years old. He worked as a classroom assistant, so I would often see him before the other students arrived, clearing up the classroom, and we would always exchange a few warm words. It was almost certainly Roger who had offered to help me on the first day as I was scrabbling to begin my class. He used language in a way that I found difficult to understand – I don't know how to describe it – but he was unfailingly enthusiastic. One day, he started talking about Newark in the 1960s, the riots of 1967, the Black Panthers, slave religion, and African languages.

In his final paper, Roger wrote what I quickly recognised as a critique of my class. Drawing on Mark's insight into *Paradise Lost*, and the idea that poetry could be bound by laws, he argued that poetry should instead be dedicated to freedom. The essay ended with an unattributed quotation:

> Nothing vast enters the life
> Of mortals without a curse

I was struck by these words. They summed up what the students had been trying to tell me about literature and its relationship to the world. They also feel true of Milton's vast poem: not as an apology for its shortcomings, but as a description of the world in which it has had a long and complex afterlife.

While I appreciated Roger's paper, I was unable to give it a good grade. There were some serious issues with the grammar, and it didn't build a coherent argument of the kind I was meant to be judging. But it was a generous and perceptive piece of writing. I gave it the highest grade I thought my colleagues would allow, and I praised it in my comments. But I felt conflicted: the situation was itself symptomatic of the problem Roger had diagnosed. In the final class, I gave the papers back, and said my goodbyes. As I was leaving, I saw Roger. He was carrying a mop and bucket towards the empty classroom. I apologised for having to give him a low grade.

'It's all right, Professor!'

I asked him where the quotation at the end of his paper had come from.

'Sophocles!' he said.

He had found the quotation in a book that a professor had given him in Trenton State Prison in the 1970s. He had kept the book ever since, he said, and will have it the day he gets out. The book said that the invention of writing had been the beginning of man's destruction. He turned to walk away, and over his shoulder let out a sudden laugh that echoed for a moment in the empty hall.

Acknowledgments

In the years of writing this book, many people have offered encouragement, advice, and support, and I am grateful to them all.

Thanks first to Kat Aitken, my agent, for her steadfast belief in this book and graceful work on its behalf. To David Milner for his warm encouragement and expert editing; to Mary Chamberlain, Jenny Dean, Bea Hemming, and everyone else at Jonathan Cape. To Deborah Ghim, for her acute comments, Ben Schrank, and the whole team at Astra House. To Ariane Bankes, Emmie Francis, Kali Handelman, and Jacques Testard for their invaluable advice.

Thanks to the scholars who read parts of the book or shared the fruits of their expertise, including Oliver Browne, Hannah Crawforth, Christian Høgsbjerg, Anna Moser, Jeff Nunokawa, Matt Rickard, David Russell, Merlin Sheldrake, Nigel Smith, Jenn Soong, Oliver Southall, Robert Stagg, Jill Stockwell, Peter Wirzbicki, Amelia Worsley, and Jeewon Yoo. All errors are my own.

Thanks to my friends and family for making the world worth living in. Especially Sofia Barclay, George Browne, Paul Graville, Matthew Holman, Ed Luker, Christopher Page, and Felix and Zenobe Reade. Nigel was a patient and generous mentor. Layla was my conversation partner for the best part of the years described in this book. My parents bequeathed to me their love of literature and helped me to deal with the consequences. At a time when I couldn't work out what was wrong with the manuscript, a certain writer heroically interceded, took each chapter apart, and told me how to put them back together.

Thanks to my students at Princeton University, the Brooklyn Institute for Social Research, and in the pandemic seminar, for sharing with me their first responses to *Paradise Lost*. Lastly, to my incarcerated and formerly incarcerated students: it was a privilege to learn from you.

Notes

Introduction: Dark Writing

1 Alex Haley and Malcolm X, *The Autobiography of Malcolm X* (Penguin, 2001), p. 249. On Malcolm X's prison years see Manning Marable, *Malcolm X: A Life of Reinvention* (Viking, 2011); Les Payne and Tamara Payne, *The Dead are Arising: the Life of Malcolm X* (Liveright, 2020).

2 On Reginald Little, see Malcolm to Philbert Little, 4 February 1949; the Malcolm X collection: papers, Sc Micro R-6270, Schomburg Center for Research in Black Culture, Manuscripts, Archives and Rare Books Division, the New York Public Library.

3 I follow the common convention of capitalising 'Black' but not 'white'.

4 *Autobiography of Malcolm X*, p. 282.

5 On Milton's life, see William Riley Parker, *Milton: A Biography,* 2 vols (Clarendon Press, 1968); Barbara Kiefer Lewalski, *The Life of John Milton: A Critical Biography* (Blackwell Publishers, 2000); Gordon Campbell and Thomas N. Corns, *John Milton: Life, Work, and Thought* (Oxford University Press, 2008); Nicholas McDowell, *Poet of Revolution: The Making of John Milton* (Princeton University Press, 2020); Joe Moshenska, *Making Darkness Light: The Life and Times of John Milton* (Basic Books, 2021).

6 McDowell, *Poet of Revolution*, pp. 57–65.

7 Ibid., pp. 82–4.

8 Ibid., pp. 8–14.

9 John Milton, *The Reason of Church Government Urg'd Against Prelaty* (London, 1641), p. 37.

10 The Milton Manuscript, Trinity College, Cambridge, 35r.

11 John Aubrey, 'Minutes of the Life of Mr John Milton', in *Early Lives of Milton,* ed. Helen Darbishire (Barnes & Noble, 1965), p. 14.

12 John Milton, *Areopagitica* (London, 1644), p. 4.

13 Ibid., p. 13.

14 John Phillips, 'The Life of Mr. John Milton', *Early Lives of John Milton*, ed. Helen Darbishire (Barnes & Noble, 1965), p. 66.

15 Lewalski, *Milton*, pp. 184–5.

16 Jonathan Healey, *The Blazing World: A New History of Revolutionary England* (Bloomsbury, 2023), p. 256.

17 Sonnet 19 ('When I consider how my light is spent') and Sonnet 23 ('Methought I saw my late espoused saint'); in John Milton, *Poemata* (London, 1673).

18 *The Memoirs of Edmund Ludlow*, vol. 2 (London, 1698), pp. 456–7.

19 Milton, *Defensio Secunda* (London, 1654), *Complete Prose Works of John Milton* [hereafter *CPW*], ed. Don M. Wolfe (Yale University Press, 1953–92), vol. IV.1, p. 672.

20 John Milton to John Oldenburg, 20 December 1659, *CPW*, VII, p. 515.

21 John Milton, *Paradise Lost,* edited by John Carey and Alistair Fowler (Longman, 2013; second edition), Book IX, line 22. Subsequent references are given parenthetically in the main text.

22 See Lewalski, *Milton*, pp. 407–8.

23 Phillips, 'Life of Milton', p. 66.

24 Edward Phillips, *Early Lives,* p. 77; see also Lewalski, *Milton*, pp. 407–9.

25 Spenser, ' Letter of the Authors expounding his whole intention in the course of this worke', *The Faerie Queene* (London, 1589).

26 Philip Sidney, *Defense of Poesy* (written *c.*1580, published 1595).

27 On epic's relationship to imperial history see David Quint, *Epic and Empire* (Princeton University Press, 1993).

28 On the failure of Milton's seventeenth-century rivals, see Nigel Smith, *Literature and Revolution in England, 1640–1660* (Yale University Press, 1997), pp. 203–49.

29 Joseph Addison, *Notes upon the twelve books of Paradise lost* (London, 1719), p. 37.

30 G. Hegel, *Aesthetics,* vol 2., trans. T. M. Knox (Oxford University Press, 1975), p. 1109. See also Franco Moretti, *Modern Epic: The World System from Goethe to García Márquez* (Verso, 1996).

31 John Milton, 'Note on the Verse', *Paradise Lost*, pp. 54–5.

1: Thomas Jefferson Isolates Himself

1 John Leonard, *Faithful Labourers: A Reception History of Paradise Lost, 1667–1970,* vol. 1 (Oxford University Press, 2013), p. 395.
2 This speculation is made in Douglas L. Wilson, 'Introduction', *Jefferson's Literary Commonplace Book* (Princeton University Press, 1989), p. 7.
3 Raymond D. Havens, *The Influence of Milton on English Poetry* (Harvard University Press, 1922), p. 71.
4 Edmund Burke, *A Philosophical Enquiry into the Origin of Our Ideas of the Sublime and Beautiful* (London, 1764), p. 101.
5 'On Milton's Sonnets', *The Miscellaneous Works of William Hazlitt* (London, 1848), p. 33.
6 Nicholas von Maltzahn, 'The Whig Milton, 1667–1700', in *Milton and Republicanism*, edited by David Armitage, Armand Himy, and Quentin Skinner (Cambridge University Press, 1998), pp. 229–53.
7 Edward Ward, *The Secret History of the Calves-Head Club* (London, 1707), p. 18; see also Samuel Wesley, *A Letter from a Country Divine* (London, 1706).
8 Thomas Jefferson to John Page, 25 December 1762, *The Papers of Thomas Jefferson*, vol. 1, 1760–1776, ed. Julian P. Boyd (Princeton University Press, 1950), pp. 3–6.
9 Diary of John Adams, November 1769; *The Adams Papers, Diary and Autobiography of John Adams*, vol. 1, ed. L. H. Butterfield (Harvard University Press, 1961).
10 The classic account is J. G. A. Pocock, *The Machiavellian Moment: Florentine Political Thought and the Atlantic Republican Tradition* (Princeton University Press, 1975).
11 Diary of John Adams, 30 March 1756.
12 Ibid., 23 April 1756.
13 Ibid., January 1759.
14 Benjamin Franklin to Thomas Brand Hollis, 5 October 1783. *The Papers of Benjamin Franklin*, vol. 41, ed. Ellen R. Cohn (Yale University Press, 2014), pp. 75–8.
15 Benjamin Franklin to Susanna Wright, 11 July 1752.

16 Annabel Patterson, *Early Modern Liberalism* (Cambridge University Press, 1997), p. 48.
17 Jefferson, 'Early Notebook', quoted in Kevin J. Hayes, *The Road to Monticello: The Life and Mind of Thomas Jefferson* (Oxford University Press, 2008), p. 92.
18 Hugh Jenkins, 'Jefferson (Re) Reading Milton', *Milton Quarterly*, vol. 32, no. 1 (1998), pp. 32–8.
19 Hayes, *Road to Monticello,* p. 120.
20 'Common Sense', *The Writings of Thomas Paine,* ed. Moncure Daniel Conway, vol. 1 (G. P. Putnam's, 1894), p. 91. The quotation is from *Paradise Lost*, IV:98–9.
21 John Adams, 'Thoughts on Government', *The Adams Papers*, vol. 4, pp. 86–93.
22 John Adams, 'Autobiography', *Adams Papers*, vol. 3, pp. 330–5.
23 John Adams to Timothy Pickering, 6 August 1822.
24 'The Declaration of Independence: A Transcript', *National Archives*, Washington, DC.
25 Thomas Jefferson to Henry Lee, 8 May 1825.
26 Milton, *The Tenure of Kings and Magistrates* (London, 1650), p. 8.
27 Thomas Jefferson, 'An Act for Establishing Religious Freedom', 16 January 1786, Manuscript, Library of Virginia, Richmond, Virginia.
28 Thomas Jefferson, 'Thoughts on English Prosody', *Thomas Jefferson: Writings,* ed. Merrill D. Peterson (Library of America, 1984), p. 618.
29 Ibid., p. 619.
30 'As Alison Morgan showed in *Dante and the Medieval Other World* (1990), Dante didn't innovate by incorporating contemporary figures in his epic. In fact, he included fewer than usual: contemporaries make up 69 per cent of the identifiable characters in popular otherworld visions, but only 36 per cent in Dante.' Barbara Newman, 'Seven Centuries Too Late', *London Review of Books,* vol. 43, no. 14 (2021).
31 George F. Sensabaugh, *Milton in Early America* (Princeton University Press, 1964), p. 124.
32 See Annette Gordon-Reed, *The Hemingses of Monticello* (W. W. Norton, 2008).
33 Thomas Jefferson, *Notes on the State of Virginia* (London, 1787), p. 271.

34 Annette Gordon-Reed, *Thomas Jefferson and Sally Hemings: An American Controversy* (University of Virginia Press, 1998), p. 60.
35 See, for example, Harriet Jacobs, *Incidents in the Life of a Slave Girl* (Boston, 1861).
36 Tony Davies, 'Borrowed Language: Milton, Jefferson, Mirabeau', *Milton and Republicanism*, pp. 254–71.
37 See Orlando Patterson, *Freedom in the Making of Western Society* (Basic Books, 1991).
38 William Murray, Lord Mansfield, quotes this phrase in the judgement that effectively abolished slavery in Britain; Somerset v. Stewart, 1772.
39 Richard B. Sheridan, 'The Jamaican Slave Insurrection Scare of 1776 and the American Revolution', *Journal of Negro History*, vol. 61 (1976), pp. 290–308; Vincent Brown, *Tacky's War: The Story of an Atlantic Slave War* (Harvard University Press, 2020), pp. 237–8.
40 James Boswell, *The Life of Samuel Johnson* (London, 1817), p. 591.
41 On Johnson's relationship to Barber, see Michael Bundock, *The Fortunes of Francis Barber: The True Story of the Jamaican Slave Who Became Samuel Johnson's Heir* (Yale University Press, 2015).
42 *Johnsoniana, Or, Supplement to Boswell: Being Anecdotes and Sayings of Dr. Johnson*, vol. 1, ed. Hester Lynch Piozzi (London, 1836), p. 32.
43 Johnson, 'Milton', *Lives of the Most Eminent English Poets* (London, 1781), p. 146.
44 Ibid., p. 255.
45 Ibid., p. 217.
46 On Equiano's celebrity, see Ryan Hanley, *Beyond Slavery and Abolition: Black British Writing,* c. *1770–1830* (Cambridge University Press, 2019); Vincent Carretta, *Equiano the African: Biography of a Self-Made Man* (University of Georgia Press, 2008).
47 *The Interesting Narrative of the Life of Olaudah Equiano, Or Gustavus Vassa, the African,* vol. 1 (London, 1789), p. 189.
48 Nicole N. Aljoe, *Journeys of the Slave Narrative in the Early Americas*, ed. Nicole N. Aljoe and Ian Finseth (University of Virginia Press, 2014), pp. 1–16.
49 On Equiano's religion see Adam Potkay, 'Olaudah Equiano and the Art of Spiritual Autobiography', *Eighteenth-Century Studies* 27, no. 4 (1994), pp. 677–92.

50 On the rhetoric of slavery in the early modern world, see Mary Nyquist, *Arbitrary Rule: Slavery, Tyranny, and the Power of Life and Death* (University of Chicago Press, 2013).
51 Thomas Jefferson to George W. Lewis, 25 October 1825.

2: Dorothy Wordsworth Brings Her Brother an Apple

1 William Cowper, 'Stanzas on the late indecent Liberties taken with the Remains of the great Milton' (1790).
2 Philip Neve, *A Narrative of the Disinterment of Milton's Coffin* (London, 1790); see also Michael Lieb, *Milton and the Culture of Violence* (Cornell University Press, 1994).
3 Horace, *Satires*, 1.4.62.
4 Jules Michelet, *History of the French Revolution*, trans. Charles Cocks (University of Chicago Press, 1967), p. 97.
5 On French translations of Milton see *Radical Voices: Revolutionary Discourses of Translation (1782–1815)*, ed. Jacob McGuinn, Rosa Mucignat, Sanja Perovic and Nigel Ritchie (Routledge, forthcoming).
6 Joseph Crawford, *Raising Milton's Ghost: John Milton and the Sublime of Terror in the Early Romantic Period* (Bloomsbury Academic, 2011), p. 27.
7 Helen Maria Williams, *Letters from France* (1796), pp. 113-4.
8 Michelet, *French Revolution*, p. 9.
9 Alexander Gilchrist, *The Life of Blake* (Macmillan, 1880), p. 112.
10 William Blake, *The Marriage of Heaven and Hell* (illustrated manuscript, 1790), p. 6.
11 Mary Nyquist, 'Equiano, Satanism, and Slavery', *Milton Now*, ed. Catharine Gray and Erin Murphy (Palgrave Macmillan, 2014), pp. 215–45.
12 'Could it be that with the increasing strength of the Abolition movement and the eventual outlawing of the slave trade, slavery became capable of functioning as its opposite, a metaphor for freedom?' Mary Jacobus, *Romanticism Writing and Sexual Difference: Essays on the Prelude* (Oxford University Press, 1989), p. 93.
13 Lucy Newlyn's wonderful book *William & Dorothy Wordsworth: All in Each Other* (Oxford University Press, 2013) honours the fruitful, strange complexity of the siblings' relationship.

14 On Milton's reception by Wordsworth and the other Romantic poets, see Lucy Newlyn, *Paradise Lost and the Romantic Reader* (Oxford University Press, 2001).
15 William Wordsworth, *The Prelude* (1805 edition), III:295–313.
16 Ibid., II:4–5.
17 Quoted in Selincourt, *Dorothy Wordsworth*, p. 84.
18 William Wordsworth, 'Written in March', *Poems, in Two Volumes* (London, 1807), p. 45.
19 On the reception of these poems, see Jared R. Curtis, *Wordsworth's Experiments with Tradition* (Cornell University Press, 1971). For an account of Wordsworth's intentions in writing this provocative poetry, see Keston Sutherland, 'Wrong poetry', *Textual Practice*, vol. 24, no. 4 (2010), pp. 765–82.
20 'Review of Wordsworth's Poems, 2 Vols. 1807', in *The Complete Works of Lord Byron* (London, 1837), p. 901.
21 William Wordsworth, 'Preface', *Lyrical Ballads* (1800), p. v.
22 On Dorothy's observational power, see Oliver Southall, ch. 4: 'Romantic Ecologies', *Rowan* (Reaktion, 2022), pp. 131–60.
23 Dorothy Wordsworth, *Grasmere Journal*, 6 May 1802.
24 Ibid., 2 February 1802.
25 Ibid., 4 October 1802.
26 On Dorothy Wordsworth's writing and domestic labour, see Anahid Nersessian, *The Calamity Form: On Poetry and Social Life* (University of Chicago Press, 2020), pp. 173–6.
27 Wordsworth, 'Sonnet 14: London, 1802', *Poems, in Two Volumes,* p. 140.
28 Wordsworth, *The Prelude,* X:13–14.
29 Ibid., X:481–2.
30 Wordsworth, *The Prelude* (1850 version), Book XII, lines 296–9. See also Warren Stevenson, 'Wordsworth's Satanism', *The Wordsworth Circle*, vol. 15, no. 2 (1984), pp. 176–7.
31 Ibid., Book XI, lines 367–74.
32 Wordsworth, 'Benjamin the Waggoner', Canto 1.
33 Byron, *Don Juan*, Canto 1, CCV.
34 See E. V. Lucas, *Highways and Byways in Sussex* (Macmillan, 1924), p. 116.
35 Mary Shelley, 'Author's Introduction' (1831), *Frankenstein* (Penguin Classics, 2003), p. 7.

36 Shelley, *Frankenstein,* p. 135.

37 William Wordsworth to Benjamin Dockray, 25 April 1840.

38 The story is told in Ralph Waldo Emerson, *English Traits* (Boston, 1856), p. 167.

3: Baron Vastey Fires Back

1 Julien Prévost, *Relation des glorieux événemens qui ont porté Leurs Majestés Royales sur le trône d'Hayti* (Cap Henry, 1811), p. 17.

2 Sudhir Hazareesingh, *Black Spartacus: The Epic Life of Toussaint Louverture* (Allen Lane, 2020), p. 11.

3 Guillaume Thomas Raynal, *Histoire philosophique et politique des établissemens & du commerce des Européens dans les deux Indes*, vol. 4 (Paris, 1774), p. 227.

4 Yanick Lahens, quoted in Hazareesingh, *Black Spartacus*, p. 11.

5 Michel-Rolph Trouillot, ch. 2: 'The Three Faces of Sans Souci', *Silencing the Past: Power and the Production of History* (Beacon Press, 2005), pp. 70–107.

6 *Mémoires de la Vie de Toussaint L'Ouverture* (Paris, 1853), p. 94.

7 William Wordsworth, *Poems, in Two Volumes* (London, 1807), p. 8.

8 Toussaint proclamation 23 August 1793; quoted in Hazareesingh, pp. 1 and 154–5;

9 Beaubrun Ardouin, *Études sur l'histoire d'Haïti,* vol. 6 (Éditions Fardin, 2004), p. 24; Dubois, *Avengers of the New World,* p. 298.

10 'The Haitian Declaration of Independence', in *Slave Revolution in the Caribbean 1789–1804: A Brief History with Documents*, trans. Laurence Dubois and John Garrigus (Palgrave Macmillan, 2006), p. 188.

11 Ibid., p. 188.

12 Jean-Jacques Dessalines to Thomas Jefferson, 23 June 1803, *The Papers of Thomas Jefferson*, vol. 40, ed. Barbara B. Oberg (Princeton University Press, 2013), pp. 597–9.

13 Dubois, *Avengers of the New World,* p. 301; Ardouin, *Études sur l'histoire d'Haïti*, pp. 16–7.

14 Trouillot, *Silencing the Past*, pp. 31–69.

15 Paul Clammer, *Black Crown: Henry Christophe, the Haitian Revolution and the Caribbean's Forgotten Kingdom* (Hurst, 2023), p. 171.

16 Ibid., pp. 138–9.

17 On Vastey's early life, see Marlene L. Daut, *Baron de Vastey and the Origins of Black Atlantic Humanism* (Palgrave Macmillan, 2017), pp. 27–62.

18 Ibid., p. 29; Laurent Quevilly, pp. 246–9, *Le baron de Vastey: La voix des esclaves* (Books on Demand, 2014), pp. 246–9.

19 Daut, *Baron de Vastey*, p. 28.

20 Ibid., p. 47.

21 Baron de Vastey, *The Colonial System Unveiled*, trans. Chris Bongie (Liverpool University Press, 1814), p. 106.

22 Ibid., p. 129.

23 Ibid., p. 109.

24 Quoted in Abbé Grégoire, *De la Littérature des nègres* (Paris, 1808), pp. 35–8. See also Winthrop D. Jordan, *White over Black: American Attitudes toward the Negro, 1550–1812* (University of North Carolina Press, 1968), pp. 453–4.

25 Thomas Jefferson, *Notes on the State of Virginia* (London, 1787), p. 108.

26 Grégoire, *Littérature des nègres*, p. 162. Grégoire is reusing an analogy made about the French Revolution in an English literary journal: 'The Dangers of the Country', in the *Critical Review* 42 (1807), p. 369.

27 M. Mazères, *Lettre à M. J.C.L. Sismonde de Sismondi* (Paris, 1815).

28 Vastey, *Reflexions on the Blacks and Whites. Remarks upon a letter addressed by M. Mazères* (London, 1817), p. 13; see also Vastey, *Colonial System Unveiled*, p. 127.

29 Vastey, *Reflexions*, p. 15.

30 Ibid., p. 29.

31 Ibid., p. 67.

32 Ibid., p. 68.

33 Anon., *L'Haitiade* (Paris, 1878), p. viii.

34 Vastey, *Essay on the Causes of the Revolution and Civil Wars of Hayti*, trans. W. H. M. B. (London, 1823), p. 108.

35 Ibid., p. 168.

36 Vastey, *Reflexions*, p. 64.

37 William Empson, *Milton's God* (Chatto & Windus, 1961), p. 146.

38 James Franklin, *Present State of Hayti* (London, 1828), p. 198.

39 William Wordsworth to Benjamin Dockray, 25 April 1840.

40 Marlene L. Daut, 'Translation for the Purposes of Indictment: Baron de Vastey in Colonial Jamaica', 18 May 2017, *Black Perspectives*, https://www.aaihs.org/translation-for-the-purposes-of-indictment-baron-de-vastey-in-colonial-jamaica.

41 Peter Wirzbicki, '"The Light of Knowledge Follows the Impulse of Revolution": Prince Saunders, Baron de Vastey and the Haitian Influence on Antebellum Black Ideas of Elevation and Education', *Slavery & Abolition*, vol. 36, no. 2 (2015), pp. 275–97.

4: George Eliot Sees Her First Man

1 The scholar is Richard Bentley; see John Leonard, *Faithful Labourers: A Reception History of Paradise Lost, 1667–1970,* vol. 1 (Oxford University Press, 2014), pp. 657–8.

2 R. D. Havens, *The Influence of Milton on English Poetry* (Russell & Russell, 1961), p. 9.

3 Joseph Wittreich, *Feminist Milton* (Cornell University Press, 1987), p. 49.

4 Karl Moritz, *Travels in England in 1782* (London, 1886), p. 35.

5 Mary Wollstonecraft, *Thoughts on the Education of Daughters* (London, 1787), pp. 52–3.

6 Ibid., p. 53.

7 Mary Wollstonecraft, *A Vindication of the Rights of Woman* (London, 1790), p. 27.

8 Ibid., p. 27.

9 *A Memoir of Ralph Waldo Emerson*, ed. James Elliot Cabot, vol. 2 (Riverside Press, 1887), p. 511; *The Journals and Miscellaneous Notebooks of Ralph Waldo Emerson*, eds. William H. Gilman, Ralph H. Orth, et al. (Harvard University Press, 1960–82), vol. 4, p. 141.

10 Kathryn Hughes, *George Eliot: The Last Victorian* (Fourth Estate, 1998), p. 59.

11 Moncure Daniel Conway, *Emerson at Home and Abroad* (London, 1882), p. 338.

12 J. W. Cross, ed., *George Eliot's Life as Related in Her Letters*, vol. 1 (New York, 1896) p. 144.

13 Hughes, *George Eliot,* p. 10.

14 George Eliot to Maria Lewis, 4 September 1839; Cross, p. 45. On Eliot's relationship with Milton see Diana Postlethwaite, 'When George Eliot Reads Milton: The Muse in a Different Voice', *English Literary History*, vol. 57, no. 1 (1990), pp. 197–221; Anna K. Nardo, *George Eliot's Dialogue with John Milton* (University of Missouri Press, 2003).
15 *The George Eliot Letters*, ed. Gordon S. Haight (Oxford University Press, 1954–78), 9 vols, 8.56–57.
16 Ibid., 2.98.
17 Phyllis Rose, *Parallel Lives: Five Victorian Marriages* (Daunt, 2020), pp. 214–15.
18 Avron Fleishman, *George Eliot's Intellectual Life* (Cambridge University Press, 2010), p. ix.
19 George Eliot, 'Life and Opinions of Milton', *The Leader*, no. 280 (1855), p. 750.
20 Ibid.
21 George Eliot to Sara Hennell, 21 July 1855; Cross, vol. 1, p. 290.
22 See David Russell, 'The Grounds of Tact: George Eliot's Rage', in *Tact: Aesthetic Liberalism and the Essay Form in Nineteenth-Century Britain* (Princeton University Press, 2018).
23 George Eliot to Maria Congreve, 22 January 1872; Cross, vol. 3, p. 71.
24 Eliot, *Middlemarch*, p. 10.
25 Ibid., p. 22.
26 Ibid., p. 78.
27 Ibid., p. 265.
28 Ibid., p. 59.
29 Ibid., p. 309.
30 Ibid., p. 755.
31 See Clare Carlisle, *The Marriage Question: George Eliot's Double Life* (Allen Lane, 2023).
32 Eliot, *Letters*, 3:22.

5: *James Redpath Tries to Start an Insurrection*

1 *Speech of Wendell Phillips, At the Melodeon, Thursday Evening, Jan. 27, 1853* (American Anti-Slavery Society, 1853), p. 28.

2 Phillips, *At the Melodeon,* p. 28.

3 Thomas Clarkson, *The Rise, Progress, and Accomplishment of the Abolition of the Slave Trade by the British Parliament* (London, 1807), pp. 44–5.

4 Manisha Sinha, *The Slave's Cause: A History of Abolition* (Yale University Press, 2016), p. 219.

5 William Lloyd Garrison, 'Milton and his Assailants', *Liberator*, 18 October 1834, p. 167.

6 'Slavery Record: Picture of American Society', *Liberator*, 5 February 1831, p. 22. On Milton and abolitionism see also David Boocker, 'Garrison, Milton, and the Abolitionist Rhetoric of Demonization', *American Periodicals*, vol. 9 (1999), pp. 15–26.

7 Frederick Douglass, 'Self-Made Men', *The Speeches of Frederick Douglass: A Critical Edition,* ed. John R. McKivigan, Julie Husband, and Heather L. Kaufman (Yale University Press, 2018), p. 436.

8 Ibid.

9 John R. McKivigan, *Forgotten Firebrand: James Redpath and the Making of Nineteenth-Century America* (Cornell University Press, 2008), p. 2.

10 Ibid., pp. 10–11.

11 Amos Gerry Beman, 'The Education of the Colored People', *Anglo-African Magazine*, vol. 11 (November 1859), p. 338; the quotation is from *Paradise Lost*, I:157.

12 On Thomas Hamilton and the *Weekly Anglo-African*, see Garland I. Penn, *The Afro-American Press and its Editors* (Springfield MA, 1891); Charles S. Johnson, 'The Rise of the Negro Magazine', *Journal of Negro History*, vol. 13, no. 1 (1928), pp. 7–21; Martin E. Dann, *The Black Press, 1827–1890: The Quest for National Identity* (Putnam, 1971); Mary Fair Burks, 'The First Black Literary Magazine in American Letters', *CLA Journal*, vol. 21 (1975), pp. 318–20; Ivy Wilson, 'The Brief Wondrous Life of the Anglo-African Magazine: Or, Antebellum African American Editorial Practice and Its Afterlives', *Publishing Blackness: Textual Constructions of Race Since 1850*, ed. George Hutchinson and John K. Young (University of Michigan Press, 2013), pp. 18–38.

13 *New York Times*, 13 April 1861, p. 1.

14 'Close Up! Steady!', *Weekly Anglo-African*, 21 April 1861.

15 Peter Wirzbicki, '"The Light of Knowledge Follows the Impulse of Revolution": Prince Saunders, Baron de Vastey and the Haitian Influence

on Antebellum Black Ideas of Elevation and Education', *Slavery & Abolition*, vol. 36, no. 2 (2015), p. 289.

16 'Phoenixonian Society', *Colored American*, 13 July 1839; Peter Wirzbicki, *Fighting for the Higher Law: Black and White Transcendentalists Against Slavery* (University of Pennsylvania Press, 2021), pp. 32–3.

17 *Institute for Colored Youth By-Laws and Rules* (Philadelphia, 1865), p. 9.

18 'Close Up! Steady!', *Weekly Anglo-African*, 21 April 1861.

19 Ibid.

20 Benjamin Fagan, *The Black Newspaper and the Chosen Nation* (University of Georgia Press, 2016), pp. 119–41; also Brian Taylor, *Fighting for Citizenship: Black Northerners and the Debate over Military Service in the Civil War* (University of North Carolina Press, 2020).

21 Debra Jackson, '"A Cultural Stronghold": The "Anglo-African" Newspaper and the Black Community of New York', *New York History*, vol. 85, no. 4 (2004), pp. 331–57.

22 Thomas Hamilton, untitled editorial, 16 March 1861, quoted in 'Weekly Anglo-African and The Pine and Palm: Excerpts from 1861–1862', *Just Teach One – Early African American Print*, http://jtoaa.common-place.org.

23 Lawrence's 'Lines to Cinque', a poem on the Amistad slave uprising, had appeared in Hamilton's earlier paper, the *People's Press*, in 1842. Brigitte Fielder, Cassander Smith and Derrick R. Spires, Introduction in 'Weekly Anglo-African and The Pine and Palm: Excerpts from 1861–1862', *Just Teach One – Early African American Print*, http://jtoaa.common-place.org, p. 4.

24 McKivigan, *Forgotten Firebrand*, p. 61.

25 Ibid., p. 64.

26 Ibid., p. 67.

27 Redpath to Hinton, 17 May 1861; quoted in ibid., p. 80.

28 Redpath to Hinton, 23 May 1861; quoted in ibid.

29 Redpath to Lawrence, 17 May 1861; quoted in ibid.

30 'Anti Haytien Emigration Meeting', *The Liberator*, 17 May 1861.

31 William Lloyd Garrison, 'Letter on Haytien Emigration', *The Liberator*, 17 May 1861. The quotation is from *Paradise Lost*, XII:646.

32 Garrison, 'Letter on Haytien Emigration'.

33 Quoted in McKivigan, *Forgotten Firebrand*, p. 73.

34 'Ethiop' has been identified as William Wilson, a Brooklyn schoolteacher. See Mia Bay, *The White Image in the Black Mind: African-American Ideas about White People, 1830–1925* (Oxford University Press, 2000), pp. 75–114.

35 James Redpath to Isaac Carey, 8 March 1862, fol. 1, p. 188, James Redpath correspondence, Sc MG 166, Schomburg Center for Research in Black Culture.

36 Redpath, *Roving Editor*, p. 4.

37 Reprinted as 'The Wicked Flee Where No Man Pursueth', *Douglass Monthly*, April 1861, p. 438. It appeared on the same page as an article lamenting Redpath's purchase of the *Anglo-African*. On this rumour, see Albert J. Von Frank, 'John Brown, James Redpath, and Revolution', *Civil War History*, vol. 52, no. 2 (2006), p. 159.

38 'The Wicked Flee Where No Man Pursueth', p. 438.

39 See Debra Jackson article, 'A Black Journalist in Civil War Virginia: Robert Hamilton and the "Anglo-African"', *The Virginia Magazine of History and Biography* (2008), pp. 42–72.

6: The Mistick Krewe Turns Carnival on Its Head

1 Isaac Briggs to Thomas Jefferson, 2 January 1804.

2 Edward King, *The Southern States* (London, 1875), p. 48.

3 Charles Gayarré, *Louisiana* (New York, 1851), p. 230.

4 Robert Tallant, *Voodoo in New Orleans* (Pelican, 1984), pp. 16–20.

5 Henri Schindler, *Mardi Gras: New Orleans* (Flammarion, 1997), pp. 10–16.

6 James H. Johnson, 'Versailles, Meet Les Halles: Masks, Carnival, and the French Revolution', *Representations*, vol. 73, no. 1 (2003), p. 90.

7 J. Mead, *Leaves of Thought* (Cincinnati, 1868), p. 47.

8 Lyle Saxon, Edward Dreyer, and Robert Tallant, eds, *Gumbo Ya-Ya: A Collection of Louisiana Folk Tales* (Houghton Mifflin, 1945), p. 68.

9 Schindler, *Mardi Gras*, pp. 28–9.

10 Joseph Roach, *Cities of the Dead: Circum-Atlantic Performance* (Columbia University Press, 1968), p. 257.

11 John Milton, *Comus*, lines 125–8.

12 James Gill, *Lords of Misrule: Mardi Gras and the Politics of Race in New Orleans* (University Press of Missippi Jackson), p. 48. On the Mistick Krewe's use of Milton, see Reid Mitchell, *All on a Mardi Day: Episodes in the History of New Orleans Carnivals* (Harvard University Press, 1995), and Richard Rambuss, 'Spenser and Milton at Mardi Gras: English Literature, American Cultural Capital, and the Reformation of New Orleans Carnival', *boundary*, vol. 2, no. 2 (2000), pp. 45–72.

13 Gill, *Lords of Misrule*, p. 50.

14 The stereotypical Southern gentleman prided himself on being conversant with literature. Bertram Wyatt-Brown, *Southern Honor: Ethics & Behavior in the Old South* (Oxford University Press, 2007), pp. 92–5.

15 *New Orleans Daily Crescent*; quoted in William Head Coleman, *Historical Sketch Book and Guide to New Orleans and Environs* (New York, 1885), p. 211.

16 Quoted in ibid, p. 212.

17 Coleman, *Historical Sketch Book*, p. 212.

18 *The Life and Letters of Charles Darwin* (London, 1887), p. 57.

19 Charles Darwin to J. S. Henslow, 24 November 1832.

20 Adrian Desmond and James Moore, *Darwin's Sacred Cause: How a Hatred of Slavery Shaped Darwin's Views on Human Evolution* (Houghton Mifflin Harcourt, 2014), p. xviii.

21 On Milton's relationship to Copernicus see John Leonard, 'The Universe', in *Faithful Labourers: A Reception History of Paradise Lost, 1667–1970*, vol. 1 (Oxford University Press, 2013), pp. 705–819.

22 Milton, *Areopagitica*, p. 13.

23 Gill, *Lords of Misrule*, p. 58.

24 Ibid., p. 60.

25 Robert Tallant, *Mardi Gras … As It Was* (Pelican, 2010), p. 122.

26 See Eric Foner, *The Second Founding: How the Civil War and Reconstruction Remade the Constitution* (W. W. Norton, 2020).

27 W. E. B. Du Bois, *Black Reconstruction in America: 1860–1880* (Atheneum, 1992), p. 178.

28 The House Joint Resolution Proposing the 13th Amendment to the Constitution, January 31, 1865; Enrolled Acts and Resolutions of Congress, 1789–1999; General Records of the United States Government; National Archives.

29 Coleman, *Historical Sketch Book*, p. 212.

30 Ibid., p. 213.

31 On the entanglement of carnival krewes and white supremacy see Justin A. Nystrom, *New Orleans After the Civil War: Race, Politics, and a New Birth of Freedom* (Johns Hopkins University Press, 2010).

32 Coleman, *Historical Sketch Book*, p. 214.

33 *New Orleans Daily Picayune*, 26 February 1873; on the carnival balls, see Jennifer Atkins, *New Orleans Carnival Balls: The Secret Side of Mardi Gras, 1870–1920* (Louisiana State University Press, 2017).

34 *New Orleans Times-Picayune*, 25 February 1938, p. 38.

7: Virginia Woolf Is Denied Access

1 This witticism is often attributed to Mark Twain, who mentions it in an after-dinner speech to the Nineteenth Century Club in New York in 1900, even though he attributes the phrase to Caleb Thomas Winchester, Professor of English Literature at Wesleyan College. 'The Disappearance of Literature', in *The Speeches of Mark Twain* (New York, 1910), p. 194. But a similar remark is also attested, a year earlier, in a detective story by the Scottish writer Fergus Hume, 'The Indian Bangle' (1899), where it already has the air of a commonplace.

2 Samuel R. Gardiner, 'Browning's Last Poems', *The Academy*, 11 January 1890, pp. 19–20.

3 James Russell Miller, *Week-day Religion* (London, 1898), p. 195.

4 Walter Alexander Raleigh, *Milton* (London, 1900), p. 88.

5 'Revolution of the Word: A Paris Group Manifesto', *Transition,* nos. 16–17 (1929).

6 Jed Rasula, *What the Thunder Saw: How* The Waste Land *Made Poetry Modern* (Princeton University Press, 2022), p. 88.

7 Rupert Brooke, 'The Old Vicarage, Grantchester', *Georgian Poetry 1911–1912*, ed. Sir Edward Howard Marsh (The Poetry Bookshop, 1913), p. 37.

8 Ezra Pound, 'I gather the limbs of Osiris', *Selected Prose: 1909–65* (New Directions, 1973), p. 35.

9 See, for example, Ezra Pound, 'Mesmerism', in *Personae* (London, 1909), p. 20.
10 Pound, *Exultations* (London, 1909), unpaginated.
11 Pound, 'I gather the limbs of Osiris', pp. 23–4.
12 Pound, 'The Renaissance' (1914), *Literary Essays*, p. 216.
13 Pound, 'Elizabethan Classicists' (1917), *Literary Essays*, p. 237.
14 Ibid., p. 238.
15 He may have been thinking of Herder's 'On the Spirit of Hebrew Poetry', which discusses Milton at some length.
16 Ezra Pound, 'The Hard and Soft in French Poetry' (1918), *Literary Essays*, p. 287.
17 Pound, 'Preface' to *The Poetical Works of Lionel Johnson* (1915), quoted in Chris Baldick, *Criticism and Literary Theory 1890 to the Present* (London, 1996), p. 40.
18 Henry Ware Eliot, quoted in *The Poems of T. S. Eliot: Collected and Uncollected Poems*, ed. Christopher Ricks and Jim McCue (Faber & Faber, 2015), p. 390.
19 Eliot, 'Introduction', *Literary Essays of Ezra Pound*, p. xi.
20 Eliot, 'Blake' (1921), *The Complete Prose of T. S. Eliot: The Critical Edition*, vol. 2, *The Perfect Critic: 1919–1926,* ed. Anthony Cuda and Ronald Schuchard (Johns Hopkins and Faber & Faber, 2014), p. 190.
21 Eliot, 'Marlowe' (1919), ibid., p. 97.
22 Eliot, 'The Metaphysical School' (1921), ibid., p. 380.
23 Eliot, 'The Love Song of J. Alfred Prufrock' (1914), line 122.
24 Eliot, 'Dryden' (1921), *Complete Prose*, p. 350.
25 Quoted in Matthew Hollis, *The Waste Land: A Biography of a Poem* (Faber, 2022), p. 262.
26 Quoted in Richard Ellmann, *James Joyce* (Oxford University Press, 1982), p. 275.
27 James Joyce, 'Drama and Life' (1900), *The Critical Writings of James Joyce*, ed. Ellsworth Mason and Richard Ellmann (Viking Press ,1959), pp. 39–45.
28 See *The Poems of T. S. Eliot*, ed. Ricks and McCue, p. 441.
29 According to Ezra Pound, quoted in *The Poems of T. S. Eliot*, ed. Ricks and McCue, p. 569.
30 Eliot, *The Waste Land*, lines 94–9.

31 Rasula, *What the Thunder Saw*, p. 191.
32 Hermione Lee, *Virginia Woolf* (Random House, 2010), pp. 112–13.
33 James Lockwood, 'Milton in the Twentieth Century', *John Milton: Life, Work, and Reputation* ed. Paul Hammond and Blair Worden, (Oxford University Press, 2010), pp. 167–86.
34 Lee, *Virginia Woolf,* p. 252.
35 Virginia Woolf to Elizabeth Cameron [Bowen], 22 July 1932; *Letters of Virginia Woolf* (Hogarth Press, 1979), p. 79.
36 I am extrapolating from two different diary entries: 24 August and 27 August 1918; *The Diary of Virginia Woolf,* vol. 1, 1915–19, ed. Anne Olivier Bell (Granta, 2013).
37 Woolf, *Diary*, vol. 1, 10 September 1918.
38 Ibid.
39 Geoff Dyer, 'Looking for Virginia Woolf's Diaries', *The Paris Review*, 12 September 2023, https://www.theparisreview.org/blog/2023/09/12/looking-for-virginia-woolfs-diaries.
40 Woolf, *Diary*, 10 September 1918.
41 Ibid.
42 Ibid.
43 Ibid.
44 Ibid.
45 Woolf, *Diary*, vol. 3, 27 October 1928.
46 Woolf, *A Room of One's Own* (Penguin Modern Classics, 2020), pp. 4–5.
47 Ibid., p. 93.
48 Virginia Woolf, 'My Father: Leslie Stephen', *Atlantic Monthly* (March 1950), p. 39.
49 Woolf, 'Four Figures', *The Second Common Reader* (Harcourt, Brace & World), pp. 148 and 142; 'Crabbe', *The Captain's Death Bed: And Other Essays* (Hogarth Press, 1950), p. 31.
50 Virginia Woolf to Ethyl Smith, 1 February 1941; *Letters of Virginia Woolf* (Harcourt Brace, 2011), vol. 6, p. 466.
51 Woolf to Smith, 1 February 1941.
52 Virginia Woolf, *Mrs Dalloway* (Oxford World Classics, 2009), pp. 149.
53 Ibid.
54 Ibid., p. 150.

55 'Milton's dislodgment, in the past decade, after his two centuries of predominance, was effected with remarkably little fuss.' F. R. Leavis, 'Milton's Verse', *Scrutiny* (1933), pp. 43–4.
56 Eliot, 'A Note on the Verse of John Milton', in *On Poetry and Poets* (Faber & Faber, 1957), p. 138.
57 Preface to *For Lancelot Andrewes* (1928), in *The Complete Prose of T. S. Eliot,* vol. 3, p. 513.
58 Eliot, 'Milton II' (Henrietta Herz Lecture, delivered to the British Academy in 1947), in *On Poetry and Poets*, p. 146.
59 Ibid., p. 161.
60 William Carlos Williams, '"With Forced Fingers Rude"', *Four Pages*, no. 2 (February 1948), pp. 1–4.
61 Christopher Ricks writes that 'the inability to prevail on oneself is a mark of the notable critic'; *Milton's Grand Style* (Oxford University Press, 1963), p. 4.
62 Canto LXVIII, *The Cantos of Ezra Pound* (New Directions, 1996), p. 395.
63 On Pound's trial and confinement at St Elizabeths Hospital see Daniel Swift, *The Bughouse: The Poetry, Politics and Madness of Ezra Pound* (Harvill Secker, 2017).

8: Hannah Arendt Begins Again

1 Milton, *Areopagitica* (London, 1644), p. 12.
2 Nigel Smith, 'Haak's Milton', *Milton in the Long Restoration,* ed. Blair Hoxby and Ann Baynes Coiro (Oxford University Press, 2016), pp. 379–96.
3 In Lessing's *Laocoon* (1766), Milton exemplifies poetry's difference from painting; in Herder's essay 'On the Spirit of Hebrew Poetry' (1782), it is an example of modern poetry that is inspired like the Hebrew Bible. See Curtis Whitaker, 'Domesticating and Foreignizing the Sublime: Paradise Lost in German', *Milton in Translation*, ed. Angelica Dura, Islam Issa, and Jonathan R. Olson (Oxford University Press, 2017), pp. 115–37.
4 Immanuel Kant, *Observations of the Sublime*, quoted in Burdick, *Kant and Milton* (Harvard University Press, 2010), p. 57. Here, Kant is probably

drawing on Meier's theory of the aesthetic shadow. See also Daniel Shore, 'Kant and Milton?' *Milton Quarterly*, vol. 48, no. 1 (2014), pp. 26–38.

5 'Goethe and Taine on Milton', *Spectator*, 18 July 1908, p. 16.

6 G. F. W. Hegel, *Aesthetics*, trans. T. M. Knox, vol. 2 (Oxford University Press, 1975), p. 1109. See also Franco Moretti, *Modern Epic: The World System from Goethe to García Márquez* (Verso, 1996).

7 S. S. Prawer, *Karl Marx and World Literature* (Verso, 2014), p. 15.

8 Ibid., p. 157.

9 Karl Marx, 'The Civil War in France' (draft), https://www.marxists.org/archive/marx/works/1871/civil-war-france/drafts/ch01.htm.

10 It wasn't actually that small a sum: a year later, Samuel Pepys bought his wife a turquoise ring with small diamonds set in it for 'near five pounds'. Diary, 18 February 1668.

11 Karl Marx, 'Theories of Surplus Value' (1861–3), quoted in Christopher Hill, *Milton and the English Revolution* (Faber & Faber, 1977), p. 354.

12 Jenny Marx, 'From London's Theatre World', *Marx & Engels: On Literature and Art* (Progress Publishers, 1976), https://www.marxists.org/archive/marx/letters/jenny/reviews/75_11.htm.

13 Friedrich Nietzsche, *Human, All Too Human: A Book for Free Spirits* (Cambridge University Press, 1996), p. 247.

14 I draw on Joachim Radkau's extraordinary *Max Weber: A Biography* (Polity, 2013), trans. Patrick Camiller, and on Marianne Weber's remembrance of her husband, *Max Weber: A Biography* (Routledge, 1988).

15 Radkau, *Max Weber*, p. 85.

16 Ibid., p. 117.

17 Ibid., p. 121.

18 Max Weber, *The Protestant Ethic and the Spirit of Capitalism* (Routledge, 2005), trans. Talcott Parsons, pp. 28–31.

19 Ibid., p. 3.

20 See Alexandra Walsham, 'The Reformation and "The Disenchantment of the World" Reassessed', *Historical Journal* 51 (2008), pp. 497–528.

21 Weber, *Protestant Ethic*, p. 46.

22 Ibid., p. 47.

23 Weber, 'Politics as a Vocation' in *The Vocation Lectures*, trans. Rodney Livingstone (Hackett, 2004), p. 93.

24 In this account, I draw on Elisabeth Young-Bruehl, *Hannah Arendt: For Love of the World* (Yale University Press, 1982), Elżbieta Ettinger, *Hannah Arendt / Martin Heidegger* (Yale University Press, 1995), and Samantha Rose Hill, *Hannah Arendt* (Reaktion Books, 2021).

25 Hannah Arendt, 'Martin Heidegger at 80', trans. Albert Hofstadter, *New Yorker*, 21 October 1971, pp. 50–4.

26 Hill, *Arendt*, p. 97.

27 Heidegger had made his commitment to Nazi ideology explicit in his public and private writings, although he started covering them up soon after the war. See Richard Wolin, *Heidegger in Ruins: Between Philosophy and Ideology* (Yale University Press, 2023).

28 Hill, *Arendt*, p. 120.

29 Ettinger, *Arendt / Heidegger*, p. 69.

30 Hill, *Arendt*, p. 121.

31 Paul Celan, 'Todtnauberg' (1970).

32 Otto Poggeler, quoted in Wolin, *Heidegger in Ruins*, p. 26.

33 Hill, *Arendt*, p. 123.

34 On Arendt and the Cold War, see Louis Menand, *The Free World: Art and Thought in the Cold War* (4th Estate, 2021); Samuel Moyn, *Liberalism against Itself: Cold War Intellectuals and the Making of Our Times* (Yale University Press, 2023).

35 Hannah Arendt, *The Human Condition* (University of Chicago Press, 1998; second edition), p. 99.

36 Ibid., p. 134.

37 Ibid., p. 99.

38 Ibid., p. 238.

39 Ibid., p. 240.

40 Ibid., p. 241.

41 Quoted in Hill, *Arendt*, p. 143.

42 Quoted in ibid., p. 144.

9: Malcolm X Startles His Visitor

1 Malcolm X to Philbert Little, September 1949, the Malcolm X collection: papers, Sc Micro R-6270, Schomburg Center for Research in

Black Culture, Manuscripts, Archives and Rare Books Division, the New York Public Library.

2 Alex Haley and Malcolm X, *The Autobiography of Malcolm X* (Penguin, 2001), p. 247.

3 Lee and Tamara Payne, *The Dead Are Arising: The Life of Malcolm X* (Penguin, 2020), pp. 222–3.

4 *Autobiography of Malcolm X*, p. 247.

5 Clark Rupp Doering, ed., *A Report on the Development of Penological Treatment at Norfolk Prison Colony in Massachusetts: Official Manual of the State Prison Colony* (Bureau of Social Hygiene, 1940).

6 *Autobiography of Malcolm X*, p. 248.

7 Dawn-Marie Gibson, *A History of the Nation of Islam: Race, Islam, and the Quest for Freedom* (Bloomsbury, 2012), pp. 13–26.

8 Erdmann Doane Beynon, 'The Voodoo Cult Among Negro Migrants in Detroit', *American Journal of Sociology*, vol. 43, no. 6 (1938), p. 895.

9 Quoted in ibid., p. 899.

10 Malcolm X, 'We Arose from the Dead!', *Moslem World & the U.S.A.* (August and September 1956), p. 24–7 and 36.

11 *Autobiography of Malcolm X*, p. 268. See Louis A. DeCaro, Jr., *On the Side of My People: A Religious Life of Malcolm X* (New York University Press, 1996) and Jed B. Tucker, 'Malcolm X, The Prison Years: The Relentless Pursuit of Formal Education', *Journal of African American History*, vol. 102 (2017), pp. 184–212.

12 Malcolm to Philbert Little, February 4, 1949. Quoted in Marable, *Malcolm X*, p. 71.

13 On Malcolm's reading of Sufi poetry, see the contributions in Maytha Alhassen, ed., 'The Black Stone of Mecca', in *Khayál: A Multimedia Collection by Muslim Creatives* (Pillars Fund, 2023), pp. 15–26.

14 *Autobiography of Malcolm X*, p. 282.

15 In his important survey of African American writers' appropriations of Milton, Reginald Wilburn passes quickly over Malcolm X's actual interpretation and instead argues for the similarities between Malcolm X and Milton's Satan; *Preaching the Gospel of Black Revolt: Appropriating Milton in Early African American Literature* (Penn State University Press, 2014), pp. 327–34. See also Carolivia Herron, 'Milton and Afro-American Literature', in *Re-Membering Milton: Essays on the Texts and Traditions*,

ed. Mary Nyquist and Margaret W. Ferguson (Methuen, 1987), pp. 278–300. See also Michael Lieb, *Children of Ezekiel: Aliens, UFOs, the Crisis of Race, and the Advent of End Time* (Duke University Press, 1998), p. 155n; Mark Christian Thompson, *Phenomenal Blackness: Black Power, Philosophy, and Theory* (University of Chicago Press, 2022), p. 162.

16 Elijah Muhammad, *Message to the Blackman* (Chicago: Muhammad Mosque of Islam, No. 2, 1965), p. 103; see also Claude Andrew Clegg III, *The Life and Times of Elijah Muhammad* (University of North Carolina Press, 2014).

17 Malcolm X to Philbert Little, 29 September 1949.

18 *Autobiography of Malcolm X*, p. 276.

19 In a striking anticipation of Virginia Woolf, Cooper argues that the ability to earn money would allow women a freedom from marriage, allowing them to 'revel in the majesty of Dante, the sweetness of Virgil, the simplicity of Homer, the strength of Milton.' Anna Cooper, *A Voice from the South* (Xenia, Ohio, 1892), p. 69.

20 Garrett Felber, *Those Who Know Don't Say: The Nation of Islam, the Black Freedom Movement, and the Carceral State* (University of North Carolina Press, 2019), p. 51.

21 Malcolm X to Commissioner MacDowell, 6 June 1950, quoted in Felber, *Those Who Know Don't Say*, pp. 27–8.

22 Marable, *A Life of Reinvention*, pp. 150–3.

23 Malcolm X made the comment at the end of a speech entitled 'God's Judgment of White America', 4 December 1963; for a transcript of the speech, see *Malcolm X: The Man and His Times*, ed. John Henrik Clarke (Trenton: Africa World Press, 1990), pp. 282–7.

24 The reference is to the commentary of Abdullah Yusuf Ali; on Malcolm X's relationship with Ahmed Osman, see 'Malcolm X and the Sudanese', dir. Sophie Schrago (2020), https://vimeo.com/394471323.

25 DeNeen L. Brown, 'Martin Luther King Jr. met Malcolm X just once', *Washington Post*, 14 January 2018.

26 See Louis A. DeCaro, *Malcolm and the Cross* (NYU Press, 1998), pp. 178–96.

27 On the developments in his political thought, see William W. Sales, *From Civil Rights to Black Liberation: Malcolm X and the Organization of Afro-American Unity* (South End Press, 1994).

28 Malcolm X, 'Message to the Grassroots' (1963), in *Malcolm X Speaks: Selected Speeches and Statements*, ed. George Breitman (Grove Press, 1965), p. 16.
29 Malcolm X, 'The Ballot or the Bullet', *Malcolm X Speaks*, p. 38.
30 Malcolm X, 'The Black Revolution', *Malcolm X Speaks*, p. 49.
31 Alex Haley, 'Foreword', *The Autobiography of Malcolm X*, p. 17.
32 On the FBI campaign against the Nation of Islam, see Mattias Gardell, *In the Name of Elijah Muhammad: Louis Farrakhan and the Nation of Islam* (Duke University Press, 1996).

10: C. L. R. James Is Deported

1 C. L. R. James, *Beyond a Boundary* (Yellow Jersey Press, 2005), p. 39.
2 Ibid.
3 Cedric Robinson, *Black Marxism: The Making of the Black Radical Tradition* (Penguin Classics, 2021), p. 250.
4 C. L. R. James, 'Bloomsbury: An Encounter with Edith Sitwell', in *The C. L. R. James Reader,* ed. Anna Grimshaw (Wiley Blackwell, 1992), p. 46.
5 John L. Williams, *CLR James: A Life Beyond Boundaries* (Constable, 2022), p. 117.
6 C. L. R. James, 'The Case for West Indian Self-Government', *The Future in the Present: Selected Writings* (Allison & Busby, 1977), p. 32.
7 Quoted in Robinson, *Black Marxism*, p. 265.
8 Williams, *CLR James,* p. 158.
9 C. L. R. James, *The Black Jacobins: Toussaint Louverture and the Saint Domingo Rebellion* (Vintage, 1989; revised second edition), p. ix.
10 Ibid., p. 28.
11 Ibid.
12 Ibid., p. 291.
13 Ibid., p. 373.
14 C. L. R. James, *Notes on Dialectics: Hegel, Marx, Lenin* (L. Hill, 1980), p. 99.
15 Williams, *CLR James*, pp. 232–3; see also Alan M. Wald, *New York Intellectuals: The Rise and Decline of the Anti-Stalinist Left from the 1930s to the 1980s* (University of North Carolina Press, 1987) p. 232–3.

16 Williams, *CLR James*, p. 205.

17 See Leon Trotsky, *Where is Britain Going?* (Allen & Unwin, 1926).

18 James, *Notes on Dialectics*, p. 185.

19 C. L. R. James, 'Cromwell and the Levellers', *Fourth International* (May 1949), pp. 143–8, https: / /www.marxists.org /archive /james-clr / works /1949 /05 /english-revolution.htm.

20 Leon Trotsky, *Literature and Revolution*, trans. Rose Strunksy (Haymarket, 2005), p. 24.

21 C. L. R. James, 'Ancestors of the Proletariat', *Fourth International*, vol. 10, no. 8, September 1949, pp. 252–5, https: / /www.marxists.org / archive /james-clr /works /1949 /09 /english-revolution.htm.

22 The text of the lectures does not survive, so I base these remarks on the other works from this time, including *Mariners, Renegades, and Castaways* and 'Three lectures: Human Personality in Great Tragedy, Birth of the Modern Personality, The Artist in the Caribbean', audio recordings of a lecture at the University of the West Indies, C. L. R. James Papers, Columbia University.

23 Vincent J. Cannato, *American Passage: The History of Ellis Island* (HarperCollins, 2009), p. 352.

24 Ibid., pp. 360–76.

25 Bill Schwarz, 'C. L. R. James's *American Civilization*', *Atlantic Studies*, vol. 2, no. 1 (2005), pp. 15–43.

26 Paul Buhle, *C. L. R. James: The Artist as Revolutionary* (Verso, 2017), p. 124.

27 C. L. R. James, *Mariners, Renegades and Castaways: Herman Melville and the World We Live In* (Allison & Busby, 1985), p. 23.

28 Ibid., p. 151.

29 C. L. R. James to Jay Leyda, 7 March 1953, in *The C. L. R. James Reader*, p. 231.

30 James, *Mariners*, p. 172.

31 Fidel Castro, *History Will Absolve Me*, translated by Pedro Álvarez Tabío & Andrew Paul Booth (Editorial de Ciencias Sociales, La Habana, Cuba, 1975), https: / /www.marxists.org /history /cuba / archive /castro /1953 /10 /16.htm.

32 C. L. R. James, 'Lenin and the Trade Union Debate in Russia', in *You Don't Play with Revolution: The Montreal Lectures of C. L. R. James*, ed. David Austin (AK Press, 2009), p. 212.

33 Ibid.

34 The historian Christopher Hill gave Milton pride of place in his famous history of the English Civil War, *The World Turned Upside Down* (1972), which gave the post-1968 Left a new image of England's revolutionary past.

35 Frank Reynolds, *Freewheelin' Frank: Secretary of the Angels, as told to Michael McClure* (Grove Press, 1967), p. 92.

36 Ibid., p. 93.

37 Jonathan Lethem and Pamela Jackson, eds, *The Exegesis of Philip K. Dick* (Orion, 2012), 15:47.

38 *The Exegesis of Philip K. Dick,* 18.29.

39 Lawrence Sutin, *Divine Invasions: A Life of Philip K. Dick* (Hachette, 2005), p. 228.

40 Mary Shelley, *Frankenstein* (Penguin Classics, 2003), pp. 224–5.

41 *Arena: Upon Westminster Bridge*, dir. Anthony Wall (1982); 'Michael Smith documentary with Linton Kwesi Johnson', *YouTube,* https://www.youtube.com/watch?v=NE3kVwyY2WU. On the documentary, see also John Merrick, 'Good Bourgeois Subjects', https://www.softpunkmag.com/criticism/good-bourgeois-subjects.

42 Oliver Browne, 'The Philistine Revolution: Literary Culture and the Uncultured in Postwar Britain' (unpublished PhD dissertation, Princeton University).

43 C. L. R. James, 'How I Wrote the Black Jacobins', *small axe* 8 (2000), p. 72.

11: *Jordan Peterson Gets Lost*

1 Rosa Flotats, 'Translating Milton into Catalan', *Milton Quarterly*, vol. 36, no. 2. (2002), pp.106–23.

2 'Milton in Serbian/Montenegrin: Paradise Lost from Behind Bars', *Milton in Translation*, ed. Angelica Duran, Islam Issa, and Jonathan R. Olson (Oxford University Press, 2017), pp. 366–79.

3 Islam Issa, *Milton in the Arab-Muslim World* (Routledge, 2017), p. 42.

4 Ibid., pp. 11–14.

5 Ibid., p. 41.

6 Ben Garcia, '"Paradise Lost" Leads to Bookshop Closure', *Kuwait Times*, 6 June 2013; see also Islam Issa, 'The Online Revolution: Milton and the Internet in the Middle East', in *Digital Milton*, ed. David Curran and Islam Issa (Springer, 2018), pp. 181–206.

7 Anne C. Krendl, 'Jordan Peterson: Linking Psychology to Mythology', *Harvard Crimson*, 26 April, 1995, https://www.thecrimson.com/article/1995/4/26/jordan-peterson-pharvard-students-may-know.

8 Jordan Peterson, *Maps of Meaning: The Architecture of Belief* (Routledge, 1999), p. 247.

9 Jason McBride, 'The Pronoun Warrior', *Toronto Life*, 25 January 2017, https://torontolife.com/city/u-t-professor-sparked-vicious-battle-gender-neutral-pronouns.

10 '2017/05/17: Senate hearing on Bill C16', *YouTube*, uploaded by Jordan B Peterson, https://www.youtube.com/watch?v=KnIAAkSNtqo.

11 Peterson, *12 Rules for Life: An Antidote to Chaos* (Allen Lane, 2018), p. 20.

12 Ibid., p. 17.

13 'Peterson: What We Should Learn from Milton's *Paradise Lost*', *YouTube*, uploaded by PhilosophyInsights, https://www.youtube.com/watch?v=DyHIqbJudcU.

14 Peterson, *12 Rules*, p. 149.

15 Ibid., p. 210.

16 Ibid.

17 Ibid., p. 17.

18 Ibid., pp. 241–2.

19 Ibid., p. 154.

20 Carl Jung, 'Introduction' to R. J. Zwi Werblowsky, *Lucifer and Prometheus: A Study of Milton's Satan* (Routledge & Paul, 1952).

21 *The Rise of Jordan Peterson*, dir. Patricia Marcoccia, 2019.

22 On Milton's Hell as an image of social media see Katie Kadue, 'Suspended Hell', *n+1*, 30 July 2021.

23 On Milton's defence of penal slavery see Mary Nyquist, *Arbitrary Rule: Slavery, Tyranny, and the Power Over Life and Death* (University of Chicago Press, 2013), pp. 137–46.

24 On the relationship between capitalism's demand for labour and the growth of mass incarceration, see Ruth Gilmore Wilson, *Golden*

Gulag: Prisons, Surplus, Crisis, and Opposition in Globalizing California (University of California Press, 2007); Jackie Wang, *Carceral Capitalism* (Semiotext(e), 2018).

25 Garrett Felber, *Those Who Know Don't Say: The Nation of Islam, the Black Freedom Movement, and the Carceral State* (University of North Carolina Press, 2019), p. 82.

26 Jefferson, 'Early Notebook', quoted in Kevin J. Hayes, *The Road to Monticello: The Life and Mind of Thomas Jefferson* (Oxford University Press, 2008), p. 92.

12: My Students Teach Me About Disobedience

1 On the history of this connection in poetry and the theory of poetics, see Andrea Brady, *Poetry and Bondage: A History and Theory of Lyric Constraint* (Cambridge University Press, 2021).

2 To take just one example: John Witherspoon, a Scottish Presbyterian minister and President of the College of New Jersey (later Princeton University), was a signer of the Declaration of Independence, a slave owner, and a theorist of criminal law. See 'Lecture X: Of Politics', in *The Works of John Witherspoon* (Edinburgh, 1815), pp. 75–86. He was also conversant with *Paradise Lost*.

3 George F. Sensabaugh, *Milton in Early America* (Princeton University Press, 1964).

4 On changing attitudes to incarceration, see Caleb Smith, *Prison and the American Imagination* (Yale University Press, 2009); Angela Davis, *Are Prisons Obsolete?* (Open Media, 2003).

Permissions

v: Epigraph from Paul Celan, 'The Conference Project: "On the Darkness of Poetry"', *Microliths: Posthumous Prose*, trans. Pierre Joris (Contra Mundum, 2020), p. 128.
128–9: Quotations from T. S. Eliot, *The Waste Land*, courtesy of the T. S. Eliot Estate and Faber & Faber Ltd.

List of Illustrations

and with funds donated by Betty Adler Schermer in honour of her great-grandfather, August M. Bondi.
113 Invitation to the 1857 Comus ball. Tulane University Special Collection.
117 The 1867 Mistick Krewe of Comus parade. Engraving after a sketch by James E. Taylor. Granger Historical Picture Archive/ Alamy.
131 Virginia Woolf and her father Leslie Stephen. Science History Images/ Alamy.
136 Virginia Woolf by Ottoline Morrell (1924). Album/ Alamy.
143 Max Klinger, *Eve from the Future* (1898), Opus III, Plate V. The Metropolitan Museum of Art, New York. Public domain.
148 Hannah Arendt as a young woman, c. 1930. Granger Historical Picture Archive/Alamy.
159 Administration building, Norfolk Prison Colony, circa 1934. Norfolk Prison Colony Collection, Robert S. Cox Special Collections and University Archives Research Center, UMass Amherst Libraries.
166 Malcolm X speaks at a rally in Harlem, 1963. Everett Collection Inc. / Alamy.
172 C. L. R. James speaks on behalf of the International African Friends of Abyssinia at a rally in Trafalgar Square, 1935. Keystone-France via Getty Images.
177 Manhattan, with Ellis Island and the Statue of Liberty in the foreground (*c.* 1934). Underwood Archives via Alamy.
183 William Blake, *The Rout of the Rebel Angels* (1807–8). Public domain.
193 White supremacists march through the University of Virginia the night before the Unite the Right rally, Charlottesville, VA, on 11 August 2017. Zach D. Roberts / NurPhoto SRL/ Alamy.
210 Alan Best, *Adam and Eve Enter the World* (2024). Courtesy of the artist.

Index

Page references in *italics* indicate images.

About the Author

Orlando Reade studied English at Cambridge and Princeton, where he received his PhD in English literature in 2020. For a period of five years, he taught in New Jersey prisons. His writing has appeared in publications including the *Guardian*, *frieze*, and *The White Review*, where he also served as a contributing editor. He is now an assistant professor of English at Northeastern University London.